**HOW TO START
A HOME-BASED
WRITING BUSINESS**

HOW TO START A HOME-BASED WRITING BUSINESS

2nd edition

by Lucy V. Parker

The Globe Pequot Press

Old Saybrook, Connecticut

Cover and text design by Nancy Freeborn

Library of Congress Cataloging-in-Publication Data is available.
Parker, Lucy V.
      How to start a home-based writing business / by Lucy V. Parker. —2nd ed.
            p.   cm. — (How to start a home-based business series)
      Previous ed. published under title: How to open and operate a home-based writing business. c1994.
            Includes bibliographical references and index.
            ISBN 1-56440-998-8
            1. Authorship—Vocational guidance. 2. Desktop publishing—Vocational guidance.
3. Report writing—Vocational guidance. 4. Home-based businesses. I. Parker, Lucy V. How to open and operate a home-based writing business. II. Title. III. Series.
PN153.P37 1997   97–17530
808'02—DC21   CIP

Manufactured in the United States of America
Second Edition/Second Printing

For Mike

CONTENTS

ACKNOWLEDGMENTS

My thanks to Betsy Amster, of Betsy Amster Literary Enterprises, Los Angeles, for suggesting this book and having faith in me as its author, and to my editors, Bruce Markot and Mace Lewis, at The Globe Pequot Press. Thanks also to the professionals who gave generously of their time and experience to provide profiles for this book and to the many other writers and desktop publishers I talked with in doing my research. Cat Volkmann offered background on the home-based business field. Stephen Morrill was helpful in sharing marketing techniques. Judith Broadhurst provided insightful information about writing online. Newsletter design consultant Polly Pattison provided much-appreciated advice and resources. Thanks to online marketer Katie Lachance, sales trainer John Klymshyn, and creative services consultant Maria Piscopo, for permission to draw on their material. Special thanks for reviewing sections of this book go to Derek Anderson, former Sports Information Director, Chapman University, Orange, CA, and attorney Blair W. Clark of St. Petersburg, FL. Any errors that may remain are mine, not theirs.

INTRODUCTION

THREE WAYS TO USE THIS BOOK

1. **Leaf through the pages.**

    You'll see that writing from a home office can be a viable and profitable venture—and you will be encouraged to start your own home business.

2. **Skim for specific information.**

    Study the "hidden market" for writing jobs listed in Chapter Three, along with the list of potential clients; the marketing techniques described in Chapter Seven; the sales techniques discussed in Chapter Eight; and the pricing strategies explained in Chapter Nine. You'll get new ideas about services to sell and proven, effective ways to market and price them.

3. **If you are really serious about starting your own home business as a writer, read Chapter One this week.**

    Then line up one or more mentors—friends or associates *who have been successful at running a creative home business for several years*. If you don't know an appropriate mentor, see if you can get an introduction to one. Most people enjoy helping others by sharing their experiences.

    Over the next two months or so, read Chapters Two through Ten—one chapter each week. Dip into the Source Directory and complete the worksheets. Then meet on a designated day for an hour with one of your mentors to discuss that week's topic and your own plans. If weekly meetings seem too frequent, try meeting every other week or once a month. It's not unusual to spend a year or more planning a new home business.

Do you know any other writers or creative professionals who are thinking about starting their own business? If so, consider inviting them to join your meetings. In my experience, "making it seem real" is one of the biggest hurdles to clear in starting a business. These discussions will help you leap that hurdle, while providing useful information and personal feedback. Remember that you must *always* take feedback with a grain of salt, comparing several opinions and measuring them against your own judgment.

After you have completed the reading, research, and planning involved in Chapters One through Ten, sit down and write your business plan. Share it with everyone involved, including your spouse or significant other. If appropriate, use it to obtain loans and leases. Then follow the directions for keeping your business plan up-to-date as your business gets under way.

While your plans are taking shape, treat your mentors to a good meal or some other favor. Good businesspeople always acknowledge favors and pay professional debts promptly—although the best repayment you can make for this help will be to advise some fledgling writer or creative professional years from now, when you are well established.

CHAPTER ONE

GETTING STARTED AS A HOME-BASED WRITER

"Until you make it, fake it."
That's what they say.
"Until you make it, fake it."
There is no other way.

I don't mean "buy a new Mercedes"
If the payments would come hard.
I don't mean "put three-hundred-dollar dresses
On your MasterCard."

But fake a little confidence—
Just fake the way you feel.
'Cause fakin' now will teach you how
And soon it will be real.

"UNTIL YOU MAKE IT, FAKE IT"

No, this lyric never made it to the "top forty." But composing it and other topical ditties kept me in touch with writing as I drove the southern California freeways, tape recorder in hand, calling on my printing sales clients during the early 1980s.

Supporting myself as an outside sales rep was part of my plan to make the transition from higher education public relations to freelance writing and graphic designing. And it worked.

This particular selection from my heretofore unpublished and unproduced "Sales Success Song Cycle" may help you, too, as you step off the diving board into your own home-based writing business.

Let me share a secret: At first, it doesn't seem real. You may even feel as though you are pretending to be in business—an imposter "playing office" with a toy telephone and a kiddie computer. That's OK. Don't worry about it. *"Until you make it, fake it."*

Acting like a professional will set you apart from equally talented writers who, in reality, are between jobs—who don't have a compelling vision of themselves as self-employed and won't be there in two years when a client wants them to rewrite an early project.

You *will* be there to handle such an assignment! By that time, you will have become a real entrepreneur—part of the vast small-business backbone of every free economy. You will be a real businessperson with real clients, real jobs to do, real cash flow, real equipment that probably needs upgrading, and dreams that are really coming true.

I did it—and so can you!

WHAT THIS BOOK OFFERS—AND ASSUMES

Before we go any further, I want to make it clear that this is a book about commercial writing, business writing, nonfiction writing. It is a book about obtaining practical, often unglamorous assignments that can pay the bills. The glamorous part is being your own boss, earning a living at a craft you enjoy—that's what I assume you're looking for as you read these pages.

Throughout the book, I have used many examples from my own experience and from the careers of writer friends. But what if you can't relate to these examples? After all, every writer is different. To broaden my research and to help you visualize yourself as a home-based writer, I have provided profiles of ten successful professionals—one at the end of each chapter.

The ten writers represent a variety of specialties. A few have gone the traditional magazine article and nonfiction book route, but most earn their living from what I describe later on as "the hidden (or corporate) market." They come from a wide geographic region. Some are older, some are younger—although the kind of writing discussed in this book normally requires some staff experience, or at least a little life experience. If you can go directly from being a full-time student to being a full-time home-based business writer, more power to you!

HOW I GOT STARTED AS A HOME-BASED ENTREPRENEUR

No one in my immediate family had ever worked for anything but large employers—the Chicago school system, United States Steel, the U.S. Department of Agriculture, the Navy—that kind of employer, that size. It was my former husband's Naval career that brought us to California from the Midwest, and I went to work for the state university system. It was all I knew—benefits, a monthly paycheck, security in numbers.

If you have a relative who is self-employed, count yourself lucky and start soaking up small-business ambience in Cousin Harry's restaurant or Aunt Betty's beauty salon. Virtually my entire career after graduating from Northwestern University's Medill School of Journalism had been spent in public relations, publications, and grant writing for public and private colleges and universities. Not only did I know nothing about self-employment, I knew nothing about business itself.

In 1975 my experience as the public relations representative and journalism instructor on a semester-long study voyage to Europe, the Middle East, Africa, South America, and the Caribbean forever changed my typically academic, out-of-touch view of business. Until that mind-blowing three months at sea, I had irrationally (but conveniently) conceived of the business world as being overwhelming on the one hand and unworthy of my efforts on the other. Seeing street vendors in every culture we visited—so like the swapmeet culture then emerging in the United States—demolished my ivory tower perspective. It made me understand that business—*the exchange of goods and services*—is a basic endeavor that sustains and will always be part of human life.

As my new understanding evolved, I began to dream of freelancing and controlling my own schedule. In 1978 I sold an op-ed piece to the *Los Angeles Times* about a liberated single mom (me) taking a part-time vacation to see how staying home would feel (heavenly).

"Perhaps our work-crazy American system, even with its incredible wealth, just can't allow institutional time to become human time," I concluded. "We single mothers, juggling the demands on us, may be only the tip of an iceberg of discontent—the frenzied fringe of an entire generation that is frantic to earn more and more money looking for Mr. Goodlife. . . . In my own case, it's taken me [years] to catch on, but finally I stopped racing long enough to smell my rosebush this morning."

Leaving my college job in 1980, I made a 180-degree turn to outside commissioned sales. As a printing buyer in higher education, I had watched scores of sales reps make their pitch and thought: "I could do that." I knew the move was transitional, but I decided that outside sales would teach me about the business world and force me to structure my time.

Well, I still struggle with structuring my time (Charles Hobbs's *Time Power* tapes and my Day-Timer have helped). But I did learn to feel at home in both large and small corporations, and I did achieve an understanding of what business is about. I built a printing clientele largely through networking in professional organizations, and I helped my clients by designing and editing for them on the side. When I made the leap to full-time freelancing in 1986, my printing clients provided a base.

While sadly many of my corporate friends have learned that in a downsizing economy, their professional loyalty does not guarantee them job security, I'm glad I have learned to scramble and survive. In addition to providing me with financial adaptability during the recession of the late 1980s, my home-based business also improved my sense of physical well-being. For years, in high-pressure public relations work and occasionally during a printing sales crisis, I got terrible headaches. I couldn't help noticing that periods of extra stress were often followed by periods of pain. In the ten years I have been self-employed, I've experienced lots of stressful deadlines, but almost no headaches. I'm not sure why. I guess I just feel more comfortable with stress I can control.

In 1994, just as the first edition of this book was being published, family commitments brought me to central Florida from southern California to care for an elderly relative—and again my business served me well. Since home-based writing is not only adaptable, but portable, I was soon able to find clients in Tampa Bay. In 1996, with more time available after my relative's death, I have adapted to new market needs, refocusing part of my business on Webpage design. And I've also undertaken a long-deferred fiction project that may or may not bring me money but has already brought me great satisfaction.

So, as you can see, a home-based writing business is nothing like the nine-to-five job you come to, go away from, and eventually leave—something separate from your "real life." It *is* your real life. At least, it has become mine.

WHY WORK AT HOME?

Why *not* work at home? Especially if you can earn a good living, be your own boss, and work on projects you enjoy. Today, in the words of management expert Tom Peters, "We're in the midst of an earthshaking change in the way business gets done." In 1900, Peters reports, 50 percent of U.S. workers were self-employed. With the rise of giant corporations, that number had shrunk to 7 percent by 1977. You are part of the small-business revival that is slowly reversing that trend. By 1993, Peters states, 13 percent of our workforce was self-employed.

And the number of people working at home is rising, too. According to Link Resources, which tracks home workers, forty million people (both self-employed and those working for others) were working at home in 1996, up sharply during this decade and still climbing. *Business Home* magazine predicts that there will be fifty-five million "homeworking households" by the year 2000.

About twenty-five million of the forty million home workers are home-based entrepreneurs, says Cat Volkmann, head of the Tampa Bay Chapter of the American Association of Home Based Businesses and a national leader in AAHBB, which is headquartered in Rockville, MD. Cat and her husband, Tom, operate The TomCat Connection. They are "In the Business to Promote Business", which they do through networking, education, resources, and building clients' images on paper and on the Web. She says that research done by the association verifies Link's numbers.

"Link Resources estimates that 8,000 home-based businesses are started every day in the United States," Cat points out, "and these businesses have tremendous staying-power. After five years, our research indicates that only one in five home-based businesses has failed. Compare that with figures from the United States Small Business Administration which shows that only one in five small businesses lasts five years." Cat cites a nine-year study of home-based businesses by the University of Wisconsin that has also found better-than-average survival.

"We just don't quit," she says. "We have such stamina and drive because everything is riding on it." Cat and Tom are a case in point. A nurse-turned-writer, she opened her first home-based business, Health Education Associates, in 1977. Tom, now doing graphic design, opened a home-based consulting business in mechanical design engineering in 1968. The two formed TomCat in 1986.

Computers, faxes, modems, E-mail, and online services have made home-based business incredibly convenient, especially for writers. Today a well-run home office is every bit as professional as a cubicle in some high-rise business center—and a lot handier for *you*. But there's still another reason to work at home. If you can avoid the pitfalls of home business (see Tips for Managing Your Business and Yourself, in Chapter Ten), your costs will be significantly less than those of public relations, advertising, and marketing firms, which must add office rent, utilities, and employee benefits to the basic expenses of equipment, supplies, and marketing. That makes you an economical alternative—exactly what clients are looking for.

The layoffs and downsizing of the nineties have caused both pain and pleasure for creative workers. Companies and organizations everywhere are seeking to meet their writing needs without maintaining staff members who draw salaries whether they're busy or not, and whose skills may not be well suited for every project.

The downside of this situation is well summarized by the following example. One successful writer I interviewed for this book told me about a friend who had been working full-time for a national publishing firm, producing a newsletter. The company abruptly laid the editor off and, in less than a week, hired the dazed woman back to continue putting out the newsletter—for less money and with no benefits. She accepted, thinking it might be the start of a freelance career, but with no preparation for freelancing and a nearly full-time job producing the newsletter, she could not find time to organize or market her business.

With the help of this book and your own research and planning, you can avoid such a trap and tap into what I call "the hidden market" for writing: businesses, government agencies, retailers, restaurants, hotels, hospitals, professional groups, universities, and many other local clients who buy services like yours in every community.

Of course, these clients could and often do meet their needs by hiring an advertising, public relations, marketing, or design agency—but they can't do it at the prices *you* can charge working out of your home—although, as we'll see in Chapter Nine, really lowballing your prices cannot lead to long-term success.

With effective marketing and a professional approach, you can gain important and lucrative jobs from very large clients—sometimes snatching them away from well-established agencies and sometimes serving as an agency subcontractor. I've done both—and so can you!

WHAT KINDS OF WRITING JOBS ARE WE TALKING ABOUT?

Throughout this book, we are talking about assignments you can realistically expect to receive as a new freelance writer—assignments that are available to you in most communities and that can add up to a full-time income.

We're talking about such meat-and-potatoes jobs as producing newsletters, product sheets and brochures; creating press releases and press kits, ad copy, speeches, and company magazine articles. We're talking about developing instructional and technical manuals, creating audiovisual and video scripts, editing, even writing resumés. In other words, this book will teach you how to be your own boss while doing what other writers do in salaried positions.

Such writing is often called "business" or "corporate" writing, and it's almost always done as "work-for-hire." You produce a specific piece of work and your client owns all rights to it.

As you read this, new kinds of writing are emerging at the heart of the electronic/online revolution. No one today can fully predict the future of this evolving technology, but everyone who cares about communications can grasp the significance of the digital buzz-phrase: "Content is King!" Some of this writing is straight work-for-hire. Some is entrepreneurial, with the writer putting material online and requiring payment to access it or selling space to online advertisers. Some is freelance, with the author selling agreed-upon rights—although obtaining appropriate compensation for electronic rights has become a hotly contested issue with the National Writers Union, the American Society of Journalists and Authors, and other advocate groups.

Whatever form this new communication takes and however it is compensated, writers are needed and opportunities are plentiful for those who develop an understanding of new interactive media.

This book also talks about traditional freelance article writing—but not for *Esquire* or *Cosmopolitan*. Rather, we're looking at writing for newspapers, newsletters, and regional or specialized magazines, including a vast array of trade journals—publications that won't be found at a supermarket checkout stand, but where opportunities abound.

Similarly, opportunities exist writing nonfiction books such as how-to's and guides. These categories are by far the easiest to break into. But be forewarned: Unless you are paid for your work up front—the way a manual writer, textbook writer, or ghostwriter might be—writing books on a royalty basis is rarely profitable until you have several steady sellers in print. One writer who fits this description is Sylvia McNair, a seventy-two-year-old travel writer who began her writing career at fifty-seven—a wonderful encouragement to other late bloomers. (You'll find a profile of McNair at the end of Chapter Eight.)

McNair and two other writers profiled in this book, Steve Morrill and Judith Broadhurst, work primarily in these traditional areas—and many business writers find it worthwhile to seek freelance assignments along with their work-for-hire jobs. However, because so many books and articles are already available on how to succeed writing articles and nonfiction books, this book gives much greater emphasis to marketing and selling in the work-for-hire world. Entering this world remains a mystery to those who have not studied its techniques, and, even more to the point, this world is readily available to beginning professionals in every part of the country, as well as online.

A business writer friend, for example, doing Internet research for her vacation in France, received an unexpected online assignment to publicize a French inn to American travelers. Jack Fehr, a Vermont writer profiled at the end of this chapter, responded to an ad for freelance financial writers in one of CompuServe's communications forums and received a series of newsletter assignments from a publisher in Boston. Technical writing/design broker Joy White of California, profiled in Chapter Two, joined an online forum called Military Brats of America because she grew up as an Army brat. Much to her surprise, the forum founder turned out to be a New York designer who was looking for a West Coast supplier where he could refer business. White was more than happy to comply.

Such connections become more common every day.

Being your own boss is a major achievement—the goal of a lifetime for many people. But if your dreams go further, *keep those dreams!* One of the benefits of being a home-based freelancer is the opportunity to do personal creative projects—and as a businessperson, you'll make every creative project profitable if you can.

It's true that some writers support themselves at home writing novels, movie scripts, or articles for national magazines. Not many, but some. Aim high, and while you grow, let meat-and-potatoes jobs pay the bills.

Perhaps your dreams are more entrepreneurial: You'd like a high-profit home business writing and producing your own products for sale to retailers, business buyers, or consumers. Examples might be a line of greeting cards, a subscription newsletter, a series of independently published books. Such ventures require additional capital but can significantly increase your return on money and time invested. Many of the business practices you'll learn in this book will help you if you decide to go in that direction.

THE CASE FOR COMBINING WRITING AND DESIGN

In addition to describing the kinds of jobs that are available, this book explains how to set up your business and your office, how to market and sell, and what to charge—with worksheets to help you develop and evaluate your plans. I started my freelance career when the home-based business was less recognized as a significant entrepreneurial option. But because of recent trends toward downsizing and hiring freelancers, you couldn't be starting your business at a better time. You have more credibility. You have better resources, with instant online research and E-mail access to your clients. And best of all, you have more demand for your work.

I am assuming that you already know your craft—how to write—although the next section of this chapter offers suggestions for strengthening your skills. At the same time, however, I invite you to consider adding desktop publishing and/or Webpage design to your arsenal, if you have the talent and interest. Even more important, I urge you to *offer* these services to your clients from the start by building relationships with other freelancers.

Desktop publishing is an inspired marketing term, but something of a misnomer. It's not really publishing in the sense that a book, magazine, or software publisher produces and markets a product. For the purposes of this workbook, I define desktop publishing as *the process of combining text and graphics into page layouts on a computer screen and outputting the pages on an imaging system so that they are ready for reproduction.*

In my opinion, the access that we have to affordable professional typesetting and page layout tools through the use of a personal computer qualifies as one of the most important developments in the history of the printed word. Many of us in the communications field have practiced this new technology, learned the rules, and can now fly with unprecedented freedom and creativity.

Unfortunately, desktop publishing has been oversold. "Just buy our products," say the ads, "and you can produce your own instant newsletters and brochures!" Like good writing, good design takes talent, skill, and experience—not just good hardware and software. That's why we are in business!

Since its introduction in the mid-eighties, desktop publishing software has revolutionized prepress print production. More recently, software for producing slides and overhead transparencies and multimedia software, which combines video and sound with text and graphics, have launched similar revolutions in the areas of spoken and audiovisual presentations. Even more recently, the exploding popularity of the World Wide Web has created entirely new opportunities to combine interactive writing, images, and sound. While this work requires some programming skills, Web authoring software is making it ever more accessible. Thus, for virtually every form of visual communication, planning, writing, and designing content have become a nearly seamless process. Using today's software, it's just another program on the computer to move from text to finished graphics—whether the final product will be printed material, an audiovisual presentation, or a Website.

As a result of this new technology, more and more clients expect to make a one-stop purchase—and if you can offer a one-stop service, you will get more business. It's as simple as that. By dealing with only one vendor—you—your buyer can save time and money.

Being able to handle all phases of the writing and production process is also helpful when clients want to share their files. For example, since I do both writing and desktop publishing, many clients have given me text files, using either disk or modem, and my task is to turn the text into a newsletter or brochure. Usually, editing and writing headlines and captions are part of the job. For one major corporation, I wrote short articles and sent them via modem to their staff designer. (Now, such a job would be delivered by E-mail.)

Today both writers and graphic designers *must* be computer literate. But that doesn't mean you should try to sell both writing and desktop or Webpage design unless you can do both well. For several years now, the business world has been bandying about a new buzzword: *virtual corporations.* Virtual corporations are temporary networks of companies and individuals brought together for a specific project.

When market opportunities appear, companies are finding it faster and less costly to partner with other businesses than to develop additional expertise in-house.

This is what home-based creative professionals have been doing all along. When we have a project that requires special skills, we draw on a group of trusted colleagues.

It's kind of neat to be in the vanguard of American business practice. Maybe some home-based writers and designers should be lecturing to Harvard M.B.A. candidates.

RESOURCES FOR GAINING SKILLS YOU DON'T NOW HAVE

If you want to become a professional writer but are not at that level now, accept the fact that gaining new skills will take serious effort and time. We are not talking about going back to college to earn a new degree or spending years learning on the job, but we *are* talking about steady concentration, practice, evaluation, and revision—a solid learning process.

There are ways to short-circuit traditional methods of mastering a craft to build the sense of authority you need in order to offer your services to the public. One is to focus very specifically on learning how to write only the type of thing that you most want to sell—or that is most often called for by the clients you serve. As you scan the many types of writing discussed in Chapter Three, ask yourself which of these you might learn to do. Once your skills in that area reach a professional level, you can concentrate on adding others.

I have a degree in journalism, I've taken endless workshops and seminars, and I've racked up some thirty years of experience as a writer, but there are still areas of writing—profitable ones—that I pass up when they are offered to me because I don't feel I do them well. Offering for sale only what you do well is professional. Offering to write "anything" and charging your clients for it is amateur behavior at best.

Classes and workshops

Looking for classes in writing? Try community colleges and evening adult schools first. Costs are minimal, and over a semester's time you will become familiar with the material, even if the instructor is not commercially oriented. You can also take a class to brush up on basics, such as grammar or computer techniques.

Your computer instructor will be happy to advise you on what equipment to buy. Also read computer catalogs and magazines. The only thing you must never do as a would-be home-based writer is show up at a computer store with your checkbook open, relying on the salesperson to equip you—unless, of course, you want to get rid of excess cash.

Once you've mastered the basics, advanced courses at a local professional school or university might be your next step. In the meantime, watch for short-term workshops and seminars. Some are priced in the Fortune 500 stratosphere, but others are more affordable. If you are not on mailing lists for such offerings, check with your library or computer store. And don't be too shy to ask professionals in the field—advertising copywriters, public relations practitioners, corporate communicators. These worthy souls get seminar mailings by the bushel and should be only too glad to pass them on to you.

Personal coaching and observation

Personal coaching and observation are like a self-administered internship. A local, noncompeting professional may let you observe for free and might even let you help in her office if you are willing to commit serious time to the project. This can be a good way to get feedback from a professional on your early efforts.

For an ongoing coaching arrangement, however, expect to pay a reasonable consulting fee. It's an uncommon, but totally natural way for someone in your situation to learn—by spending time, one-on-one, with someone who knows a lot about what you are studying. Approach people who are active in professional associations—a good indication of their desire to help others.

A variant on this idea, in the graphics area, is to visit places where the work you are interested in is being done. List the kinds of vendors you may be using—such as desktop publishing service bureaus, graphic film shops, lettershops, commercial printers, Website providers—and arrange to tour typical establishments. Some firms will give you a tour just because you ask for it. If that doesn't work, perhaps a regular customer could arrange for you to visit. To help understand the process, ask to be shown the steps a job takes as it goes through the shop. Ask to be shown examples of good and bad work and have the differences between the two explained. Ask what you, as a graphic designer, can do to make it easier for the vendor to serve you and to save money.

Volunteer projects

Get your feet wet as soon as possible by doing volunteer writing projects. You can learn much more from planning and completing a real project than from doing a made-up one—and you don't need professional-level skills to volunteer. Bob Brenner, a writer and publisher profiled at the end of Chapter Ten, used this technique. As a retired military officer with an engineering background, he volunteered for projects to teach himself to write and again served as a volunteer to learn desktop publishing.

Your church, club, or fraternal organization will be grateful for whatever you come up with. Then call on the network of professionals you are establishing to critique your work and find out how you could have made it better. Save your best volunteer efforts to start your personal sample file.

Reading and sample collecting

Read. Read. Read. The Bibliography in this book will start you off. Rely on periodicals to give you the "feel" of the specialty you want to master, reveal current trends, and point out major players. Rely on books to give you solid historical and technical grounding. Ask writers you respect what books and periodicals they find useful.

From the moment you decide to master your new skill, start collecting samples of work you like. As you gain more theory and experience, ask yourself why a particular piece works. Sometimes it's a good idea to collect samples of work you don't like, too. You can't help but hone your skills if you keep your eyes wide open.

TOWARD A BUSINESS PLAN

Success Worksheet One

Expand your capabilities.

Providing writing, desktop publishing, and Webpage design services from a single source will increase your business.

- Do you have the professional skills you need to sell your services as a home-based writer?

  _____

- If not, how do you intend to develop these skills? Learning options include classes, individual study, private consultant training, and practicing with volunteer projects. Can you think of other methods?

  _____

  _____

  _____

- Do you plan to be a desktop and/or Webpage designer, as well as a writer?

_____

- Do you currently have professional-level skills in these areas?

_____

- If not, how do you intend to develop these skills? Learning options include classes, individual study, private consultant training, and practicing with volunteer projects. Can you think of other methods?

_____

_____

_____

- If you do not want to develop additional skills, do you plan to locate designers with whom you can work? (Success Worksheet Seven in Chapter Two suggests ways to find reliable associates.)

_____

WHAT'S YOUR NEXT STEP? WAYS TO GET STARTED

The sooner you start making concrete plans for your new business, the sooner you will be a full-time home-based writer. If you are already or have at one time been self-employed, you must still make the transition to a new type of business. But you are far ahead of the game! For most of us who are accustomed to working for a regular paycheck, the transition is long and complex, often as wrenching as it is exhilarating. But careful planning can help. And that includes a written schedule projecting what steps you will take and when you will take them.

All of the profiles in this book sketch in the process by which the writer made his or her transition. See if one of them fits your situation.

Starting part-time vs. full-time

Some writers have started out by combining part-time regular employment and part-time freelancing. Others have established an "outsource" relationship with their present employers, continuing to do the same work, but as an independent contractor. I used commissioned sales to nudge me toward freelancing, and I was emboldened to leave selling when one of my printing clients offered me the equivalent of a half-time salary to carry out a specific writing project. That was the "nut" I knew I must have to pay the bills for the next few months.

Dividing your time between freelancing and regular employment probably takes its biggest toll on your marketing efforts. It's hard (but possible) to push into new market areas and follow up every lead, when four or more hours a day are committed elsewhere. For this reason, some writers take the instant full-time plunge, relying on savings or a loan or another family member's income to survive.

Financing

The talented director Spike Lee is reported to have financed his early films on credit cards. That takes guts or maybe desperation, but I don't recommend it for commercial writers. A more conventional option is to borrow on your home or to liquidate or borrow on other assets—but consider this option carefully and use it as a last resort. Typically, writers finance their start-up costs from savings, the income of a spouse, or help from other family members.

Getting some money coming in

I believe it is far better to get some small amount of real business income trickling in as soon as possible—income you can (and probably must) use to pay the light bill or the dentist—than to draw on a savings account temporarily fattened by a mortgage loan. That borrowed money isn't real. You didn't scramble and sweat for it, and it's more likely than earned money to go for an elegant oak desk or an elaborate capability brochure. Wait to buy those refinements with income from your new career. Your business will be a lot healthier for it!

Health insurance (and peace of mind)

If you are in reasonably good health, giving up your employee benefits is nothing like the big deal many salaried people fear when they consider self-employment. You can replace all your necessary benefits at relatively affordable rates. It may be a jolt to your budget at first, but I've done it and so have millions of others.

Health insurance policies, including traditional fee-for-service plans with an annual deductible, preferred provider plans, and health maintenance organizations, are widely available to individuals. Your one-person business may also qualify for a business health insurance plan (mine does). A major medical plan, covering only catastrophic costs, is another option. You may get better rates or better coverage by joining a professional organization that offers group insurance. Individual vision-care and dental plans are also available. Be aware that insurance companies are rated by standard industry ratings and by consumer advocates such as *Consumer Reports,* and check before you buy.

Until recently, if you or your spouse or child had a serious health problem, individual coverage might be denied you—a cruel reality in this richest of all societies. Federal legislation to make health insurance portable has changed that for many Americans. If you are currently employed and covered, check with your provider. Check also to see if your state has an assigned risk pool.

Disability insurance

You probably have life insurance or own some assets that would at least partially provide for your family if you should die suddenly. But what about the far more likely possibility that you may be injured or ill and unable to maintain your customary income? Disability insurance will help you through such a period, and, depending on the coverage you select, it can also help retrain you for a new career, should that become necessary—or even help care for you if you are totally disabled.

A very wide range of options is available, including credit card or mortgage loan insurance, so do some research and talk to several agents before you decide. While you don't want to be "insurance poor," and you can't protect yourself against everything, a reasonable amount of disability coverage will give you and your family protection and peace of mind—and rates for writers are among the lowest.

TOWARD A BUSINESS PLAN

Success Worksheet Two

Have a transition plan.

A carefully planned transition to your full-time home-based business will give you a solid start.

- How will you make the transition from outside employment to a full-time home-based business?
  __ Part-time employment, part-time freelancing?
  __ "Outsourcing" work for your present employer?
  __ Living on savings or a loan as you build up your business?
  __ Living on someone else's income as you build up your business?
  __ Other options? _____

  _____

- Discuss the plan you have selected.

  _____

  _____

- How will you replace employee benefits such as health and disability insurance?

  _____

  _____

LIFE AS A HOME-BASED FREELANCER

The following worksheet enumerates key benefits that have drawn many creative people into freelance careers. But every coin has two sides. Negative aspects of freelance life have kept other writers from starting their own home businesses—or have convinced them to abandon their efforts at self-employment. Ironically, what some people view as a benefit, others may perceive as a liability.

In order to evaluate your own motivations and potential problem areas as a freelance writer, checkmark the benefits you find most attractive and the liabilities that most concern you.

TOWARD A BUSINESS PLAN

Success Worksheet Three

Understand your motivations.

The benefits of freelance life must outweigh the liabilities for you if you are to succeed in a home writing business.

- Which of these benefits appeal to you most strongly? (Check all that apply.)

  __ Independence.

  __ Opportunities to earn more than a predetermined amount.

  __ Convenience—no commuting.

  __ Control of your time.

  __ Control of which clients you serve.

  __ Control of what kinds of business you go after.

  __ Control of your own ethics and business standards.

__ Integration of your business and personal life.

__ Freedom from office politics and gossip.

__ Opportunities for family involvement.

__ Opportunities to do personal creative projects.

- Which of these liabilities are likely to trouble you? (Check all that apply.)

  __ Having to be a "self-starter" every day.

  __ Uncertain income, cash-flow problems.

  __ No paid benefits.

  __ Having to market your own services.

  __ Having to be aggressive in collecting money.

  __ Work space that may be inadequate or lacking in privacy.

  __ No time off without financial loss.

  __ Difficulty getting credit.

  __ Having to do everything yourself. No executive perks.

  __ Loneliness.

  __ May have to take whatever work comes in the door.

  __ Family members may exert a negative or disruptive influence.

  __ Unpredictable work schedules may disrupt family and personal plans.

  __ May have less time for personal creative projects than when you were on salary.

- Do the benefits outweigh the liabilities for you?

  _____

- How can you overcome the liabilities you have identified?

  _____

  _____

  _____

  _____

  _____

GETTING SUPPORT ON THE HOME FRONT

Family members often make significant financial contributions to the start-up of a home-based writing business, but there is another kind of family support that is much harder to measure yet even more critical to your business's success. That support is "buying into the idea," caring about your dream, hoping you will succeed, being willing to endure inconvenience on your behalf.

There's a hierarchy to this kind of support. Some of it is nice to have. Some of it is just about essential. Your parents, siblings, grown children, or close friends may not share your enthusiasm for risking your financial and professional future on a home-based writing venture. That's too bad, but you can survive without their approval. Do not—I repeat, *do not*—fight or argue with them. Instead, while you are in your fledgling stage as an entrepreneur, avoid discussing your business with them. Get professional advice instead from people who are truly informed about your industry and who know that a well-run home-based writing business is a viable way to make a living.

In most cases, your success will bring these special folks around. Very likely they just had no mental model for what you planned to do and saw you stepping off into an abyss. When your business is running smoothly, risk showing them where and how you work and what you produce. Their praise will be among the sweetest you receive.

Now for the really hard part.

If your spouse or the significant other with whom you share your home is actively against your plans, you have a much more serious problem. To a great (and unavoidable) extent, a home business is a family business, and as you make your inevitable mistakes, that person's daily criticism and fault-finding can damage your self-confidence and even drive the two of you apart.

There are many excellent guidebooks on relationships and communication, as well as many supportive third parties—from friends to pastors to psychologists. Take this problem seriously and use all the help you can get. Remember that for many entrepreneurs running a home business is a deep source of joy. So can it be for you—and for those you love!

TOWARD A BUSINESS PLAN

Success Worksheet Four

Make sure your players want to be on the team.

Personal support from those closest to you can spell success or failure in a home-based business—especially one involving creative work.

- Which people are part of your vital inner circle? Do they support your plans?

- If any members of your inner circle do not support your plans, what will it take for you to obtain their support?

- If you cannot obtain their support, can you succeed without it? If so, how?

HOW TO USE THE WORKSHEETS TO BUILD YOUR BUSINESS PLAN

Success Worksheets accompany each chapter of this book—thirty-two worksheets in all. As you complete them, you will be gathering virtually everything you need to write your business plan.

I suggest you tear the worksheets out of the book or make copies of them. Then complete each worksheet in turn, using additional paper if necessary, and file them in a loose-leaf binder. As you move toward starting your business, you will begin to collect all kinds of information—ideas relating to the writing that you want to do; marketing ideas and information about possible clients; specifications, sources, and cost of equipment and software you may need; income and expense projections; regulations that apply to starting a business in your city and state; tax information.

Add it to your notebook. If the notebook begins to overflow, start a second one or set up some file folders. If you are meeting regularly with a mentor or colleagues—a procedure I strongly suggest—make your notebook and the worksheets you are currently completing the basis of that day's discussion. Starting a business takes time and planning, and these steps will help you stay on course.

Writing Your Business Plan

Many writers open and operate their businesses without a written business plan, but no one opens a business without a mental plan. Without a plan you wouldn't know what to sell or to whom—let alone what to charge. A written business plan is a normal requirement for a business loan, and no doubt that's why many entrepreneurs develop one. (Good thing, too, because producing them sometimes provides employment for writers.) The reality is, however, that in a creative start-up like yours, you will probably not be applying for an initial business loan. So why write a business plan?

No one should have to tell a writer the value of writing something down. Writing forces you to think it through, clarify it, put it in order, eliminate conflicts and contradictions. When completed, your strategies for success, based on an analysis of the market and your business's strengths and weaknesses—along with your tactics and timing for implementing each strategy. You will be doing this planning as you use the Success Worksheets throughout this book.

Another vital aspect of your busines plan is your strategy for *using it* as a working document. For establishing a timetable and adjusting it to keep it realistic. For taking out what doesn't work and adding new elements that do. It's your strategy for believing in the plan, living by it, and updating it on a regular basis—every six months or oftener for the first two years and at least annually thereafter. This plan is for *you*—not for your mentor, your spouse, your former boss, a loan officer, or a teacher who will give you a good grade. It should be your most useful business tool.

That said, I want to stress that a business plan is not too fluid or too personal to share. It's written and clearly organized so that you can share it and get feedback on it—especially from your mentor and any other trusted colleagues. As Napoleon Hill pointed out decades ago in his classic business success book, *Think and Grow Rich* (1937), sharing your ideas and plans with what he called your "Master Mind group" sharpens your focus and increases your commitment.

What should a business plan contain?

At this point, obviously you are not yet ready to write your business plan. You will be invited to return to these pages when you have completed the book. But reading this outline now will provide a valuable overview—a kind of long-range guide.

There is no set pattern or length for a written business plan, but there is general agreement on the topics it should cover. I like this seven-part formulation:

1. *The executive summary.* Though often written last, this comes first for the convenience of busy readers. Keep it under three pages. It contains your mission statement and a brief description of your business—what services you will perform for what clients. This is covered in Chapters One, Two, and Three, and further refined throughout the book.

2. *The management plan.* This section covers personnel—your resumé and those of any other key staff. Explain important areas of responsibility. If appropriate, include one or more associates who can provide design or other services to increase your business opportunities. If resumés are lengthy, summarize them and include the full documents in an appendix. If additional training is a key part of your plan, explain it here. This section also covers your basic management systems. (See Chapters One, Two, Four, and Ten.)

3. *The organizational plan.* This section covers business structure—the way your business is licensed and organized. It also covers your office setup—including major equipment and software—as well as maintenance plans and plans for obtaining outside services. Finally, it should include your timetable for get-

ting your business started and the initial phases you expect to go through. (See Chapters One, Four, Five, Six, and Ten.)

4. *The service and product plan.* What services and products do you plan to sell? Describe them here, pointing out special features and discussing pricing. (See Chapters Two, Three, Seven, and Nine.)

5. *The marketing plan.* This section summarizes the results of your marketing research. What is the demand for your services and the outlook for the future? What is your competition? What are your strengths and weaknesses in entering the market? How do you plan to get the business you're seeking? Describe your procedures for marketing and selling. (See Chapters Seven and Eight.)

6. *The financial plan.* This key part of your business plan includes the following:
   - A balance sheet showing your business's assets and liabilities
   - An analysis of your start-up costs and your anticipated sources of funds
   - Anticipated monthly sales and expense figures for at least the first year
   - Monthly profit-and-loss statements for at least the first year
   - A monthly cash-flow statement for the first year, showing whether you will have enough cash on hand to meet expenses and how cash will be utilized
   - Your personal financial statement, showing all your personal assets and liabilities as well as your net worth (See Chapters One, Five, Six, Seven, Eight, Nine, and Ten.)

7. *The forecasting plan.* Here you explain your plans for keeping your business on course. On what do you base your forecast of anticipated sales and expenses? Do you have contingency plans? When will you review and revise your Business Plan? (See Chapters One, Seven, Nine, and Ten.)

What format to use

A business plan can be as brief as twenty-five or thirty pages, but many run much longer. Business plan software is available and should be especially helpful as you develop the financial section of your plan. (See Source Directory.) Books are also devoted to this subject (see Bibliography), providing suggested formats. Again, they're especially useful for presenting your financial data. The plan should have a cover page and a table of contents. Detailed resumés and reports (such as a marketing survey) are often included in an appendix.

Jack Fehr
Jack Fehr Associates, Shelburne, Vermont

Escaping to a New Life

In 1988, between jobs and fed up with city living, former sportswriter and marketer Jack Fehr "escaped" from New York with his wife and three young daughters to a small town in Vermont. He soon found work in corporate communications with a Vermont insurance firm, but, two years later, downsizing threatened his position. After some careful planning, Fehr decided to open his own home-based writing business.

"During my first year," he says, "I had a variety of clients by using my New York contacts. I did a statistical newsletter for Avon Products, a white paper for Simon & Schuster, and a by-lined article for an insurance company. But I wasn't marketing myself very well, and I thought we were going to starve when my severance package ran out."

To find new clients, Fehr read "everything under the sun." He developed a mailing list of senior public relations executives, later realizing that most were government affairs specialists and not potential clients. He also targeted small local businesses. "I was calling on people who didn't have advertising budgets," he explains, "telling them I could give them agency-quality work for half the price. That just didn't ring true.

"Another mistake I made," Fehr recalls, "was trying to be everything to everybody. I claimed I could do speeches, AV scripts, anything—not realizing there are specialists who do each of these. I was going to be a generalist to Fortune 500 companies. But the more I decided that, the more I kept getting dragged into insurance expertise. After about a year, I decided I'd better accept it. Then everything just started clicking."

Now focusing on large films, Fehr does ghostwriting for executives, writes articles for trade journals and company magazines, and produces such nonadvertising marketing materials as capability brochures, descriptive product pieces, and annual reports.

Growing his business, he has branched out from insurance into the related fields of personal finance and mutual funds and has begun writing consumer articles for single-sponsor magazines—published for clients by insurance and investment firms.

After briefly considering desktop publishing, Fehr decided writing was more profitable for him. He brings in a designer when he needs one and has the designer bill the client directly.

Fehr enjoys working at home and having control of his time. "I put in forty-plus hours a week, but twenty hours might be on a rainy weekend," he points out. "If I've got an article to write and the temperature is ninety degrees, I'd just as soon jump in the lake with my kids and write the article at night."

With his flexible schedule, Fehr has found extra time for fatherhood, coaching his daughters in basketball. "They're teenagers now," he observes. "They'll be going soon. It won't be that long." The former sportswriter has also volunteered for other coaching jobs and admits he loves doing it.

"I reached a point about four years into my business where I was making what I made when I was a manager in a corporation, and I haven't gone much higher than that," he observes. "I think I'm just not willing to put in that much time right now, and that's a freedom I wouldn't have if I were still working for someone else."

Fehr stresses that the online revolution has been a research boom for him, living as he does in a small Vermont town far from major libraries. "I haven't stepped into a library in two years," he says. He also has become heavily involved in CompuServe's many communications forums, where he has made friends with other professional writers. He's tried America Online, but says, "as a writer, CompuServe is more valuable to me."

Having gone through a lean period a few years ago when several stable clients disappeared, Fehr refuses to neglect his marketing. "I had been working with so many faceless people that I went out on the road to Boston and New York and New Jersey. It takes six months to develop leads into prospects and into clients.

"Now," he continues, "even if I've had a 12-hour day, I'll spend another hour and type up letters to a few people and send them some samples." A Webpage is not in his marketing plans. "It's still like the Wild West out there [the Internet] and I'm not sure how anybody would get to me or what it would do," he says.

Fehr admits he "started out learning by trial and error," but says he has "a much better idea now about how to approach people who buy corporate freelance writing."

He also advises: "When you're marketing yourself, you can't take anything personally. If someone is not receptive, it just means they don't have time to be receptive today, but they might be receptive tomorrow. I've had people who refused to answer my calls contact me later with a job. I've had others tell me they'd love to hire me and I never got any work from them. I've given up trying to understand it. Now I just go with the flow."

CHAPTER TWO

WHAT WILL YOU DO AND FOR WHOM?

Building on Your Strengths and Teaming with Other Professionals

WHY DEFINE YOURSELF?

"I can write anything" is the brave cry some writers issue to the world. Willing to tackle any work they can find, these fledgling entrepreneurs assume that a broad focus will bring them more business than a narrow one. Not so.

Dig deeper and you will probably discover that such home business operators have not done their homework. They don't know what they are best at or what they really want to do. Don't let this happen to you. An unfocused person is hard to remember and does not inspire confidence.

I think the real reason we creative types often fudge when asked to define ourselves is that we don't want to be locked into one definition. Many times we have a hidden agenda. The person writing a press release secretly wants to be a screenwriter. The person editing a computer manual would rather be creating an interactive fiction game. And why not? Dreams are what keep us alive. Moreover, your home-based business is an ideal way to bring your daily work closer to your dream occupation—if you do it in small, carefully focused steps.

Developing a direction for your business will take time, and over the years your emphasis may change. The important thing is to start *somewhere*—stake out a claim and start working it. If you don't find gold, try another claim.

The Writer's Essential Desk Reference (Writer's Digest Books 1991), a volume I highly recommend to both writers and desktop publishers, offers an exercise that can help you as you begin to ask, "What will I do, and for whom?"

Take a conscious look around you today at written copy, wherever you are, beginning with what's right in front of your eyes—a calendar that has photo captions; an advertisement on the back of a cereal box; a button or T-shirt with a cute slogan on it—and continue throughout the day, wherever you are. Don't overlook the flyers posted on telephone poles by a local theater company, signs on the backs of benches or high up on billboards, and your own mail, especially your direct (also called "junk") mail.

Do you see the point? As *The Desk Reference* suggests, all of this material was painstakingly written, designed, and prepared for production by someone—possibly a freelancer. Maybe it could be you.

MY SEARCH FOR A BUSINESS IDENTITY

When I first started thinking about freelancing, I was making a professional transition from higher education public relations and publications into printing sales. As a sideline, I dreamed up a business called Logos Unlimited, designing logos and business letterheads. My service was focused—too focused, as it turned out.

Of course, I had a wonderful logo for my new business, with gold-foiled business cards and letterhead that I could ill afford (I'm still using up that clay-colored letterhead for scrap paper). As a new part-time freelancer, I knew I lacked the experience and credibility to market high-ticket corporate identity programs. And, to be honest, I also lacked the confidence. So I went after more modest clients—new businesses and nonprofit agencies, as well as individuals—and I received quite a few logo assignments.

The problem was that a new business needs one logo and one set of stationery and maybe a flyer, and for a while, at least, that's it. What I had staked out for myself was endless marketing for a fairly inexpensive product with little repeat business—from clients who were very ego-involved in the product, who had little to spend, and whose credit was often impossible to check. It's true that some designers make this type of work pay handsomely—but they usually aim at higher-paying clients.

Another early business idea of mine that fizzled on the launchpad (even though Logos Unlimited had designed a clever logo for it) was Growth Greetings. The greeting cards I envisioned were virtually unavailable in the late seventies—cards to celebrate non-traditional events like receiving a divorce, losing weight, getting sober, or having a spiritual experience. I still think it was a good idea, but working at it part-time, I lacked the funds to print cards in quantity and the know-how to develop distribution—to say nothing of the confidence to go out and get financial backing.

A friend who was a Ph.D. historian by training, Ashleigh Brilliant, did all of these things successfully when he established his offbeat greeting-card line, Pot Shots. Ashleigh passionately wanted to get what he then called his "unpoemed titles" out into the world—and he has done so! His firm in Santa Barbara, California, is now known as Brilliant Enterprises. I wasn't that passionate about either my logos or my greeting cards, but these ventures did teach me two things.

First, I learned to take the grim truism that *"most new businesses fail during the first year"* with a very large grain of salt. Those "failures" often represent a determined entrepreneur learning his or her craft, making a beginner's blunders, and bouncing back with new and better ideas. Colleges and universities are now offering theoretical courses in "being an entrepreneur," but I believe the best training is your own careful observations and inevitable mistakes when *your* capital is at risk.

The second thing I learned was the importance of identifying a market that I knew how to reach—one that spent serious money, paid on time, and had an ongoing need for my services. As a printing sales rep, I was selling to corporate and hospital communicators—people I already had a lot in common with. It was only natural that I turn to them for freelance work. At first I did whatever came to hand—articles for employee magazines, press releases, brochure and flyer designs, product literature, newsletters, workbooks, even logos.

With such assignments I managed to survive, and my list of corporate and hospital clients began to sound impressive, but I felt fragmented. It took me about two years to realize that newsletters were what I wanted to specialize in. In the first place, I like newsletters. I will always marvel at the persuasive power these homely, unobtrusive little publications have when they are done well. Newsletters called on both my writing and designing skills, giving me an advantage over freelancers who don't do both. Because they repeat regularly, I could spend less time marketing. They also matched my previous experience in designing and selling two- and three-color printing. And they let me do what I do well—identify and fit in with my clients as a part of their teams.

Before I left California for Florida in 1994, newsletters accounted for about three-quarters of my work. Writing the first edition of this book brought me closer to my lifetime interest in writing fiction and nonfiction, which drew me to a writing career in the first place. Today I have been able to scale back and undertake a long-planned fiction project, while I develop new skills in Webpage authoring.

FINDING YOUR BUSINESS FOCUS

As you begin your new home-based business, you will probably have a similar journey, defining and redefining what it is you want to do and for whom. Fortunately, some techniques are available to speed up the process.

You may have already done some freelance writing that can provide a starting point—or you may want to get away from those assignments and turn to others. The key is to find the types of writing projects that you feel comfortable with and are interested in. This will help you answer the question, *"What will I do?"*

At the same time, you need to identify the industries or subject areas that you would enjoy working in, such as banking, entertainment, real estate, medicine, local government, food service, or fashion. This will help you answer the question, *" . . . and for whom?"* Your client may be a business that provides goods or services in a certain area, an agency that provides services to such businesses, or a firm that produces printed or electronic material in the same field. You can serve all three.

If you choose an industry or field with care, you will be able to write well in these areas and enjoy your work over the long haul. Equally important, you will be on the same wavelength with your clients. They will feel easy with you and trust you with their ideas and goals.

Using your education

Review your educational background, including subjects you have studied but have not used in your work. For example, you may have studied biology in college, then switched to communications and wound up doing public relations for a government agency. If you still have a scientific bent, your background in biology can open doors to writing for laboratories, hospitals, and medical groups. You don't have to master the subject, but it's important that you have a feel for it.

Make a list of the subjects you have studied, including short courses you have taken as an adult, and see what fields of writing they suggest. Did you do any writing as a student? If you enjoyed editing your yearbook, for example, you might also enjoy putting together community directories.

Using your work experience

Even more important than your education is your work experience. Your most recent experience is the most viable, but go all the way back. I had done medical writing early in my higher education public relations career. Some twenty years later I trotted out those skills, very profitably, for freelance clients. (And the new edition of the medical dictionary I had once paid $15 for now cost me $75.)

Make a list of the industries in which you have worked and any tasks you have done that relate to writing. Have you had experience proofreading, designing or taking surveys, writing reports, preparing marketing materials? Write them down. They may help you focus on an appropriate specialty or an industry where you will find clients.

Using your personal, family, and volunteer experience

When they are establishing their expertise, entrepreneurs often overlook areas where they have not had formal training or work experience. Do you speak a second language? If so, you have an edge with certain clients. Are you a member of an ethnic group? Special business or social organizations where you can meet clients may be open to you. Are you a member of a minority? A certain percentage of federal contracts must go to minority firms. Seeking this business requires a minority business certification. (Unfortunately, the federal government doesn't consider women a minority, although some states do.) Do you have a disability or a past experience that gives you knowledge and a special ability to work with clients who serve these populations?

How about your interests? Did you ever study music or play in a local group? If so, you can talk to music stores, bands, nightclubs. Did you grow up helping out in your father's restaurant? Then you are a food service insider. Your experience editing or designing your church newsletter, writing press releases for a battered women's shelter, or preparing handouts for your garden society also give you inside knowledge. In addition to the practical experience, you already have a special camaraderie with religious, social service, and horticultural clients.

Exploring new areas

Now is a good time to start building expertise in areas that have long intrigued you but in which you have little expertise. Writing skills are needed in every corner of our society. If you are fascinated by the worlds of sports or politics, if you would like to help the homeless, or if you would like to hang out with theater folk—whatever your interest—you can build up your knowledge through the learning techniques presented in Chapter One for improving your professional skills. These techniques include classes and workshops, special-interest organizations, personal interviews and observation, reading, and sample-collecting.

Your initial contact may be on a volunteer or low-paying basis—especially in nonprofit areas and highly competitive "glamour" areas—but you will find that with a careful study of the territory, your freelance skills can take you almost anywhere you want to go.

Florida writer Steve Morrill, profiled in Chapter Six, disagrees with the common wisdom: "Do volunteer work. Write for free just to get clips [samples]." He insists: "Assuming you're capable of writing professional work, you may as well get paid, even if it's only a nickel or ten cents a word."

START WITH A REALITY CHECK

If you know—or can arrange an introduction to—people who are doing the kind of work you are interested in doing, ask for a little of their time or offer to take them to lunch for a brief reality check. Does it really work out, being a home-based freelancer? This query from new or potential entrepreneurs is very familiar to established home-based writers. We did the same thing when we were starting out, and when we are not too busy, most of us are happy to advise beginners.

Find out how established freelancers got started, what kind of work they do, where they get clients, and, if possible, what they charge. Be tactful. Since these people may eventually be your competitors, they may be less than forthcoming with specific details. And be cautious about believing everything you're told. Your mentor may be having a bad day and feel negative about his work. Or he might decide to discourage competition by telling you the field is too crowded. Don't base important decisions on the input from only one or two individuals.

TOWARD A BUSINESS PLAN

Success Worksheet Five

Build on your past skills and experience.

You already have knowledge and experience. Use them to help you focus your writing business.

- What education have you had relating to writing? Consider both the fields you have trained for and the types of writing you have studied.

- What interested you the most?

- What job experiences have you had relating to writing? Consider both the industries you have worked in and the types of work you have done.

- What interested you the most?

- What personal, family, or volunteer experiences have you had that may translate into writing specialties? Again, consider both the fields you were in (for example, sports, religion, community government) and the types of work you have done.

- What interested you the most?

- What other types of writing would you like to do? What other industries or fields would you like to be involved in?

- Based on your knowledge, experience, and interest, what could you specialize in as a writer?

- What can you do to gain the knowledge and skills you lack?

SETTING UP RELATIONSHIPS WITH OTHER SUPPLIERS AND ASSOCIATES

If you are not proficient in desktop publishing and online design, you may decide to master the missing skills—or you may not. But in either case, you will soon be dealing with some clients who want to buy these additional services. You can leave them on their own to find a designer, running the risk that a new vendor will try to snatch away the whole job. Or you can set up relationships with competent vendors you can trust and offer their services in combination with your own. It's well worth the effort for the marketing advantage you will achieve by being a "full-service" supplier.

While you're thinking about other professionals, don't overlook the benefits of having a cooperative relationship with one or more colleagues who have capabilities similar to your own. Sure, they're competitors, but if you're sick, experiencing an overload, or facing a family emergency, a trusted colleague could be a godsend.

TOWARD A BUSINESS PLAN

Success Worksheet Six

Find reliable associates.

This list will become one of your most valuable databases. You'll need several dependable vendors to call on in case your first choice isn't available or isn't quite right for a particular job.

- Referrals are your best source when seeking reliable associates. Check with clients and with other writers. Check with desktop publishers and Webpage designers; advertising, marketing, and public relations agencies; photographers; printers and publishers; desktop service bureaus; and Website providers.

List some sources you might draw upon:

_____

_____

■ Professional associations and directories can put you in touch with vendors, but you will have to verify their reliability.

List some you might check with:

_____

_____

■ When you see work you admire, find out who did it and the vendor's price range. Can you think of any such sources to investigate?

_____

_____

■ Advertising can connect you with needed services—both responding to ads and placing them. Don't overlook Internet and online bulletin board postings, which are normally free.

Where would you look for such ads?

_____

_____

■ If you are placing an ad, what kind might you run? Where? When? What would it cost?

_____

_____

■ In selecting your associate vendors, here's a checklist of factors to consider:

_____ Quality of work.

_____ Experience and interests. Do they fit your clients?

_____ Price range. Is it comparable to yours?

_____ Business style. Is it similar to yours? Are they comfortable with formal or informal agreements? Do they have similar policies in handling deadlines, revisions, extra expenses?

_____ Reliability. Check references; try a few small jobs.

_____ Ethical standards. An ethical associate will not steal your client, cheat you, or automatically blame you if there is a problem. What is the vendor's professional reputation?

Handling a disaster

When a disaster occurs on a job—regardless of which vendor was at fault—never, never blame your associate when dealing with a client. The only professional thing to do is to present a unified front. After all, you agreed to team up, and one of you told the client that the other was reliable.

Privately, discuss the problem and your available options with your associate and identify points of negotiation you can agree upon. Then meet with the client, define the problem clearly, negotiate any financial or other adjustments, and concentrate on getting the job done right as soon as possible.

Bidding and billing

When bidding on jobs together, there are basically two ways to present your estimates—as two separate bids or as one combined bid. The same applies to billing—two separate bills or one bill covering both services.

If you see yourself as a one-person operation and have no desire to expand, you will probably be more comfortable with the former. Some writers would rather not worry about collecting from the client in time to pay a subcontractor or collecting any taxes due for the subcontractor's portion of the work.

But there is significant money to be made in buying a service or product at one price and selling it for more. That's what business is usually about! Many corporate writers take advantage of this opportunity to increase their incomes. If you expand beyond your own capacities, you will often be hiring subcontractors, and it is certainly fair for you to profit by marking up their prices.

Working with the client

You can handle all dealings with the client yourself, even though the bidding and billing may be handled separately, or you can introduce your associate to the client and have the associate deliver his portion of the job directly.

As a rule of thumb, keeping your associate in the background is best for maintaining strong, personal client relationships—but it's not always best for every job. Some clients want to give you an assignment and receive back a finished product with as little in-between contact as possible. Don't bother bringing your associate to meet this customer. Other clients want to be involved in every step of the job, playing a major part in the creative process and often waiting to see the product before they decide whether it's really what they want. If such a client's instructions to the other vendor are complex, subtle, or vague, you will save time and needless aggravation by bringing your associate into this picture early.

It's your *client*

However you handle the details, remember that the work is being done for *your* client and you want his or her entire experience to be pleasant and profitable. Stay in touch and in control. Make sure your associate's work is of the style and quality expected. Keep track of costs and see to it that the final bill is as agreed upon. If not, make sure your client has agreed to any added costs. When the job is being done for your associate's client, show both of them the same respect.

TOWARD A BUSINESS PLAN

Success Worksheet Seven

Increase your business through joint ventures, but guard against potential problems.

With the proper safeguards and a cooperative spirit, working with other independent professionals can help your business grow.

- Does the idea of teaming with other professionals fit your business plans— assuming the other vendor will provide skills you lack?

  _____

  _____

- Would you be willing to use a colleague to handle an overload on your own work?

  _____

  _____

- What kinds of business might you be better able to obtain if you offer more than writing services alone? Examples might be newsletters, catalogs, Web-pages, product launches, and direct-mail packages.

  _____

  _____

- What services might you require?

  ____ Graphic design—desktop publishing, Webpages, other?

  _____

  ____ Illustration—realistic, cartoon style, other?

  _____

  ____ Photography—portraits, catalog shots, news photos, other?

  _____

  ____ Computer services—database, Website providing, other?

  _____

  ____ Marketing, Internet marketing, marketing research

  ____ Media relations

  ____ Special events planning and production

  ____ Lists

  ____ Printing, duplicating

  ____ Addressing, mailing

  ____ Other services _____

- What could go wrong in a joint venture, and how can you protect yourself? In the examples below, I've suggested some steps to take. To be safe, think about this in advance.

- Vendor's work is substandard.

  ____ Check vendor's work samples carefully and discuss expectations.

  ____ Check on job progress.

  ____ Other? _____

- Vendor misses a deadline.

  ____ Stay on top of the job at all times.

  ____ If warranted, build a late penalty into the agreement.

  ____ Other? _____

■ Vendor becomes unable to do the job.

_____ Have a backup in mind.

_____ Other? _____

■ Client and/or vendor disagrees over fees.

_____ Put fees in writing in advance.

_____ If, during the job, changes occur or are requested that will affect final costs, bring this to the attention of all concerned promptly.

_____ Other? _____

■ Dissatisfied client threatens legal action.

_____ Carry liability insurance.

_____ Use vendors who carry liability insurance.

_____ Look into mediation services.

_____ Know of an attorney experienced in business law and check his references in advance.

_____ Other? _____

■ Vendor steals your client.

_____ Reach an agreement with the vendor on this matter in advance.

_____ Stay close to the client throughout the job.

_____ Meet with the client and try to win back her business.

_____ Let other independent writers know that this vendor is not to be trusted.

_____ Other? _____

Success Worksheet Eight

Set up joint work agreements.

When you team up with another vendor, be sure to establish an agreement about each party's responsibility and liability.

- It's preferable to have joint work agreements in writing. At minimum, you should discuss and reach consensus on key issues. Here's a checklist to make sure the most important issues are covered.

- What is the relationship of the vendors to each other? Contractor, subcontract, or or co-equal? If you're doing a job, whose job is it?

  _____

- Apart from this joint venture, would it be acceptable for the vendors to work independently for the same client or clients? Put another way, what would "stealing a client" mean in terms of this relationship?

  _____

- How will fees be set?

  _____

- What are the responsibilities of each vendor? For a long-term relationship, this could be a general statement. For an individual job, it could be a specific list of tasks.

  _____

  _____

- What are the deadlines each vendor must meet? What is the penalty for not meeting a deadline?

  _____

  _____

- What are the legal and financial responsibilities of each vendor?

  _____

  _____

- How will job-incurred expenses be handled?

  _____

  _____

- How will invoicing and collection of payments be handled?

  _____

  _____

- What it the period of time covered by the agreement?

  _____

  _____

- How may the relationship be terminated?

  _____

  _____

Joy Mieko White
InfoTeam, Inc., Lake Forest, California

Meeting a Need

"Engineering firms pooled their resources to build Hoover Dam because one firm couldn't do it alone, so why couldn't we do the same thing as communications professionals?"

This was the idea buzzing in Joy Mieko White's brain during the mid-1980s, as she struggled to put together teams of writers, illustrators, and word processors for CalComp, a large computer hardware manufacturer. Because of a hiring freeze at the southern California firm, White, as technical documentation manager, was forced to call on independent contractors. "I had to spend days trying to find people who could work together," she says. "It was ridiculous. I felt that I should have been able to place just one call."

White began thinking about starting her own business, and she and her husband "worked lean and mean" putting a year's worth of net pay into their credit union. In 1986 she "took the big leap out of the corporate world."

Since White's background includes a communications degree, teaching credentials, and two years of high school teaching, she initially hung out her shingle as a seminar broker. At night she taught technical writing at the University of California, Irvine, and local colleges. She also purchased an IBM PC system and began developing desktop publishing skills.

"To keep the business alive, I moved into technical writing," White recalls, "but as I started meeting other freelancers and understanding their capabilities, I finally acted on my real goal."

In 1989, the year her daughter was born, White refined her procedures, researched laws and regulations, studied the market, hand-picked ten writing and desktop publishing professionals, and invited them to become part of her organization. All but one signed up.

On Valentine's Day 1990, she incorporated InfoTeam, a consortium of writers, editors, and workgroup publishers. "What a valentine!" she says.

Per a written agreement, all members must be in business and must satisfy a twenty-point set of criteria. Any member may withdraw or be asked to leave at any time. White handles most marketing and sales, calling on the technical skills of other members as needed, and earns a 10 percent commission. If another member brings in a sale, that person earns the commission. InfoTeam charges 15 percent for overhead.

The consortium members are encouraged to continue serving their own clients. "If InfoTeam provides more than 80 percent of any consortium member's livelihood, that person would be viewed legally as an employee," White explains.

The consortium holds monthly teaming meetings to share technical expertise, make plans, and talk things over. Each project has its own teaming agreement, which details the work expected, fees, and a timetable. Each project also has a manager—a job that rotates between White and several consortium members.

Since White's mother is Japanese and part of her heritage is Native American, she applied for and received federal certification as a minority business owner along with certification as a woman business owner in California. "Being a minority or woman-owned firm doesn't get you the job. You have to prove your technical skills," she stresses. The certifications, however, may have helped her firm earn several large contracts.

After six years in business, InfoTeam has settled into a combination of government and commercial high-tech work. Under a government contract, White's firm provides marketing collateral material for minority-owned firms in southern California. Commercial jobs often involve manuals or trade journal articles. The consortium has tightened down from ten to five members, drawing on independents for illustrations and specialty expertise.

Three years ago White seriously considered moving her business into an outside office, but new computer technology has made the move unnecessary.

She has added a complete voicemail system with a fax-back capability. E-mail enables her to send graphic files and even complete manuals back and forth to clients. "We have three PC systems in the house now," she says, "and we're thinking about putting up our own Website."

Corporate downsizing and the bankruptcy of Orange County, California, hit White's business community hard. As a result, she says, "We find a lot more independents out there, working for very low fees." However, when she hears, "I can get this technical writer down the street for ten dollars an hour," her firm's track record helps her frame a response.

"Yes," she tells the prospect, "but he's probably looking for full-time work. If something better comes along, who will finish your job?"

As the local employment scene improves, White has modified her marketing to turn some of the newly emerging permanent positions into contract jobs for InfoTeam. She also receives referrals from brokers with services similar to hers.

"They always say, 'You seem to have the bodies," White reports, "and I say, 'Thank you, I love that reputation!' They leave their prospects' phone numbers and say, 'Just tell them I gave you the lead.' When we land a job, I always provide a finder's fee, and the broker is shocked to get a check in the mail."

White often meets other brokers through the independent contractor's stem of the Society for Technical Communication. To connect with writers and brokers in this field, she suggests checking STC's Webpage and technical writers' forums on CompuServe and America Online.

CHAPTER THREE

WHERE THE WORK IS

Key Writing Products and Clients

WRITERS AND THE ONLINE REVOLUTION

In preparing my revision of this book, originally published in 1994, I asked each of the successful home-based writers being profiled, "How has the online revolution changed your working life?"

The answers confirmed what I already believed—that a commerical nonfiction writer cannot be successful today without being online. All of these writers were using E-mail to communicate with clients and to transmit material. Most were using the Internet and commerical online services for research. Many were schmoozing in forums and chatrooms to keep up with their fields and, occasionally, to find new clients. Several were planning Websites to market some aspect of their business. Only a few had actually completed writing assignments for the World Wide Web or online services, but most expected to see such assignments coming their way.

"It's changed everything. I've gotten heavily involved with it," said Jack Fehr. "I haven't stepped into a library in two years!"

"I join quite a few technical writers' forums," stated Joy White. "What we've discovered is that someone will talk about a subject and if you bring up your solution, people will start to ask you, 'Well, what is your business?'"

"It's changed my life a lot," said Donna Donvan, who was involved early on as a writer of "those annoying advertisements they used to have across the bottom of the Prodigy screens." She added, "I'm using E-mail to transmit files and it's instantaneous, which means that things can move a lot more quickly. But," she admitted, "there's a downside to this because people get used to 'faster than a speeding bullet.'"

Alan Horowitz observed: "For me the biggest thing is E-mail. I used to walk over to the post office once a week at least to send overnight mail. I haven't done that for a year!"

Jan Franck reported forming alliances with Internet marketing firms in Des Moines. She handles traditional collateral materials for their clients while they build Webpages for hers, to her targeted specifications. "The Webpages I'm helping with are being created for a specific marketing purpose, rather than just 'Well, everybody else has one,'" she stressed.

"I'm making contacts all over the world," said Ilene Schneider, adding that she finds online research especially useful in writing grant proposals. "You can learn specifically online what different government agencies and foundations are soliciting and write to a framework."

"I was one of the first writers to get a computer, back in '82," recalled Steve Morrill. "I belonged to CompuServe back when it was called The Source." He's tried all the online services but thinks "CompuServe edges out America Online in terms of research capabilities"—even though he teaches writing courses for AOL.

As a book-writer, Sylvia McNair communicates much less frequently with her book-editor clients than corporate writers or freelancers writing articles do. However, she has started using E-mail and plans to begin doing online research—"once I get a little easier with it."

"I got online in 1989 or 1990, and I was such a klutz," said Judith Broadhurst, author of *The Woman's Guide to Online Services* (McGraw–Hill, 1995). "I had never been online and I didn't know about auto-reader programs and all that sort of thing. I spent more money on online fees the first two months than I did on groceries because I kept doing everything wrong." Those days are long gone for Broadhurst, who also established and recently sold a newsletter for writers, *Freelance Success,* delivered both electronically and in print. Leading up to the newsletter were the two and a half years she spent as a volunteer leading the public freelancers' section of CompuServe's Journalism Forum.

Robert Brenner has found numerous ways to use online resources, among them collecting data for his *Pricing Guide to Desktop Publishing* and doing nearly instantaneous research for his consulting clients. "We've got fourteen universities and colleges around here [San Diego]," he said, "and when you go out to do research, you locate a particular article, a particular book, and you find the pages torn out. People are not that considerate. So we've learned to use the sources of information that are online."

As I write this, I have collected mountains of articles and books and logged numerous hours online, partly in preparation for explaining to you, as a reader of this new edition, how important the online revolution will be in your professional life.

Now I believe the other writers have said it for me. The purpose of this book is not to explain how the Internet works or to help you log on to the Library of Congress. There are many excellent sources of such information, including Judith Broadhurst's book, and you can avail yourself of them just as I have done. But the very best way to do it is just to jump in. Broadhurst did that in 1989, long before online books and magazines were taking up several aisles at your local Barnes & Noble—and look how much she has accomplished!

Steve Morrill summed it up when he said, "Anybody who, number one, hasn't got a computer and, number two, isn't online has about as much chance [of succeeding as a commercial writer today] as a monk doing illuminated manuscripts.

"Some people aren't getting this message yet," he added when I asked him to amplify his remark. "I don't know which way the electronic revolution is going, but it isn't going to involve cutting down more trees."

WHAT IS THE "HIDDEN MARKET"?

The more jobs you can do for the same clients, the more you will benefit from your marketing efforts. The key is identifying work you enjoy doing—and for which you can charge a profitable fee—and the clients who have a steady need for such work. Many writers start out by taking any jobs they can get—and you may do so, too—but if you know which jobs and clients you really want, you will soon be guiding your business toward higher profits and greater satisfaction. This chapter will help you make your selection by analyzing "the hidden market" that exists in virtually every community.

The "hidden market" consists of a wide range of local assignments that allow you to be your own boss while doing what many writers and graphic designers do in salaried positions. I think of these as the meat-and-potatoes jobs. These are jobs that can start you off as a home-based writer and sustain you for a lifetime, if you choose to stay with them. In general, these assignments meet three criteria:

1. They are assignments you can realistically expect to receive as a new freelance writer.

2. They are available in most communities.

3. They can add up to a full-time income.

To start you thinking across a wide range of options, this chapter lists sixty such jobs alphabetically. You'll notice that articles and short stories for general-circulation magazines, nonfiction books, genre and mainstream novels, plays for stage and screen, poetry and song lyrics, essays, syndicated columns, and comedy writing are not included in this list. Why? Because these popular specialties are discussed in many excellent books on writing—to say nothing of writers' magazines, newsletters, and workshops, *ad infinitum*.

Of course, the big bucks and ego rewards to be achieved in these specialties can be mind-boggling—so by all means, as your time and finances permit, purchase the books, take the workshops, and try your hand.

But remember that the money available for the plain-Jane tasks we are talking about here is often more substantial—and certainly more reliable—than the money earned writing even moderately successful books or plays. For example, it's not unusual for a good friend of mine, an experienced freelance writer, to make $3,000 writing one twenty-minute speech for the CEO of a locally based international corporation. Although doing high-profile writing can bring personal satisfaction, it is often at the expense of your bottom line—at least in the short term.

In the list of writing jobs that follows, look at each project description with these questions in mind, and checkmark as you go:

- Which assignments would I like to do?

- Which assignments can I do now?

- Which assignments could I do with additional knowledge and experience?

SIXTY KEY ASSIGNMENTS FOR HOME-BASED WRITERS

1. *Advertising copy.* A big area with lots of opportunity. Both advertising agencies and the in-house advertising departments of large companies use help for their overloads. Occasionally they need special expertise not available on their staffs. In addition, small companies and professionals in solo and group practice often turn to outside professionals for advertising copy—and your rates can beat those of a full-service ad agency.

   _____ *like to do*   _____ *could do now*   _____ *could learn to do*

2. *Anniversary materials for corporations, organizations, institutions, municipalities.* Writing and producing company and organizational histories is a specialty that requires astute, long-range marketing, but one or several projects can provide a year's income. A California-based specialist in corporate histories told me that she looks for good-size, privately held companies founded by strong, charismatic figures, with significant anniversaries coming up. Companies, universities, hospitals, trade associations, churches, cities, and other organizations also produce collateral materials such as calendars, flyers, and souvenir items in celebration of their anniversaries. Depending on the staff workload, the entire anniversary project may be bid out to a cooperative freelancer.

   _____ *like to do*   _____ *could do now*   _____ *could learn to do*

3. *Annual reports.* Producing annual reports for large, publicly traded corporations is not a place for a beginner to break in, although independent designers and writers are often employed for these prestigious, big-ticket jobs. Smaller companies and other organizations, however—community service agencies, colleges and universities, water districts, and government departments—often produce annual reports for their constituents that new freelancers can profitably produce.

    _____ *like to do*   _____ *could do now*   _____ *could learn to do*

4. *Articles for employee magazines.* While the techniques for writing an article for an employee (or other internal) magazine are essentially the same as for any other magazine, the method of selling such articles is far less speculative. Basically it is work-for-hire, with the client owning all rights. Editors come up with the idea and assign the work for an agreed-upon price. One or more rewrites are included in the price; additional rewrites are extra. Often the fee is comparable to what a larger magazine would pay. Since the editor generally has confidence in the writer, outright rejection of the completed work is rare.

    _____ *like to do*   _____ *could do now*   _____ *could learn to do*

5. *Articles for single-sponsor magazines.* The best-known magazines in this category are in-flights. Others are published and sent to customers by insurance companies, investment firms, health maintenance organizations, and others. Quite often an outside publisher produces the magazine under contract to the sponsor. A variant on this is the magazine or newsletter in your doctor's or dentist's office—produced for the specific purpose of selling copies to professionals for their offices. All of these publications use articles that are related to the sponsor's interests but that are indistinguishable in style from major consumer magazines. They're a good place to hone your skills while being paid for it.

    _____ *like to do*   _____ *could do now*   _____ *could learn to do*

6. *Articles for trade journals and small magazines.* Payment is generally low for these articles, but your income can be multiplied if you rewrite the material and sell it to a noncompeting publication, something you should consider doing whenever you write an article. The credibility you will attain from being published in a trade journal or small magazine will help you get jobs from other clients, and building a long-term relationship with an editor can result in repeated assignments or even a monthly column. If you want to sharpen your

article-writing skills, you will find endless books and articles on how to write articles of all kinds. Whole books are devoted just to writing query letters to get article assignments. Another important market for business and trade journal articles is public relations and marketing specialists, who will pay you very well to write articles about their clients. They, in turn, will try to place the articles with appropriate publications. If you are a writer who specializes in publicity, you can place your own work.

_____ *like to do* _____ *could do now* _____ *could learn to do*

7. *Brochures.* The workhorses of communication in every field, brochures provide work for both writers and desktop publishers. All organizations and businesses need brochures, as do seminar promoters, hospitals, medical groups, educational institutions, community and government agencies, churches, and fund raisers. The list is endless, as are the opportunities. Brochures are typically described by their format, such as a two-fold brochure or a three-fold brochure.

_____ *like to do* _____ *could do now* _____ *could learn to do*

8. *Calendars.* Some desktop publishers have made a specialty of personalized calendars based on a standard format, but with the client's individual dates (birthdays, anniversaries, etc.) included. Personalized calendars are printed on a laser or inkjet printer and individually bound. Of course, many businesses and organizations distribute promotional calendars each year to their constituents. National calendar companies have traditionally served such customers, selling standard calendars imprinted with the client's name, but local writer and desktop publisher teams can capture some of this business. In addition, nonprofit organizations and associations often produce calendars themselves for promotional and fund-raising purposes, but such calendars are far more successful when produced by professional writers and designers.

_____ *like to do* _____ *could do now* _____ *could learn to do*

9. *Capability brochures.* Certain kinds of businesses, such as engineering firms, consultants, and management companies, need this specialized type of brochure as the core of their business solicitation. Capability brochures are usually more extensive than typical brochures in terms of text and illustrations, as well as more expensive in terms of graphics and printing.

_____ *like to do* _____ *could do now* _____ *could learn to do*

10. *Catalogs and product sheets.* A lucrative workhorse of the business world offering plenty of business for both writers and designers. Businesses everywhere need catalogs and individual product sheets, with regular updates and reprints. If this work interests you, establishing a link with competent product photographers would be a plus. Business can come from individual firms, advertising agencies, photographers, or printers. The more you specialize in this area, the more business you are likely to receive.

_____ *like to do* _____ *could do now* _____ *could learn to do*

11. *CD–ROM/interactive media writing.* In a July 7, 1996, America Online chatroom for business writers, Gloria Stern, a Hollywood literary agent with a special interest in interactive multimedia, wrote: "Journalism is about to boom. There is a confluence of disciplines in entertainment and education. Fiction and nonfiction are almost interchangeable. We will have entertainment centers in malls and news programs around the clock. There will be work for writers everywhere." But how to take advantage of new-media opportunities? The June 1996 issue of the writers' newsletter *Freelance Success* details how one freelance writer, Sara Godwin, moved from print media to video scripts to scripts for CD–ROMs. Basically, she learned by studying examples of good work and modeling her writing after what she saw. She urges writers to get into multimedia as soon as possible. Find out who is producing the kinds of CD–ROMs you'd like to do and sell yourself to them, either presenting your own ideas or seeking an assignment on one of their projects. An agent who, like Stern, specializes in multimedia is another way to go. Check directories of agents. Alternatively, if you own the rights to, say, a how-to book or series of columns you have written, you might turn the material into a CD–ROM and sell it yourself or through a distributor.

_____ *like to do* _____ *could do now* _____ *could learn to do*

12. *City and newcomer guides.* Publishers of city guides need both writers and designers—or an enterprising writer might develop a guide for a city that lacks a good one. Selling advertising covers the costs and provides the profit. City maps carrying ads are another option. If you are good at illustration or work with an illustrator, "cartoon-style" city maps are popular and profitable.

_____ *like to do* _____ *could do now* _____ *could learn to do*

13. *Collateral materials. Collateral* is an advertising term that covers all the printed materials relating to a product or project—order forms, spec sheets, invitations, whatever may be needed. Such work may come from business firms or advertising and marketing agencies and requires the skills of both writers and designers. If you are assigned to one part of what appears to be a more complex project, ask about doing the "collateral."

_____ *like to do*   _____ *could do now*   _____ *could learn to do*

14. *Conference and trade show materials.* Sales managers, associations, meeting planners, and other event specialists need a wide range of materials—including posters, programs, audiovisual and video scripts, workbooks, flyers, brochures, tickets, badges, and more—for the conferences and trade shows they produce. Writers and designers going after such business will find that local hotels and convention centers may help put them in touch with potential clients.

_____ *like to do*   _____ *could do now*   _____ *could learn to do*

15. *Consultation.* Your expertise can be valuable to both individuals and organizations. I have been paid to help staffers plan a newsletter, to provide advice and training on desktop publishing, to critique and guide the redesign of an employee magazine. If, as this book assumes, your major emphasis is on selling your services as a writer, consulting assignments will usually come to you through networking and referrals. If you like doing this kind of work—analyzing your clients' needs and advising them on what to do and how to do it—you may want to move toward communications consulting as your primary focus, once you are well established in the field. If you can speak publicly on the subject, so much the better.

_____ *like to do*   _____ *could do now*   _____ *could learn to do*

16. *Contributing editor assignments.* Becoming a regular contributing editor for a local newspaper or magazine, a business publication or a trade journal in the field of your specialization can provide a regular monthly stipend—plus constant exposure to potential clients.

_____ *like to do*   _____ *could do now*   _____ *could learn to do*

17. *Critical reviewing.* If you have or can acquire knowledge of theater, dance, a musical specialty such as classical or rock, art, books, CD–ROMs, or computer software and hardware, you may obtain assignments from local newspapers and magazines to review local performances and exhibits, as well as whatever books, interactive media, software, or hardware appeals to the publication in question. (Consider a local parenting magazine, for example, a rock fanzine, or a computer publication.) A friend who grew up in Poughkeepsie, NY, parlayed such local reviewing into a phenomenal opportunity to review and go backstage at every major Broadway musical when he was in his early teens. His only compensation was tickets and expenses, and that may be the case for you as well. However, freelance reviewers are often paid for their critiques, and the local exposure helps establish their names for other assignments.

    _____ *like to do*   _____ *could do now*   _____ *could learn to do*

18. *Direct-mail packages.* Another biggie. There's plenty of good money to be made by both writers and designers who can master the subtle and demanding skills of this results-oriented specialty. Experts in direct marketing love knowing within a few weeks exactly how successful their efforts have been and delight in analyzing such measurements as cost-per-response. If you can write or design packages that pull, you will have plenty of clients. Direct marketers believe that only specialists in their field know how to produce winning packages, so study the many excellent books on the subject, take classes, network in direct-marketing organizations, attend conferences, snag any assignments you can to prove yourself, and eventually choose a specialty: financial, consumer, business-to-business, subscription sales, and fund raising are some of the possibilities. Work is available on local, regional, and national levels—and many of the best pros are freelancers.

    _____ *like to do*   _____ *could do now*   _____ *could learn to do*

19. *Directories.* Like city guides, directories require the efforts of both writer/researchers and desktop publishers. Business can come from directory publishers, chambers of commerce, associations, and institutions such as hospitals, colleges, and churches. If you do a good job, directories repeat on a regular basis.

    _____ *like to do*   _____ *could do now*   _____ *could learn to do*

20. *Editing.* Who does writing or deals with it? Book publishers, authors, and agents; undergraduate and graduate students; people preparing proposals, technical reports, newsletters, and employee benefits kits; consultants and engineers issuing studies for their clients; physicians, attorneys, and other professionals writing articles. The list goes on and on. Any of these nonwriters (and some writers as well) could be in the market for your editing skills. Editors specialize to some extent, so focus on the kind of editing you want to do. Editing can stay at the level of grammar, syntax, and clarity—or it can extend all the way to complete revision, with your price varying accordingly. Be sure you have agreement on what kind of editing is needed.

_____ *like to do* _____ *could do now* _____ *could learn to do*

21. *Employee benefit materials.* If you have expertise in this specialized area, or are willing to develop it, you can find work writing employee benefit materials. Clients can include employers, as well as insurance companies and agents. This sort of work is ideal for a writer who prepared similar materials as an employee and is now seeking freelance work. You may need to team with a designer.

_____ *like to do* _____ *could do now* _____ *could learn to do*

22. *Environmental materials.* This is another area for experts. As with medicine, investments, or any other specialized area, if you're a writer with experience in the environmental sciences, you can capitalize on your background as a freelancer. You can draft or help draft environmental reports, policies, guidelines, and informational brochures for companies, organizations, and government agencies. You can also write articles on environmental topics for a wide range of publications. If you lack specialized knowledge but want to become involved, editing environmental materials for a consulting firm might be a place to start. A similar specialty for medical writers is the preparation of documents required for government approval of pharmaceutical and medical devices.

_____ *like to do* _____ *could do now* _____ *could learn to do*

23. *Family histories and genealogies.* A growing specialty that uses both writing and desktop publishing skills. If you are a genealogy buff, so much the better. A fully researched, custom-written, professionally typeset and designed family history might be worth several thousand dollars to a client—even before the printing or duplicating charges. But simpler projects based on completion of

a detailed questionnaire—either on paper or on a software program—can yield a more affordable product. Audiovisual specialists are also getting into the act, recording the memories of older family members and editing them into a videotape. Advertising in senior citizen and genealogy publications is a good source of business—as are local media publicity and networking in churches and other organizations.

_____ *like to do* _____ *could do now* _____ *could learn to do*

24. *Flyers.* Most of what was said about brochures also applies to flyers. Though the terms *flyer* and *brochure* are often used interchangeably, a flyer is basically a single sheet, carrying a simple message, while a brochure contains folded panels with more detailed information. Every organization and individual involved in communication with the public will need a flyer eventually. Residential and commercial real estate are especially voracious markets. Contact successful brokers to offer your writing and production services.

_____ *like to do* _____ *could do now* _____ *could learn to do*

25. *Fund-raising materials.* Prior experience can get you assignments here, but if you lack experience, you can gain it over time through study, networking, volunteer work, and careful observation. Clients include large nonprofits such as colleges and universities, hospitals, zoos, museums, and performing arts centers, as well as fund-raising consultants. Materials needed include brochures, flyers, annual reports, posters, invitations, letters of solicitation, volunteer instruction and motivation, newsletters, forms, and direct-mail packages.

_____ *like to do* _____ *could do now* _____ *could learn to do*

26. *Ghostwriting and collaboration.* Many people want or need to write books and articles but lack the skill, the time, or both. Celebrities are an obvious example, but the list is much longer. Executives in both the public and private sectors require speeches and articles. Professionals publishing scientific papers often need much more than just editing to get their manuscripts in shape. Such clients can be reached through universities, professional associations, and professional journals. Working with them usually requires some familiarity with the material as well as with the target publication's style. Ghostwriting books is a specialty in itself.

_____ *like to do* _____ *could do now* _____ *could learn to do*

27. *Greeting-card writing.* According to a recent *Writer's Market,* nearly 50 percent of all first-class mail consists of greeting cards, and while three large companies dominate 85 percent of the market, many smaller firms are serving special interests and breaking new ground. Read trade publications, locate lines of cards that appeal to you, and write to the companies for their catalogs and submission guidelines. Many card companies also buy ideas for gift products related to their cards.

   _____ *like to do*   _____ *could do now*   _____ *could learn to do*

28. *Indexing.* This specialty can be profitable for writers with a good eye for organization and detail. Clients include book authors, book publishers, and software publishers. Good computer skills help, since advanced word-processing programs provide indexing tools.

   _____ *like to do*   _____ *could do now*   _____ *could learn to do*

29. *Industry-specific writing.* This is another way of slicing the pie. Many writers specialize almost exclusively in aviation/space, medicine, travel, science, computers, investments, petroleum, food, or some other specific industry. Professional organizations, such as the Associated Business Writers of America, the Association of Petroleum Writers, or the Aviation/Space Writers' Association, bring these writers together. Membership in such organizations helps build your knowledge, increases your credibility, and brings you referrals. Clients sometimes go through directories of such associations looking for writers and call you directly. I've received such calls as a member of the International Association of Business Communicators (which includes both corporate staff communicators and freelancers).

   _____ *like to do*   _____ *could do now*   _____ *could learn to do*

30. *Instructional materials.* A good area for writers, but you may need special expertise or on-the-job experience to qualify for assignments. Clients include textbook publishers, business and professional trainers, companies doing internal training, manufacturers providing instruction for customers, government agencies, religious organizations, and health care providers. (Schools, colleges, and universities are less likely clients.) Locating clients will require well-focused marketing efforts, but once a relationship is established with a vendor, repeat business is often forthcoming.

   _____ *like to do*   _____ *could do now*   _____ *could learn to do*

31. *Investor-relations materials.* A profitable subspecialty in the corporate communications world. Previous on-the-job experience and financial expertise help qualify writers for such assignments, as does extensive knowledge of the industry involved. You would need to establish your credibility before a firm would give you investor-relations materials to prepare.

_____ *like to do*   _____ *could do now*   _____ *could learn to do*

32. *Letter writing.* The sales letter is a vital part of most direct-mail packages, and successful direct-mail copywriters are highly compensated for letters that pull a strong response. But there are other opportunities for writers to sell letter writing to clients. A firm might want standardized letters of all sorts written or updated. A marketing department might want letters that could be customized to accomplish various sales objectives. A writer with consulting and teaching skills might combine such projects with a contract to evaluate a firm's overall letter-writing performance or to train executives and middle managers in business writing. Individuals in business—such as architects and other professionals, independent sales representatives, and financial consultants—might also need sales letters. Models for standard sales letters have long been provided in books and booklets on business methods, and the same kinds of letters are now available in software programs.

_____ *like to do*   _____ *could do now*   _____ *could learn to do*

33. *Manuals.* A solid source of income for technical writers who specialize in these long jobs. Writers may need special expertise to deal with certain topics. It's wise to build expertise and contacts within specific industries. Repeat and referral work is often forthcoming from such frequent manual producers as manufacturers, software publishers, and government agencies.

_____ *like to do*   _____ *could do now*   _____ *could learn to do*

34. *Menu writing.* An interesting specialty for writers who have connections with the restaurant world and with printers who specialize in menus. When I talk with food and menu copywriters, I marvel at the number of enticing ways they find to say something tastes good.

_____ *like to do*   _____ *could do now*   _____ *could learn to do*

35. *New-product regulatory writing.* Firms—such as pharmaceutical and medical equipment companies—attempting to introduce new products must prepare massive documents to satisfy government regulations both in the United States and abroad. Some use outside writers to turn the reams of research data into readable reports. Background in the industry or tech writing experience would be expected.

_____ *like to do*   _____ *could do now*   _____ *could learn to do*

36. *Newsletters.* An important source of income for many business writers—and an especially good niche for those with a good command of both writing and desktop publishing skills. Newsletters come and go, so marketing must be constant in this specialty, as in any other. However, some newsletters provide steady business for years. Clients include trade associations, private clubs, residential communities, businesses of all kinds, human resources departments producing employee newsletters, professionals seeking to market their group or solo practices, hospitals, colleges and universities, large nonprofit organizations, and government agencies. Some entrepreneurs become so successful at newsletters that they expand beyond one-person, home-based businesses and open offices where they employ staffs of writers, designers, and salespeople. Often they they sell advertising, which allows them to offer a newsletter to a client very inexpensively or even free. Another approach is to produce a generic newsletter where only one page or one section is customized for individual clients. An informative generic newsletter can be an effective marketing tool for a real estate broker, a financial planner, a chiropractor, and others. The newsletter publisher signs up as many noncompeting clients as possible, usually on a regional or national basis. The publisher may mail the newsletter, using client-supplied lists, or may ship a certain number of customized copies to each client for distribution. Yet another angle is to write for an entrepreneur who publishes a subscription newsletter on some specific topic, such as the oil industry, stock investments, wines, or travel. Be aware that many subscription newsletter publishers prefer to do all their own writing and often their own production in order to maximize profits.

   Newsletters are not always printed with a copy for each potential reader. They may be posted on workplace bulletin boards or delivered by fax. Video is another nontraditional medium that can be easily viewed by workers in offices, shops, or employee cafeterias. Newsletters have also moved online, traveling almost instantaneously by E-mail. This medium's strict graphic limitations are circumvented by saving the newsletter in a PDF (portable document format) with a program such as Adobe Acrobat. The resulting file can be opened with full graphics and can even be printed from any computer, regard-less of software and fonts available, using Acrobat Reader, a widely distributed free program. Many other newsletters are being published on the World Wide Web—often as the "What's New?" section of a larger Website. Online media are forcing newsletter publishers and writers to redefine the concept of an "edi-tion"—a group of pages printed at one time for distribution on a specific date. Especially on the Web, updating can be done continuously.

_____ *like to do*   _____ *could do now*   _____ *could learn to do*

37. *Newspaper feature writing, reporting, and stringing.* A source of extra income for writers skilled in journalistic techniques. While payment from all but the larger dailies may be low, published bylines give you credibility and may impress potential business or organizational clients. Being out and about cov-ering stories, especially in a specific field of expertise, keeps you well informed and gives you an edge over other writers. But beware of conflicts of interest. Should a newspaper ask you to write about one of your clients, better pass.

_____ *like to do*   _____ *could do now*   _____ *could learn to do*

38. *Packaging design and copy.* A specialty that can be profitable. Every manufacturer who puts out a product requires words and design on the package. You will need contacts with manufacturers, advertising and marketing agencies, and packaging firms—and you should be familiar with relevant government regulations.

_____ *like to do*   _____ *could do now*   _____ *could learn to do*

39. *Policies and procedures writing.* Previous on-the-job experience can qualify writers for these corporate and government assignments. Topics might include disas-ter planning as well as safety, quality, and environmental compliance and employee policies. Your assignment might also come from a consultant hired to assist the client.

_____ *like to do*   _____ *could do now*   _____ *could learn to do*

40. *Political campaign writing.* Candidates and party organizations at all levels need compilations of research on opponents as well as effective policy and program statements in a wide range of formats—from speeches to mailers to brochures to ads—providing both paid and volunteer assignments. Hook into local polit-ical groups to make contacts if this kind of writing appeals to you.

_____ *like to do*   _____ *could do now*   _____ *could learn to do*

41. *Press releases and press kits.* A profitable public relations activity for writers. Elaborate press kits may also require desktop publishing skills. You may produce material according to your client's direction. If you are responsible for public relations strategy and media placement, you should also guide content and design. Clients may be individuals, corporations, organizations, public relations firms, or advertising and marketing agencies.

_____ *like to do*   _____ *could do now*   _____ *could learn to do*

42. *Proofreading.* Writers should not overlook this source of extra income when assignments are few. Earlier I mentioned a writer friend who receives $3,000 for a corporate speech. Early in her freelance career, I well remember seeing her in the offices of a typesetter we both used in those pre-desktop-publishing days, making extra money as a proofreader. Anyone who produces large quantities of printed material may need a freelance proofreader—including typesetters, printers, publishers, consultants who issue long reports, and organizations preparing directories.

_____ *like to do*   _____ *could do now*   _____ *could learn to do*

43. *Proposals.* Another specialized area for writers with previous on-the-job experience or special training. Good teamwork and organizational skills, logical thinking, and clear writing are essential, as is security awareness, since you will often deal with confidential information. Clients include fund-raising consultants, large nonprofit organizations, and a broad range of businesses. Payment varies widely.

_____ *like to do*   _____ *could do now*   _____ *could learn to do*

44. *Public relations services and materials.* We have already discussed press kits, but other public relations materials might include letters, ads, speeches, newsletters, brochures, educational materials, posters, and many other devices. This writing specialty often involves desktop publishing as well. Public relations is an excellent field of opportunity for the home-based entrepreneur—especially in the present economy, when many corporations have reduced or eliminated their in-house public relations staffs. With the right clients, you can be as effective as a large agency—and a lot cheaper. Solo public relations practitioners usually specialize in a particular area, such as entertainment, medicine, high tech, sports, social services, or fine arts. Narrowing your focus allows you to develop solid, long-term relations with media, government officials, and others whom you seek to influence.

Don't overlook the new area of Internet exposure for your clients. Getting users to absorb your clients' message by visiting their Websites is a delicate art, involving much more than listing them on search engines (a new specialty now done automatically by online firms for a a flat fee). It can involve newsgroup participation and conventional media publicity.

Payment is handled as a monthly fee for ongoing services or as an hourly or per-job fee for such specific assignments as a special event or the development of a public relations plan. There is a vast number of businesses, organizations, and individuals who need and can afford the services of a small public relations firm—either occasionally or on a regular basis. The challenge is reaching them and convincing them that they need and can afford you.

_____ *like to do* _____ *could do now* _____ *could learn to do*

45. *Radio and TV ads and promotions.* If you are a writer with previous experience in broadcasting or advertising, you can put that knowledge to work freelancing in this special area. Your clients will be radio and TV/cable stations, advertising agencies, advertisers, and independent producers. If you want to get into this area, take a class in broadcasting or advertising copywriting, or contact other broadcast copywriters through professional groups.

_____ *like to do* _____ *could do now* _____ *could learn to do*

46. *Researching.* If you are a writer with good research skills and are comfortable using primary sources, libraries, and especially online databases, you may be hired to help a marketing team, a scholar, a publisher, a law firm, a government agency, or any other client with special research needs. To build a career in this specialty, you will seek clients and referrals through networking and advertising in appropriate journals. Payment is by the hour or the project. Skilled use of online databases is an exciting new specialty.

_____ *like to do* _____ *could do now* _____ *could learn to do*

47. *Restaurant reviewing and writing.* In virtually every community, there are restaurant reviewers who produce local restaurant guides and often conduct radio talk shows about the local restaurant scene. Even if you choose not to make such an all-out commitment to restaurant reviewing, doing a column for a local newspaper or magazine could be a gastronomically enjoyable sideline that might also bring you to the attention of prospective clients in the restaurant field and beyond. Restaurants and restaurant chains require a wide range

of promotional materials and media publicity. Some restaurants produce promotional newsletters for their clientele. If you are a restaurant critic who includes food service accounts among your freelance clients, guard against conflicts of interest.

_____ *like to do* _____ *could do now* _____ *could learn to do*

48. *Resumé writing.* Check your Yellow Pages to see how many fellow writers are already toiling in this vineyard—there's probably room for one more. Local and national firms hire writers to produce resumés, but individuals can compete effectively in this market. Directory, classified, and display ads are a vital source of business. Networking and referral programs are also effective. Speaking on resumé preparation before local groups and writing articles on resumé preparation for local business and organizational publications can also pay off.

_____ *like to do* _____ *could do now* _____ *could learn to do*

49. *Retail and mall promotions.* Brochures, flyers, posters, point-of-sale displays, and more are involved in retail and mall promotions produced every day in every community. As a home-based writer—possibly working with a desktop publisher colleague—you can produce this material for retail stores and malls in your region. When a good relationship has been established, there's lots of repeat business.

_____ *like to do* _____ *could do now* _____ *could learn to do*

50. *Sales presentations.* Writers who specialize in marketing materials and who have a strong relationship with a company or marketing firm may be assigned the job of preparing a sales presentation. Based on marketing research and product information, the presentation could include a verbal text plus a variety of audiovisual aids. Charge plenty.

_____ *like to do* _____ *could do now* _____ *could learn to do*

51. *Scripts and storyboards.* Rates for scripts to be used in audiovisual presentations and industrial or instructional videos and films are reckoned by the minute and vary widely, from really high to really low. Unless you are doing the work for little or no money, you will be expected to have solid experience in this specialty. If nothing in your previous employment and educational history has prepared you to write scripts but you would like to enter this fascinating field, allow time to get yourself up to speed. Take classes. Ask professionals for information interviews. Volunteer to help crews on student and low-budget shoots.

Check to see if your local cable station offers free technical training for public-access video. Your clients will be independent producers and in-house production teams.

_____ *like to do*   _____ *could do now*   _____ *could learn to do*

52. *Speeches.* An all-purpose public relations writer is expected to be able to write speeches, but specializing in speechwriting for corporate executives, politicians, and other public figures can be a lucrative business. The best opportunity to make money is in the corporate world, but you will need to build credibility with the speaker and his or her public relations people first—perhaps by doing other kinds of writing for them.

_____ *like to do*   _____ *could do now*   _____ *could learn to do*

53. *Sports materials and services.* Local athletic teams need team books, programs, and other materials at the start of each season. The news media sometimes pay freelancers to report scores and do seasonal writing in areas their regular sportswriters can't cover. You won't make much for this kind of writing, but you'll enjoy doing it, and the contacts could lead to other business.

_____ *like to do*   _____ *could do now*   _____ *could learn to do*

54. *Teaching writing.* Teaching can supplement your income while it builds your credibility and occasionally brings you an assignment. One approach is to teach adults through your local community college or any other adult education program. Or if you have a master's degree or the equivalent, you might become a part-time instructor for a local university or college, teaching a regular writing course for credit. The huge amount of work required to develop materials for your first class may discourage you, but freelancers who persist as regular college and university teachers find the experience both profitable and emotionally rewarding. And, of course, you will have no financial risk and little or no responsibility for recruiting students. The downside is that halfway through the semester, when a big freelance assignment comes your way, you must continue to serve your students. A more entrepreneurial approach is to offer short-term workshops or seminars on writing, financing and promoting them yourself. If you're good enough, eventually you can go on the road as an instructor for a business training firm. Since such programs usually attract working professionals, they may bring you a significant amount of business. (Don't overlook the burgeoning opportunities to teach writing online, as Steve Morrill and Judith Broadhurst, both profiled in this book, have done.)

_____ *like to do*   _____ *could do now*   _____ *could learn to do*

55. *Technical writing.* Many of the formats we have already looked at, such as manuals, brochures, and proposals, exist in the specialized area of technical writing. If you are familiar with (or are undaunted by) computer, scientific, and engineering jargon, technical writing can be a profitable specialty for you. Producing manuals is an especially lucrative part of this work.

_____ *like to do*   _____ *could do now*   _____ *could learn to do*

56. *Telemarketing scripts.* Have you ever been a telemarketer—or are you willing to familiarize yourself with the large body of literature available in this growing field? Telemarketing firms and other advertisers who use this powerful sales technique need scripts for their telemarketers to follow. Some scripts are written by knowledgeable freelancers. Advertise your services through direct mail, or network in professional organizations to meet those who buy telemarketing scripts. Or try telemarketing yourself.

_____ *like to do*   _____ *could do now*   _____ *could learn to do*

57. *Transcriptions and other forms of word processing.* If you are reading this book, transcriptions and other word-processing jobs are not your long-range goals. But while you're getting started as a writer, you may take on such work to make ends meet—especially if the work could lead to assignments that require your writing skills. Make sure the work does not prevent you from doing your regular marketing. Then charge the going rate—which will be lower than your rate for writing—and do the work to the best of your ability. Finally, let your client know about your real goals and capabilities—and ask for a writing assignment or referral. You may get it just because you did the word processing on time and with a good attitude.

_____ *like to do*   _____ *could do now*   _____ *could learn to do*

58. *Translations.* If you are proficient in a foreign language, make the most of it. Translations can provide a source of income and give you an entree among foreign companies, publishers, trade representatives, and others that may eventually lead to bilingual writing assignments in the specialty of your choosing. If you can write professionally in English and in another language as well, your skills are worth more!

_____ *like to do*   _____ *could do now*   _____ *could learn to do*

59. *Travel writing.* This can be a glamorous full-time specialty—as it is for Sylvia McNair, profiled in Chapter Eight—but not until you have solidly established yourself. At the very least, travel writing can be a way for astute writers to pay back some of the expense of their own vacations and weekend excursions. Markets are newspapers and magazines, including some membership publications (teachers' associations and auto clubs, for example), as well as general interest publications produced by airlines, insurance compaines, and financial institutions for their clients. Producing and marketing a local travel guide (*Anytown's Historic Sites, Where to Take Your Kids in Anytown*) can be an enjoyable and profitable venture.

_____ *like to do* _____ *could do now* _____ *could learn to do*

60. *Website content providing.* Being an "online content developer" was cited as one of the "Twenty-Five Hottest Careers for Women" in the July–August 1996 issue of *Working Woman.* Since writing, editing, and designing Webpages is hardly gender-specific, we can assume that such a career offers opportunities to men as well—and to *you* as a freelance writer. A related term coming into use is *Web content manager.*

Websites must have a clear focus and interest-holding value if they are to keep the attention of restless Web surfers. A body of knowledge, both theoretical and technical, about Webpages is evolving even as college courses sprout and new guidebooks appear. If you have graphic design and computer skills and can learn to do limited programming, you can do the entire job. Web authoring software is making the work much less technical. Often, however, putting up a Website is a team effort. Several writers interviewed for this book have planned and written copy to be used on Webpages without having any part in actually putting their words online.

Webpages are proving incredibly adaptable. Already they do the jobs of many traditional forms of print communication: capabilities brochures, directories, product sheets, parts lists, catalogs, press releases, annual reports, personal profiles, work samples, and calendars, just to name a few. I was impressed recently by a Website "press kit" for a forthcoming book on financial planning. It contained everything a media person would need to write about the book or interview the author—quotes from celebrities, a fact sheet, an author bio, a table of contents, chapter excerpts, interview questions, and even downloadable pictures of the book cover and the author in high and low resolutions for print or electronic use. At the same time, of course, it did a thorough job of informing an interested Web surfer about the book.

Clear purpose and organization with bite-size chunks of information and a limited number of concepts per page—these are some of the guidelines that are emerging for Web content providers. Judith Broadhurst, author of *The Woman's Guide to Online Services* (McGraw-Hill 1995) and profiled in Chapter Nine, gives more clues to the new kind of writing called for on the Web. "Stories online have to have some interactive components, something for people to do," she says. "There's a lot of talk about nonlinear writing—meaning that you don't just write one story, maybe with a couple of sidebars as you would for a women's magazine, but you write a lot of things related to that story and you give people other places to go and other ways to follow up on that kind of information. That's what the whole Web is all about—hypertext links. You need to think in a different way when you write for online publications. You have to write short, declarative kinds of things and use simple words. More and more and more [material] is going to be online, and professional writers are going to be expected to be able to do both kinds of writing."

If you are a writer whose primary experience is in print—a very linear medium—you are going to have to start thinking not only in terms of linked chunks of related information but also in terms of sound and moving images. Audio, animation, and video may convey your message more clearly and/or more interestingly than silent, static graphics and type. These capabilities are becoming more common on the Web every day. When improved transmission systems become available, multimedia will be an everyday feature.

Where to find Web content work? Any of your regular clients may have a Website or want to develop one. If your client's Website is being provided by an advertising, public relations, or marketing agency, or by a site provider, ask to be referred to them. Websites have an ongoing need for new material, and, as a writer already familiar with the client, you may be able to subcontract some writing assignments.

Another source of business is companies in the new Website provider industry. They often have writing and design jobs for freelancers—and may end up listing you as a staff writer on their own Websites—part of the Web's bent toward virtual corporations. You'll find listings of these companies online, using search engines like Yahoo. Nearby site providers may advertise in local business journals and will eventually be listed in your city's Yellow Pages and business directories. One of the most exciting aspects of Web content providing is the disappearance of geography. You can serve a client anywhere in the world—and if you have a second language, count that as a major plus!

_____ *like to do* _____ *could do now* _____ *could learn to do*

ZERO IN ON YOUR AREAS OF SPECIALIZATION

Review the above list of writing specialties and look for patterns in your responses—those you would like to do, those you can do now, and those you can learn to do. What common threads do you see among the kinds of jobs you want to do? If you *can* do something but don't *want* to do it, should you eliminate it? Probably you should, if your feeling against it is strong. If you want to do something but are not currently qualified to do it, what will it take to become qualified?

TOWARD A BUSINESS PLAN

Success Worksheet Nine

Define your niche

Having a business focus (one or more areas of specialization) will give you credibility and better access to clients.

Here are some ways to establish your business focus. Based on your responses *(like to do, could do now, could learn to do)* to the key assignments for home-based writers listed in this chapter—and to other types of work that may occur to you—answer the following questions.

- What types of writing work would you like to do?

  _____

- Based on your knowledge, experience, and interest, what could you specialize in as a writer?

  _____

- Is this type of work going to be profitable? Can it predictably provide a satisfactory return for the time you must invest?

  _____

- How much competition is there for this type of work in your community? You'll learn more about how to evaluate the competition when you study marketing in Chapter Seven, but for now, what is your best educated guess?

  _____

- Will this type of work lead to repeat or related business?

  _____

- Is the work seasonal? Is it related to popular trends that may shift?

  _____

- What is the long-range outlook for this type of work? Is it related to growing or at least stable industries or technologies?

  _____

- Will you need additional knowledge or training in order to succeed at this type of work?

  _____

- How will you get the knowledge or training you need?

  _____

WHO BUYS THE MEAT-AND-POTATOES JOBS?

Once you have focused on the kinds of work you will do, you can define your marketplace and begin to identify and make contact with potential clients. The following list gives you a cross section of many businesses, organizations, and individuals in your community who may buy services from professional home-based writers.

Recall that in Chapter Two you analyzed your education; your work experience; your personal, family, and volunteer experience; and the areas you would like to know about—in terms of both the work you would like to do and the clients you would like to serve.

As you go through the following list, rate your interest in serving each client. Then look for a pattern in the clients you have rated "high."

If you would like to serve a client category but do not feel qualified to do so, highlight that field for future study. For example, attorneys often attract clients by sending out informational newsletters, but a writer would need some background in legal terminology and procedures in order to write a newsletter for an attorney. This is just one more reason for specializing. When you have special knowledge in a field, you can work more quickly and accurately—and you can charge more.

SIXTY KEY WRITING CLIENTS

Interest in Serving Such Clients

	High	Average	Low
1. Accountants, architects, attorneys	____	____	____
2. Advertising agencies	____	____	____
3. Art galleries, public and private	____	____	____
4. Associations	____	____	____
5. Athletic teams, sports promoters	____	____	____
6. Book publishers	____	____	____
7. Churches, denominations, religious organizations	____	____	____
8. City guide publishers	____	____	____
9. Colleges, universities, private schools	____	____	____
10. Concert promoters	____	____	____
11. Conference planners	____	____	____
12. Consultants	____	____	____
13. Convention centers	____	____	____
14. Corporate human services departments	____	____	____
15. Corporate marketing departments	____	____	____
16. Corporate public relations/communications departments	____	____	____
17. Corporate purchasing departments	____	____	____
18. Design firms	____	____	____
19. Direct-marketing firms, especially direct mail	____	____	____
20. Directory publishers	____	____	____
21. Engineering firms	____	____	____
22. Fitness centers	____	____	____
23. Fund-raising departments and consulting firms	____	____	____
24. Government departments—federal, state, county, township, city	____	____	____

25. Goverment-funded special agencies, such as water districts, school districts, and libraries ____ ____ ____

26. Greeting-card and gift companies

27. Health clubs ____ ____ ____

28. Health insurance firms, health maintenance organizations ____ ____ ____

29. Hospitals, medical centers ____ ____ ____

30. Hotels, resorts, casinos ____ ____ ____

31. Importers, exporters ____ ____ ____

32. Individuals, families ____ ____ ____

33. Labor organizations ____ ____ ____

34. Laboratories ____ ____ ____

35. Magazines/newsletters—business and trade ____ ____ ____

36. Magazines/newsletters—consumer, including single-sponsor publications ____ ____ ____

37. Magazines/newsletters—employees, alumni, organizations ____ ____ ____

38. Marketing agencies ____ ____ ____

39. Medical professionals, including physicians, dentists, psychologists, chiropractors, nutritionists, and more ____ ____ ____

40. Museums, public and private ____ ____ ____

41. Newspapers—community and regional ____ ____ ____

42. Newspapers—business and trade ____ ____ ____

43. Performing arts centers, theaters, performing groups ____ ____ ____

44. Political parties and candidates ____ ____ ____

45. Private clubs—yachting, golf, etc. ____ ____ ____

46. Producers—of industrial/educational/ promotional films, video, broadcast, CD-ROMs ____ ____ ____

47. Public relations agencies ____ ____ ____

48. Research organizations ____ ____ ____

49. Restaurants ____ ____ ____

	High	Average	Low
50. Resellers	____	____	____
51. Retail stores	____	____	____
52. Shopping centers, malls	____	____	____
53. Small businesses	____	____	____
54. Social service agencies	____	____	____
55. Software publishers	____	____	____
56. Theme parks, recreation centers	____	____	____
57. Transportation/shipping firms and agencies	____	____	____
58. Travel agencies	____	____	____
59. Website providers	____	____	____
60. Wholesalers	____	____	____

WRITING-RELATED AGENCIES

While some employment agencies specialize in communications skills and may be able to place you in a temporary job, in my experience, they are a last resort for a freelancer—use them only to keep the wolf from the door. Unless you learn valuable new skills or make new contacts, such a job is a setback because working in an employer's environment will keep you from seeking new business. Only in technical writing is it common practice—and the stuff of which a freelance career can be made—to take temporary full-time assignments.

There is, however, another type of agency that brokers freelance writing and design services. Often these writing-related agencies specialize in technical communications, as does The Write People in Dayton, OH, and Joy Mieko White's firm, Infoteam, Inc., in CA. Some writing-related agencies or groups emphasize medical, public relations, or other specialties. Some have a broader focus. Cincinnati-based Creative Consortium, Inc., is a full-service marketing communications agency dealing with associated writers and graphic artists across the nation.

Writing agencies may provide you with work for a percentage of your fee, or, like an advertising agency, they may pay you for your work and bill the client directly. Either way, they will require that your work meet their professional standards and that you follow their business practices. Check your regional Yellow Pages and other directories under such headings as "writing," "graphic design," and "marketing communications" to see if you have such a resource in your area.

Rank your interest in working with a writing-related agency. Is it high, average, or low?

MATCHING JOBS AND CLIENTS

At this point, go back over your responses on the list of jobs and the list of clients and compare the kinds of work you would like to do with the kinds of clients you would like to serve. Do the clients you like buy the jobs you prefer? If not, what jobs do they buy? Let your mind float over the material and look for connections you may not have seen before. Look for patterns that will help you decide *what you will do—and for whom.*

TOWARD A BUSINESS PLAN

Success Worksheet Ten

Identify your market.

Identifying your potential clients is vital to your home business success.

- Have you already done some independent writing (either free or for payment)? Who were your clients?

_____

- Would it be profitable for you to continue serving these clients and others like them? (If not, samples of your work for them and testimonials from them may help you approach more profitable clients.)

_____

- Within which industries do you plan to seek business?

_____

- Will you need any special preparation in order to work in these industries?

_____

- Within these industries, what types of clients do you plan to serve? Consider all the individuals who customarily buy printed presentation or online materials—owners, marketing directors, communications specialists, art directors, human services directors, and purchasing agents. Which ones can you work most effectively with?

_____

- How can you prepare yourself to call on buyers whose specialties may be unfamiliar to you?

  _____

- How creditworthy are the clients you are interested in serving?

  _____

- How promptly will they pay?

  _____

- Do they offer repeat or related business?

  _____

- How much competition are you likely to encounter in serving these clients?

  _____

- Is the business seasonal or dependent on trends that may shift?

  _____

- What is the long-range economic outlook in your region for the industries you are considering?

  _____

Donna Donovan
Really Good Copy Company, Glastonbury, Connecticut

Finding Yourself Through Your Business

"Self-employed people have often held a lot of different jobs in their careers," observes Donna Donovan. "It's the 'finding oneself' process." Donovan, who founded her home-based writing and desktop publishing business in 1981, is a case in point. "I've been in business for myself longer than any job I ever had," she says.

Donovan's first position after college was as a newspaper reporter. She became a copy editor, did some page layout, switched to corporate communications, and attended law school but didn't finish—most of this as a single mother. Her last job was writing industrial advertising copy. But when Donovan describes how her business has evolved, a pattern of incremental change appears.

She first planned to specialize in industrial accounts, building on leads from her last employer. "I was going to give industrial advertising a consumer spin," she recalls. But during her first two years, she found selling engineers on her approach "a real uphill battle."

She joined organizations, networked, and did a lot of thinking. "I was trying to fit in," she says, "but I didn't feel comfortable in a navy blue suit, so I decided to be myself." With this in mind, Donovan chose her company's name, Really Good Copy Company, because she found it "memorable and unusual" even though it didn't sound corporate.

Building a new client base, she began writing copy for real estate developers. "I enjoyed the challenge of creating 'a sense of place' about a place that didn't exist yet," she says, "but the economy changed that."

In a shrinking economy, Donovan was convinced that "clients were looking for new options." Drawing on her newspaper design experience plus knowledge gained from her father, a graphic designer, she began desktop-publishing newsletters.

Now desktop publishing has given her a profitable niche in the thriving catalog business. Clients send Donovan a designed document, and she writes and fits the copy on-screen. "I know what else is on the spread, so I can avoid repetition," she explains, adding that "some firms produce four, eight, even ten catalogs a year. Unless I screw up, they'll be back, leaving me time to do fun projects."

These have included composing board game cards and writing stories to be made into jigsaw puzzles. Donovan's legal background has helped her work with law firms and small businesses. "I enjoy it because a Yellow Pages ad or a direct mail piece is so important to them," she says.

Donovan often joint-ventures with designers—usually on a verbal agreement.

To complete a recent assignment for the *Readers Digest*, a New York agency paired her successfully with an independent designer from their database. She also participates in a creative writing group, following *The Artist's Way*, a study guide, and says, "I think it's really helped me in my business. It's made me more open to options, not just in my writing but in the way I interact with people."

Downsizing has hit Donovan's region hard, she says, observing, "It's more and more difficult to maintain a local base of business. It used to be you could be a generalist and find enough business in your own backyard. Now I think you need to be a specialist and you need to look further afield to keep your schedule filled."

To solve this problem, Donovan has built relationships with catalog firms around the country. A self-professed online "junkie," she once subscribed to Prodigy (a former client), CompuServe, and America Online but now uses only AOL. "I find it to be the most comprehensive resource," she says. Online research helps her gather background material for catalog writing. For example, information on current Broadway shows enables her to write savvy copy about T-shirts bearing the shows' logos, sold by one of her clients. "That information might not be available yet in the library," she says.

A "morning person," the Macintosh-based writer-designer averages sixty-hour weeks in her glass-walled office overlooking the wooded acreage she and her semiretired husband own. She says her years of catalog writing— "getting a lot out of fifty words or less"—have been good practice for the World Wide Web assignments she has begun to receive. She's considering putting up her own Webpage as a marketing device.

For the first edition of this book, Donovan told me about being recruited for a job that appeared to offer security. "I turned it down," she said then. "The only security is what you create yourself. I could pack up and go anywhere in the country and within two months, I would be up and running with a good flow of business."

When we talked recently to bring her profile up-to-date, she described her plans to move with her husband to California. "I've had enough terrible winters," she told me. "I want some sunshine. So I'm going to bet on what I said!"

CHAPTER FOUR

MAKING YOUR BUSINESS LEGAL

THE BASICS OF SETTING UP A BUSINESS

Many writers start selling services out of their homes part-time—and even full-time—without ever taking a serious look at the fundamentals of choosing a suitable form of business organization, selecting an appropriate business name, and obtaining the necessary business licenses. *Not a good idea!* Be serious about your business from the beginning. Your customers will sense the difference—and, down the road, you will avoid such potential disasters as property use violations, fines, back taxes, business name lawsuits, and issues of business ownership.

These factors are somewhat more important for the corporate writer who will be serving local business clients, or the entrepreneur combining writing and graphic design services, than for the freelancer dealing with distant editors by phone and E-mail. However, anyone who is in business should be familiar with these basics.

Selecting the organizational structure on which you will build your business is a vital first step, and there is no shortage of information on the subject. Most books on starting your own business explain the three basic types of business organization—sole ownership, partnership, and corporation—as well as procedures for establishing a name for your business and obtaining the necessary licenses. Since regulations in these matters vary from state to state, county to county, and city to city, what follows will be a general guide to the points with which you must be familiar. Eventually, you will have to obtain forms and file papers with specific government agencies—but the more information you have in advance, the better. Be aware also that maintaining more than one business entity can have advantages down the road in handling special business projects or problems.

For recent information about starting a business in your state and community, go to your library and ask for relevant books or pamphlets or check such online sites as the Smart Business Supersite on the World Wide Web (http://www.smartbiz.com). At http://www.smartbiz.com/sbs/cats/home.htm, you will find downloadable fact sheets on starting and operating a business in each of the fifty states—useful excerpts from the Oasis Press series *You Can Start Your Own Business,* which can be ordered from Smartbiz online.

Another good move at this point is to attend free or low-cost seminars about starting a business. Many organizations offer such training. Watch the business section of your newspaper, and check with your library, chamber of commerce, and local office of the federal Small Business Administration (SBA). SBA information is available online at http://www.sba.gov. In addition, adult education classes on starting a business are offered by many school districts and colleges. The information you obtain in these programs will be current and specific to your locality.

Often local accountants, bankers, attorneys, SBA spokespersons, and representatives of the Internal Revenue Service (IRS) are asked to address seminars and classes on starting a business. They will give you materials and be available to answer your questions, and they would not be on the platform if they were not interested in making contact with new business owners. You may find your own future accountant, attorney, or business banker this way. Talking with other new entrepreneurs in the audience may also provide you with information and resources.

As a writer, I love and live by the printed word, and I rely on books, magazines, and newspapers for much of my mental sustenance. But I am also a strong believer in networking. When you are exploring a new area, face-to-face contact is a better way to gain a foothold.

SOLE PROPRIETORSHIPS

Most of the small businesses in this country are sole proprietorships. Basically, if you do not form a partnership or file articles of incorporation, a sole proprietor is what you are. This is where you will probably start and where you may very well stay, although you can always change your form of business organization later on.

Characteristics

As a sole proprietor, you are solely responsible for your business. You are the boss. You make the decisions, pay the bills and taxes, and may keep the income that is left. Any debts or obligations your business incurs are your personal responsibility. Hiring employees to work for you does not change the status of your business. If you decide to move your residence, your business can move with you. When you die, your business will end. You may operate any number of sole proprietorships at the same time—or in addition to any role you may play as a partner in a partnership or an officer in a corporation.

You pay taxes on net earnings

As the owner of a sole proprietorship, you will pay taxes via your personal tax return, calculating the net earnings of your business on Schedule C of Form 1040 and reporting that amount as personal, taxable income. You will also be required to pay your own Social Security taxes.

You can't hire yourself

One of the most common misunderstandings on the part of individuals new to business is how an entrepreneur actually "pays" himself. A sole proprietor cannot hire himself as an employee but may withdraw any amount of money from the business as a "draw." This is not a wage and is not subject to payroll taxes or to any unemployment or disability requirements. At tax time the profit of your business, as calculated on Schedule C, is your actual wage and is reported as income, regardless of how much or how little "draw" you took during the year.

Federal Identification Number

If you have set up your sole proprietorship under a name other than your own—such as The Write Stop or Hometown Editorial Services—you will need to obtain a Federal Identification Number (FIN) from the IRS. Contact your local IRS office for the necessary form or check the Website http://irs.ustreas.gov. Clients will need this number to report the payments that they make to you. At the end of the year, you will receive statements from your clients (those who keep good books), showing the totals that they have reported. If you work under your own name, you can obtain a FIN or you can use your Social Security number.

Advantages and disadvantages

A sole proprietorship has many advantages. It is easy to start and to discontinue. Because fewer documents and no legal fees are required, it is the least expensive form of business to start. It is freer of government regulation than a corporation. And your tax rates may be lower than corporate rates.

A sole proprietorship also has disadvantages. A corporation provides a shield for your personal assets—one reason why the letterhead used by your physician in solo practice down the street may say, "Ann Smith, M.D., Inc." A sole proprietorship does not. Damages from any lawsuits brought against your business as well as debts incurred by your business can be taken from your personal assets. You will also encounter more difficulty than a corporation or partnership raising capital or obtaining business loans. Barring a major improvement in the U.S. health care system, you will probably pay more for health insurance than a large business would pay, although the federal government is finally giving self-employed persons a break on health insurance tax deductions. Lastly, a sole proprietorship "dies" when you die. You can, of course, leave your business to your survivors, but the assets of your business could be subject to inheritance taxes.

Husband-and-wife arrangements

If you are a husband and wife running a business together, you may form a partnership but you may also designate one spouse as the sole proprietor and consider the other an employee, deducting his or her wage as a business expense. The wage of the employee spouse is taxable income, and all required federal and state deductions and payments must be made. A simpler but perfectly legal option exists, however. In this scenario, the employee spouse works in the business but is not on the payroll, saving federal and state payroll taxes and avoiding all the paperwork. The "draw" taken by the employer spouse covers the needs of both. The main drawback to this simple, inexpensive solution may be a serious one at retirement time: The employee spouse earns no Social Security credits for working in the business.

PARTNERSHIPS

When two or more people go into business together but do not form a corporation, they are in partnership. From a tax standpoint, there is little difference between a partnership and a sole proprietorship except that an annual notice of the revenue distributed to the partners must be filed with the IRS, and a partnership must have its own Federal Identification Number (FIN). Partners pay their taxes in the same way sole proprietors do, and the personal assets of partners are at the same risk as those of sole proprietors to meet business debts or judgments. Since partners, like sole proprietors, cannot be employees of the business, arrangements for paying them must be agreed upon in advance. Each partner may draw a regular guaranteed payment or may share in profits—or some combination of the two.

When one partner dies or withdraws or a new partner is added, the partnership is legally terminated. The business need not be liquidated, however. All that is needed is a new partnership agreement.

Advantages

Obviously, the talents, energy, contacts, and ideas of two or more professionals can be a great asset to any business. A writing–desktop publishing or Web design team is an especially winning combination. Having a partner can even out workload peaks and valleys and make it easier for owners to schedule vacations and deal with personal emergencies. Each partner may bring different pieces of equipment into the business, reducing start-up costs. When funds are needed, a partnership will usually find it easier than a sole proprietorship to raise money, since lenders and investors see less risk when several entrepreneurs are committed to the venture. Government regulations for a partnership are less stringent than for a corporation. And partnerships are easy to start—though less easy to dissolve.

Disadvantages

Since the breakup rate for partnerships is even higher than that of marriages, a partnership poses some very real risks. Partners may not have compatible working habits and may not agree on long-term goals. Lines of authority may be in frequent dispute. Issues relating to unequal initial investments may be hard to resolve. And all partners can be held personally liable for the acts of any one partner relating to the partnership business—whether it be borrowing money in the name of the business or mishandling a job so that a lawsuit results.

Partnership agreements

From a legal standpoint, a partnership is a real entity, even if a written partnership agreement does not exist. Unfortunately, many small partnerships get under way with no written agreement—and such casualness can be costly. In their book *Working from Home* (1994), Paul and Sarah Edwards state, "Anyone entering into a partnership should have an attorney draw up a partnership agreement first and obtain partnership insurance as soon as the agreement goes into effect." Other authorities take a less extreme position, providing guidelines partners may use in drawing up their own agreements for possible review by an attorney.

Whether or not you seek an attorney's help, your agreement should cover the following:

- the nature of your business and its goals

- what each partner will contribute in labor and property

- how earnings are to be distributed, procedures for withdrawing funds and paying profits

- a clause specifying the financial and legal powers of each partner

- provisions for continuing the business if a partner leaves or dies

- provisions for adding a new partner

- procedures for mediation

- provisions for revising the partnership agreement and keeping it current

A good reference on this topic is *The Partnership Book,* published and periodically updated by Nolo Press of Berkeley, California, (800) 992-6656. Nolo has also introduced a software program, Partnership Maker, that can be used in any state to prepare a legal partnership agreement.

Partnerships in the home

When partners share a home—whether or not they are a married couple—there should be no special problems housing their business in their residence. However, when a business is housed in the home of only one partner, this significant contribution to the business—and its financial and management implications—should be carefully discussed and clarified in the partnership agreement.

Limited partnerships

A limited partnership allows investors to become partners in a business without assuming unlimited liability, while at least one general partner bears full legal and financial responsibility. Limited partners don't take part in the daily operation of the business but do share in profits. Since government regulations at the federal, state, and even county levels are much more stringent regarding limited partnerships, you should consult a tax accountant or an attorney familiar with the rules in your area before entering into an agreement.

As a writer getting started at home, bringing in a limited partner might work if you have a friend, relative, or other investor willing to help fund your new business. However, in line with the wise old business adage, "KISS: Keep It Simple, Stupid!", I would strongly advise you to handle such an investment as a loan, perhaps paying only the interest for the first few years.

Limited liability partnerships

A new partnership structure, available in at least eighteen states, is the limited liability company (LLC). An LLC is a partnership that works like a corporation with respect to liability, limiting liability to the assets of the enterprise, but when it comes to income taxes, it works like a traditional partnership. If you are considering a partnership, find out if your state offers this option.

CORPORATIONS

A corporation is a legal entity in itself. It suggests stability and strength to potential investors and can extend beyond your lifetime. The corporate form of business limits your liability and may enable you to obtain insurance benefits not available to a sole proprietorship or partnership. The days of incorporating small businesses as a tax loophole, however, ended with the Tax Reform Act of 1986. Establishing a corporation today can be expensive and time-consuming and may require the help of an attorney, unless you want to gamble the future of your business on a do-it-yourself kit or the low-cost "instant incorporation" services available in most areas. Since corporations are regulated by several levels of government, running even a small one requires extensive paperwork. Corporations are also subject to higher taxes and could increase your insurance costs.

For these reasons, very few writers will start their businesses as corporations. The only exception might be an entrepreneur who sees his or her home business as the first step in a larger enterprise. In that case, incorporating at the onset could be simpler and less expensive than incorporating later. *Small Time Operator*, by Bernard Kamoroff, C.P.A. (1996), is one of many books for new entrepreneurs that go into the specifics of starting a corporation.

NAMING YOUR BUSINESS

Even though naming your business is a marketing function, I'm going to take it up now because filing a fictitious name statement is one of the basic steps of setting up your business, and it's required in most states if you're using a name other than your own. Bearing in mind that you can modify or completely change your business name later as your business evolves, consider these general suggestions while you engage in one of the fun parts of starting a business.

Just your name

You can work under your own name—a simple "Mary Sanchez" at the top of your letterhead. This is typical of writers serving such traditional markets as magazines, publishers, and advertising agencies. If you are entering the local business marketplace, however, your business will be better accepted if its name clearly suggests what you do. You are not dealing exclusively with editors but a wide range of buyers, some of whom may never have encountered a writing service before.

Adding to your name

For a single, home-based entrepreneur, adding a term such as *enterprises* or *group* to your name suggests a larger, more permanent organization. Calling yourself *president* instead of simply *owner* has the same effect. A young friend who operates a marketing firm out of his home calls himself *vice president* to suggest an even bigger organization. I must admit that I have mixed feelings about trying to appear larger than you actually are. I have been given assignments from some very large corporations who know full well that I am just one person working out of my home, and they are happy to get good work by hiring me. On the other hand, a person working alone is less credible in soliciting a large assignment than someone who has a team backing him up—which is why some form of networking among trusted colleagues is so vital.

Multiple identities

For a different perspective, however, let me share something I learned years ago in an E. Joseph Cossman seminar for small entrepreneurs. Since most of these businesspeople were planning to sell products by mail, Cossman recommended they use multiple company names on multiple letterheads—even listing one "firm" as a "division" of another. After all, the impression made at the other end is all that really counts (along with, of course, the price, the service, and the final product). If this advice fits your operation, give it a try.

Elements of your name

One popular approach to selecting a name is to use an element of your own name followed by a business description, such as: "Wong Communications" or "Bruce Wong Public Relations" or "BW Web Authoring" (your initials) or "W & J Resumé Service" (you and your partner, Nancy Janowitz). Since I do not plan to add assistants or associates, and since I feel that *I* am what I sell, I use my full name followed by a business description—"Lucy Parker Writing/Design." But this, too, has caused problems. When a large hospital issued a check to "Writing/Design," I had to ask them to cut another check made out to me so that I could cash it.

A play on words

If your name lends itself to a play on words, you're lucky. Such tricks help clients remember your business name—as long as the moniker is not too cute! Good (fictitious) examples would be Wright Writing (owned by Jean Wright) or High Voltage Copy (owned by Sam Volt). Be careful to avoid trendy words that may soon sound dated.

General or specific?

Some writers and desktop publishers elect to sound like an organization, while not suggesting what they do—for example, Betty Jones & Associates. I understand the dilemma of a new entrepreneur who is not sure what his or her area of specialization will be, but I also believe strongly in clear communication. Vagueness may turn out to be a mistake when a potential client tries to recall what that nice woman he met at the networking breakfast really does.

A separate name

Another valid approach is to give your business a completely separate name, perhaps suggesting your locale or the quality or tone of your work, such as "Tri-Counties Copywriting" or "Word-Tech Company." This, too, suggests a larger, more permanent organization.

Being cute

Before we leave the ego-titillating topic of naming your business, let me stress again that writers seem especially prone to inventing cute names—no doubt because we like to play with words. Unfortunately, a cute name may convey an unprofessional image. If you are aiming at a market segment that will appreciate an off-the-wall name, go for it! But if corporations are part of your marketing mix, it's usually better to be businesslike than amusing.

Check for duplication

Whatever name you select, even your own, run a check of local competition in Yellow Pages and business directories to see if another firm is using something very similar. You can carry this search further by checking the sources listed below under Trademarks.

FICTITIOUS NAME STATEMENTS

As I mentioned earlier, in most states if you are doing business under anything other than your own name (that is, just "Robert Schwartz," not "Robert Schwartz Editorial Services"), you will need to file a fictitious name statement, also known as a DBA ("doing business as"). Without filing a DBA, you will probably not be able to obtain a city business license or open a bank account in the name of your business. Check, first, however, in case your state is one that permits the addition of descriptive words to the entrepreneur's own name. Often the filing of DBAs is handled at the county level.

Filing a fictitious name statement helps to protect the community from shady operators who might not want their identities known. It also helps protect your business name from use by others because it establishes the date and place you first used the name. For full protection, however, you will need to register a trademark or service mark.

Filing a DBA is a two-step process. You must obtain and register a form with the appropriate government agency, paying a nominal filing fee. And you must publish your fictitious name in a general-circulation newspaper. The easy way to do this is to observe which local papers carry fictitious name statements and then contact one. In many locations, small newspapers keep DBA forms on hand and will handle all the paperwork for you.

TRADEMARKS

Both the wording of your name and its typographic representation as well as any graphic symbol that is part of your business identity can be legally protected through a trademark or service mark (a trademark for a service). If there is an infringement, however, you must still front the legal costs to fight it. You can also trademark the name of a specific product. Some states register trademarks, giving you statewide protection. The U.S. Patent and Trademark Office (see Source Directory) currently registers trademarks nationally for $245 per category. The process is fairly lengthy. A trademark includes "any distinctive word, name, symbol, device, or any combination thereof adopted and used, or intended to be used, by a manufacturer or merchant to identify his goods or services and distinguish them [from others]." The term of registration or renewal is ten years. Since a trademark is an intangible asset, it can be sold with your business, but it cannot be depreciated, as can patents and copyrights.

Registering a trademark involves a search of existing trademarks. You can do this yourself at some libraries by consulting *The Trademark Register* on CD–ROM, containing all federally registered U.S. trademarks and those recently applied for. A trademark research firm, such as Thomason and Thomason in North Quincy, MA, or Trademark Research Center in New York City (see Source Directory), will search all state and federal trademarks plus additional sources. Fees range from $120 to more than $1,000. An online database, Trademarkscan, produced by Thomason and Thomason, is updated weekly and accessible for a charge through CompuServe.

Do you need a trademark? Most home-based writers do not—or at least not right away. However, if you offer a unique product or service, and especially if you serve a widespread clientele, registering your trademark may be advisable.

BUSINESS LICENSES AND ZONING

If you are serving your local business community, almost certainly you will be required to get a local business license, which is a permit to do business in a specific city or county. Usually this involves going to the appropriate office, filling out a form, paying an annual fee based on the volume of business you expect to do, and then renewing your license each year by mail. Often you will be required to post your license in your place of business—a small but special moment for the new entrepreneur!

Rules against home-based businesses

Unfortunately, this otherwise routine procedure holds some pitfalls when you plan to work at home: Many communities have zoning regulations against home businesses—or against certain types of home-based businesses. Also, your municipality may require you to obtain a "home occupation permit" before you can apply for a business license.

With the recent boom in home-based business, these restrictions are easing, rather than tightening. But bite the bullet and learn the rules in your area. You don't have to explain why you want to know. How is your neighborhood zoned? Single-family residential? Multiple-family residential? Light industrial? Commercial? What does that mean in terms of a home business? Can you put up a small sign? Can you have a business telephone listing? Can you advertise your home address in the Yellow Pages? What are the penalties for zoning violations? If the business licensing department does not have this information, the zoning department will. Check also with your chamber of commerce or local Small Business Development office. Or you may want to consult an attorney.

Fortunately, neither writing nor desktop publishing is characterized by the objectionable features that zoning restrictions are designed to prevent—large numbers of people coming and going, parking problems, noise, smoke, odors, hazardous materials, commercial signs, and unsightly exterior equipment or storage. Some communities also distinguish between a business and a profession in granting home business licenses, in which case you probably will qualify as a professional. If you live in an area zoned for agriculture, you're in luck! Such zones rarely ban home business.

What if home business is prohibited?

If establishing a home business is prohibited in your area, you may decide to ignore the restriction, as many home entrepreneurs do—bearing in mind that if a neighbor files a complaint, you may be vulnerable to being fined, or worse. And if your state requires you to charge sales tax on any of your products, applying for a state reseller's permit may result in your city being notified of your business address.

If you want to play by the rules, you can apply for a variance. This may also be necessary if you live in an apartment complex, condominium, or private community that has its own regulations against home businesses.

Another alternative is to obtain an address through a private mailing service, or if you work in close association with a colleague, you might use your associate's address. You could also move. Your new career as a home-based writer is very, very important, so if the obstacles in one community are too great, go to a community that is more hospitable. Two adjoining towns may have completely different regulations. Be sure to let your old community know why you had to move! As home-based entrepreneurs, we must all work to improve zoning, tax, and other regulations that affect our success or failure.

SELLER'S PERMITS

Sales taxes are imposed today by most states and some local governments. If you sell products or services on which your state charges sales tax, you are required to collect this tax and turn it over to the state annually, quarterly, or monthly depending on your volume of business. To comply with these regulations, you must apply for a seller's permit (also known as a resale permit). What is taxed varies from state to state. Writers providing copy for their clients' use are generally in the clear, since such writing would probably not be considered a taxable product. Not so, however, with desktop publishers. Camera-ready art may be considered taxable in your state. And when you supply printing to a client, you will certainly be expected to collect tax unless your client plans to resell the material.

Again, bite the bullet. It's part of doing business. Find out from your state and local governments what regulations apply to your products and, if necessary, obtain a resale permit. When you do so, you may be required to deposit cash against the taxes you will collect. Your clients will accept the sales tax as a necessary burden, and if your volume of taxable business is small, you may have to file and pay only once a year. On the plus side, when you purchase raw or finished material for resale, you can avoid paying sales tax if you put your resale permit on file with your vendors. Likewise, you must keep your clients' resale numbers on file when they purchase products tax-free from you, planning to resell them.

Success Worksheet Eleven

Set yourself up right.

Choosing the most suitable form of business organization, selecting an appropriate business name, and obtaining necessary licenses are the right way to begin.

- Do you plan to organize your business as a sole proprietorship, partnership, or corporation?

  _____

- How will you handle ownership if you are a husband-and-wife team?

  _____

- What names are you considering for your business? List your best ideas.

  _____

  _____

  _____

- How can each of these names benefit you from a marketing standpoint? (See the discussion about business names in Chapter Seven.) Do you see disadvantages to any of the names you are considering?

  _____

- Try the names out on some potential clients. Which name will you select?

  _____

- Will you need to file a fictitious name statement? Do you know how to file one? When do you plan to do it?

  _____

- Will you need a trademark? Now or later? State or federal?

  _____

- What local zoning regulations will apply to your home-based writing business?

  _____

- Do you live in an apartment, condominium, or private community that regulates home-based businesses? How will these regulations affect you?

  _____

- If any potential zoning or regulation problems exist, how do you plan to handle them?

  _____

- Do you know how to obtain a local business license? When do you plan to apply?

  _____

- Does your state and/or local government collect sales tax? Are any of the products you plan to produce taxable?

  _____

- If you will need a seller's permit, do you know how to obtain one? When do you plan to apply?

  _____

Alan S. Horowitz

Business and Technology Writer, Salt Lake City, Utah

Creating Business Opportunities

"You never know where business will come from," says Salt Lake City business writer Alan S. Horowitz. Horowitz traces the growth of his own writing career through a web of introductions and seemingly opportune connections, yet he insists that "thinking and initiative are all that are required. You don't need inside information."

Horowitz didn't start out as a writer. A native of New York City, he earned advanced degrees in both economics and theater management, but while writing theater public relations material, he realized that writing was his true love.

Horowitz worked as a writer for a Los Angeles public relations firm and an in-house ad agency, wrote academic term papers, and then got a job at *Entrepreneur Magazine*, where he met an editor who had started an investment newsletter. The editor hired Horowitz to write for him full-time, and when the newsletter business moved to Salt Lake City, Horowitz went along. But when it moved again following the 1987 stock market crash, he decided to stay put as a freelance writer, pursuing a longtime dream.

Horowitz's initial strategy was to "go all over the place," writing on health, travel, business, and theater. "But after a while," he says, "I saw the benefits of focusing on a couple of markets." Today Horowitz specializes in business, with an emphasis on small business, personal finance, and the business side of the computer industry. He writes articles and newsletters and has ghostwritten a book on personal financial planning. Recently he has begun doing press releases, brochures, and other public relations work for several high-tech firms.

A web of connections has helped his business grow. For example, a friend introduced Horowitz to the editor of Novell's *Selling Red,* a magazine for computer resellers. It was his entrée to computers. Later, he used his articles from *Selling Red* to approach *Reseller Management,* a national computer trade journal for which he still writes.

"In any industry you write about," Horowitz explains, "you build up a knowledge base along with a database of contacts, information, and quotes."

Often it is simple research that gets Horowitz the job. Reading the *Wall Street Journal,* he learned of a new entrepreneurial magazine being started by American Express. He got in touch and sold them several articles. In the local office of the Small Business Administration, he noticed *Small Business Success,* a magazine published by Pacific Bell. He called the editor, put together a query letter with three story ideas and clips of his work, and received a positive response. Recently Horowitz received a mail solicitation from a new magazine, *Self-Employed Professional.* He subscribed to study the publication, pitched some ideas, and sold some articles.

In another venture, Horowitz and a desktop publisher colleague created a marketing newsletter for an East Coast computer reseller. It was a turnkey operation, and the two divided the income based on the hours each had put in.

Horowitz, who is single, has his office in one bedroom of his apartment, equipped with a transcription machine, a fax-modem, and a venerable 486 PC that he plans to replace soon. Although E-mail has become a valued part of Horowitz's operations, he feels the Internet is overrated and has found its resources only moderately useful in his work.

"I'm not what you would call disciplined," he says, "but I try to spend up to half my time doing something that could lead to new business, whether it's sending out pitch letters or queries, researching new markets, thinking up story ideas, or calling prospective customers." I was pleased to learn, when I contacted Horowitz to update his profile, that he used his profile from this book as part of a marketing packet he sends to prospective clients. (Some of the other writers profiled do, too.)

CHAPTER FIVE

OFFICE SPACE AND EQUIPMENT

WHAT WILL YOU NEED TO GET STARTED?

This chapter deals with office space and office equipment for the home-based writer (with the exception of computer hardware and software, which will be discussed in Chapter Six). It's designed to help you determine what you will need to do a professional job from Day One without squandering precious start-up funds on nonessentials.

In areas where you are not sure ("Should I tear out the closet?" "Will I need a laser printer?"), you may wish to do some additional research. You can also collect opinions from your mentors and other knowledgeable people.

Heading into the exciting (but stressful) phase of creating and equipping your home office is like setting sail on a choppy sea in an untested boat. You're leaving dry land as you start to commit money, space, and time. And you're not 100 percent sure your plans will work. For a safe voyage, navigate by this lodestar: The goal is to be IN business, not to have your business perfectly set up. Once you start earning money, you can refine the rough edges. Until you start earning money, you have nothing to refine.

There are expenses involved in starting any business—but there are also ways to keep costs down. Remember, "conserve cash" is a vital rule of thumb for new businesses.

At the end of the next chapter, after you have given detailed consideration to space, office equipment, and computer hardware and software, take a look at Success Worksheets Eighteen and Nineteen. These worksheets will help you balance the funds you have available against your needs and start-up costs.

SPACE FOR YOUR HOME OFFICE

Back in my university public relations days, long before I dreamed of working for myself at home, my English-teacher husband and I became friends with a novelist and his wife. As a couple, they also wrote TV scripts, working in a tidy, attractive, air-conditioned building in their backyard. How we envied that creative space! It seemed the epitome of a writing life.

Later I met a friend in Orange, CA, who had successfully ghosted ten books and nine book proposals—plus four books under her own name—from a home office in an open corner of her living room, about 12 feet from her front door and 5 feet from where her young daughter often sat with neighborhood children watching TV.

As I work now at my Macintosh in my cool, quiet, albeit cluttered office—with a tropical Florida view outside and my own children grown and gone—I honestly do not know how my friend did it. But she did—with style and high-volume production!

At another extreme, *Home Office Computing* reported on a successful graphic designer in Philadelphia who shared "his two-story, 2,000-square-foot home with his wife, his brother, and his brother's wife—as well as five graphic designers, two or three regular freelancers, and a steady stream of models, photographers, print reps, clients, and other visitors." Whew! With its flexible high-tech design, this spacious home office reflected the owner's wanderlust, according to the magazine. He had moved three times in three years as his company grew.

In other words, there are as many kinds of home office arrangements as there are home entrepreneurs. And each arrangement is a compromise stitched out of five basic elements that must be taken into account:

- The space you have available
- Your existing equipment and start-up funds
- The requirements of your business specialty
- Your own work habits
- Your family's lifestyle

Keep these in mind as you go over the following topics related to office space.

BASIC SPACE NEEDS

Although a desktop publisher or Website designer needs much more equipment than a writer, there are several functions that your home office must support regardless of your specialties. Don't shortchange yourself on these requirements or you'll regret it as you struggle over the years with inconvenience and mislaid materials.

- Desk, chair, computer, and telephone for you
- The same for any other frequent workers
- Storage areas suitable for files, books and periodicals, computer materials, art materials, and office supplies
- Space for large pieces of equipment, including access to the equipment and handy storage for supplies

Be aware, also, that the Internal Revenue Service requires you to have a separate space in your home dedicated solely for office use in order for you to deduct home office costs. If necessary, this could be part of a room, even though the rest of the room is used for nonbusiness activities. But keeping the IRS happy is just one of many reasons why a separate room is preferable.

Working area and storage

Get as much square footage for your office as you can. Be aware, however, that, according to tax authorities, your office should not exceed fifty percent of the total area of your home. Consider creating an L- or U-shaped work area where you can easily reach your computer and other materials—you'll save time. For storage, a walk-in area adjoining your work area is just about ideal. It's handy and keeps clutter out of sight. A wall of cabinets (similar to those in your kitchen) will also serve— or you can even hang drapes or shutters in front of open shelves.

If your work area is too small to provide good storage, commandeer part of a guest room, garage, basement, or outside building for your needs. You must have storage—and even the inconvenience of storage in a detached building is preferable to the frustration of having no place to put things. Good storage promotes productivity. It allows you to keep and find what you need—when you need it!

Locating and relocating to suit your work style

Many new entrepreneurs don't choose the best place for their home office on the first try. The problems may be subjective. One writer sets up work in her living room, but she and her husband soon hate having business clutter "in their faces." Another writer locates his office on the street side of his apartment and finds that traffic noises break his concentration. A third writer feels claustrophobic after three months in his basement. He misses having windows with fresh air and a view.

The problems may be objective. An office may be in a family traffic path. It may lack a door, inviting children or animals to enter and do damage—or visitors to look at confidential papers. A basement may flood in winter. An attic may become a summer sauna.

Don't be surprised if you end up relocating to another part of your house, remodeling your garage—or even erecting an outside building. When I was living in California, I moved to the basement after deciding that my bedroom was incompatible with an office. Sleeping in the same room with my freelance materials and client records did not give me the sense of "going to work" that I seem to need. Moving in to look after an elderly relative in Florida, I realized I would have to take over the living room for my office. It was the only area available that was large enough, and my relative spent most of his time in the Florida room, watching TV. Now that he's gone, I love the view from my desk and wouldn't dream of a more conventional arrangement.

To avoid the cost and bother of a move, try to anticipate problems in advance, taking your work style into account. Do you like having people around? Then you may want to be in the traffic flow. Do you like taking your work to the living room or patio? Then you may need phones and small work areas in other parts of the house. Would you enjoy having a window—or would that be a distraction? The only "right" way to set up your office is the way that makes you most comfortable and most productive.

SPACE FACTORS TO CONSIDER

If you can't afford to do all the necessary construction and buy all the equipment you need for your office in advance, develop a written plan outlining each stage of the project, with materials lists and cost estimates. This is especially appropriate when converting a patio, porch, or basement; adding a dormer to an attic; or creating a loft above a high-ceilinged room. Consider seeking an architect, contractor, or handyman's advice. When you know what you're going to need, it's amazing how often you will spot low-cost supplies and equipment in ads and at garage sales.

What follows is a list of factors you can use as a planning guide in setting up your home office, based on my research and my own experience.

Bulletin boards and pegboards

A bulletin board is a practical and businesslike addition to your office. Beyond the usual wall calendar, monthly or yearly planner, cartoons, and inspirational sayings, your bulletin board can hold a job status chart or reference materials pertinent to your work, such as maps (including one showing time zones and phone prefixes), current postal rates and regulations, type samples, and printing paper charts.

For years, I have made inexpensive bulletin boards by stapling colored fabric tightly over half-inch fiberboard. Sold by building supply stores in 4-x-8-foot or 4-x-4-foot sheets, the fiberboard is easily cut to fit the space available. Or you can always buy a traditional bulletin board, framed in aluminum or wood.

For small tools and supplies—especially art supplies—a panel of the same pegboard that you use in the garage is perfect. Pegboard hooks and shelves come in a wide range of designs to fit your needs.

Your communications system

Telephones, fax and modem connections, computer networks, and intercommunication systems (if needed) must be part of your office plan. Good advance planning will help you avoid changes later on, saving you downtime and frustration. How many phone lines will you need? Tax experts often advise home entrepreneurs to install a separate business telephone line to avoid any IRS questioning of business costs. I have not found this necessary. I take half my phone costs for business and answer my phone with a business message during business hours and a personal message during nonbusiness hours. I do, however, have a separate fax-modem line so that clients and others will never have a problem faxing me and, if necessary, I can communicate with a client or vendor on my regular line while sending a document via modem. An added benefit is that I have an extra call-out line.

Where will you place phone outlets? If you have several lines, will all phone instruments be able to access them? If you have a separate line for your business, will you need phones for it in other parts of the house? Will your fax-modem require its own line? How will your computer and peripherals be networked? Do you need an intercom to other parts of the house? Do you need a listening device (such as to a child's room)? What about your front door? Can you hear the doorbell from your office? If not, will you need a special buzzer or communication line?

If you are going to do even minor remodeling, consider running phone and computer networking cables through walls or ceilings to meet a variety of future needs.

Toilets

You'll need convenient access to toilet facilities for yourself and any workers.

Exterior access and parking

If you expect to receive many clients or vendors and can arrange a separate entrance for your business, it might be worth paying for some remodeling. However, most home offices get by without such access. Since exterior signs are likely to be prohibited, make sure your address is clearly marked. If you are hard to find, make up a small businesslike map that you can supply to those who will be visiting you.

To create a businesslike impression, keep up the appearance of your entry as well as the interior areas your visitors pass through. You'll also need a place for visitors and delivery persons to park—especially if unauthorized parking could cause conflicts with your neighbors. If street parking has restrictions, be sure your visitors know what to do.

The comings and goings of visitors are a potential minefield, and complaints from nearby residents can cause serious, long-lasting problems—even in a city where home businesses are allowed! In general, it's best to be friendly with neighbors and to keep them informed, probing for and correcting any potential sore points.

Safety and emergency procedures

A few years ago I did an article on telecommuting (employees working from their homes) for a computer marketing newsletter. One of my questions was, "How do employers handle on-the-job injuries at home?" Several employers replied that they specifically define the employee's home work area and inspect it for safety, requiring that the employee correct any hazards. Then they insure the employee for the time he or she is doing company work in that work space.

Take the same approach to providing safety in your home office and you will be ahead of the game. You'll be protecting yourself as well as any employees, freelancers, vendors, customers, or other visitors from injury.

Your local library can provide you with guidebooks to home and office safety. Look them over and take an inventory of potential problems, such as stairs without handrails, poorly lighted areas, scatter rugs or slippery floors that might cause falls, low beams that might cause head injuries, bookshelves that might fall over (folks think about that a lot in earthquake-prone California), and hazardous materials. Correct problems when you can and put safety notices up when you can't—just as you would in a commercial setting.

Your office should have an emergency exit if possible. For example, a roll-down ladder can serve as an exit for an upstairs window. Your office should also be equipped with a smoke detector, a flashlight, and a fire extinguisher. (There are several types of extinguishers, so read up or talk to your vendor. Personally, I wouldn't advise calling the fire department.) Some health-and-safety authorities suggest putting a low-radiation screen in front of your computer monitor to reduce electrical emissions. Finally, you, your family, and your employees should agree on what to do in case of a fire, earthquake, flood, hurricane, or any other likely disaster and you should periodically review these procedures.

Power

I had two dedicated electrical circuits added to my basement office in California for the security of knowing that my power-hungry computer, printer, scanner, copier, waxer, space heater, and anything else I might plug in would have enough juice to avoid catastrophes. Now, in Tampa Bay, "the lightning capital of the nation," I live in fear of power surges that the best local computer experts say no surge suppressor can block. Nearly everyone here has lost a VCR or answering machine to lightning, so we plug and unplug a lot. Lightning blanked out my computer while I was signing up for CompuServe, so I started over and ended up with two accounts.

Putting in extra circuits may not be possible for you—especially if you are in an apartment. But at least study your circuits and try to equalize the power loads. You don't want to lose computer documents when your microwave and washing machine kick in at the same time. If you cannot fully protect yourself from such a disaster, my best advice is, "When using your computer, save, save, save!"

Light

Industrial research has shown that productivity drops when lighting is poor, and we usually think of an office as a place with plenty of light. But too much light can make it hard to adjust back and forth between your desk and your computer screen. Since the goal is to prevent eyestrain, a balance between ambient (room) lighting and task (area) lighting is the answer. Set up different arrangements to see how they work at different times of day before you install permanent fixtures. Like other home-based writers and designers, you may soon be meeting deadlines at 2:00 A.M., so your office must provide good lighting at all times.

Another factor to consider is the positioning of your computer screen. Place a small mirror where your screen will be. If lights are reflected in the mirror, distracting reflections will also show up on your screen. Try another angle or location.

Temperature control

An office in a spare room will probably share the existing heating and cooling system. But if you are converting a garage, attic, basement, or external building, you will have to equip it for temperature control. A small electric heater in winter and an oscillating fan in summer may do the job—but don't stint on comfort in the space where you will be living eight to ten hours a day. Remember, this is where you must perform at your best! Installing a wall heater, a ceiling fan, a room air conditioner, a humidifier, or a dehumidifier could be a very good investment.

Ergonomics

With recent attention focused on such on-the-job difficulties as carpal tunnel syndrome (a wrist disorder afflicting some computer users), ergonomics has become a hot topic. I think of ergonomics as the science of fitting form and function to the human frame. Industrial designers use it in establishing specifications for chairs, desks, counters, and other equipment. They design for average human dimensions, however, and one of the nicest things about planning your own office is that you can base your design on your own height and arm length or back problems. Your home office can be the most comfortable office you have ever worked in.

Decor

Shelter magazines, furniture manufacturers, and interior decorators have staked out home offices as a new frontier. The theory is that if an office is in your home, it should meet a higher standard of decor than in an office building. I don't buy this one bit! All my office furniture, except a very good desk chair, is secondhand, much of it from Goodwill and the Salvation Army. My U-shaped work area consists of three large hollow-core doors from Home Depot, mounted on filing cabinets. Commercial metal shelving (also preowned) sits on the doors to hold my books, periodicals, and many supplies. I do try to coordinate colors, but the fact is, I get a bigger kick out of saving money than decorating. On the other hand, I paid an electrician plenty to install recessed lighting for my eyes.

But don't let me talk you out of decorating your office. If it's in a high-traffic area, or if you have frequent visitors, or if the aesthetics of your surroundings are very important to you, go for it—assuming you have sufficient start-up funds!

Using design software or to-scale drawings

Interior design software is available to help you plan your home office. If you have a page layout or draw program you can save money by creating desk-size and file-cabinet-size boxes and moving them around a floor plan of your office drawn to scale to try out various options. Or, of course, you could also do that the old-fashioned way—on paper. Such planning will keep you from damaging the floor—or your back—as you experiment with furniture arrangements.

What if you have "no space?"

Don't give up. If you must stay where you are, convert a closet or the area under a stairway. Divide a room with a screen or a combined desk and shelf unit. You may be surprised what good lighting and a carefully planned desk surface and shelves can do to transform a cubbyhole into a businesslike space. Later, as your business prospers, you can move to larger quarters or build a room addition.

TOWARD A BUSINESS PLAN

Success Worksheet Twelve

Plan an office that suits you.

Your home office will be a compromise between your available space, existing equipment, start-up funds, and specific business requirements; your own work habits; and your family's lifestyle.

- What space do you have available to meet the following needs?

  Your personal workspace and that of other frequent workers

  _____

  Well-organized storage

  _____

  Equipment and room to use it

  _____

  Comfortable meeting space to accommodate clients and vendors

  _____

  Assembling materials

  _____

- What percentage of the square footage of your home will you use for your office and business storage?

  _____

- Will your work and storage areas be together or separate?

  _____

- What features of your office location might cause problems for you or other family members?

  _____

- In converting space for your office, what can you adapt or build yourself?

  _____

  _____

- Will you have to do significant remodeling? Can you do it in stages? Do you have a written plan or design? What outside assistance will you need?

  _____

  _____

- Have you considered the following factors?

  _____ Bulletin boards and pegboards

  _____ Your communications system: telephone lines, computer networks, and intercoms

  _____ Toilet facilities

  _____ Exterior access and parking

  _____ Safety and emergency procedures

  _____ Electrical power

  _____ Lighting

  _____ Temperature control

  _____ Humidity control

  _____ Ergonomics

  _____ Decor

- If you have "no space," is there anything you can do to create some?

  _____

  _____

- Make a list of the expenses you think you will incur in preparing your office space.

  _____

  _____

  _____

  _____

DETERMINING YOUR EQUIPMENT NEEDS

The equipment you have on hand, plus the money you can invest, will determine the equipment you have when you start your business. If you're a desktop publisher, the equipment you have will determine the work that you can do. Setting ego aside, the real goal at this point is for you to *become functional and credible* as a home-based entrepreneur. Much as you might like to have them now, a new oak desk and foil-stamped letterhead can usually wait.

Furniture, files, shelving

Let's take a look at furniture, filing cabinets, tables, bookshelves, and storage shelves first. You will probably pay too much for these items if you shop at traditional office equipment stores, geared to furnishing large offices. Go there to get ideas. Home furnishing stores, such as the international chain Ikea, also offer attractive but, to me, rather "lightweight" furnishings for the home office. Their showrooms are another good source of ideas, however. If you want to pay a little less for a wider selection, check the catalogs of large office supply mail-order houses. In my experience, you will pay even less at the big office-supply discounters, such as Office Depot. Discounters have thousands of products in stock and can order many thousands more through catalogs on file in their stores.

By the way, these stores are a great source of large, inexpensive plastic wastebaskets. Get several.

To make your money go as far as possible, consider buying used furniture, files, and shelving whenever possible. Check used office equipment stores and thrift stores such as the Salvation Army and Goodwill Industries. Look into government and corporate surplus sales. Check newspaper classified ads and "recycler" publications.

One caveat: If you can't find a used desk chair that suits you, pay whatever you must to get one that will be comfortable for you eight to ten hours a day. One friend with back trouble happily paid $400 for a lumbar support chair at an office discount store. Other back-pain sufferers also experiment with special cushions, available from orthopedic suppliers. Still others swear by "knee chairs," where body weight is said to be better balanced. A knee chair with casters will scoot you around in style.

As you lay out your office floor plan, remember that using lateral files (similar in shape to bookshelves) are sometimes preferable to traditional file cabinets, which require an open area for their pull-out drawers. Plastic crates designed to hold hanging files and sturdy cardboard "transfer" files and storage drawers can also help handle file storage. Rolling carts can hold frequently used files or supplies—or materials related to a current project.

Adjustable metal or plastic bookshelves, available at hardware and home supply stores, are a good investment. These shelves typically are ivory, black, or gray, 3 feet wide by 1 foot deep, with uprights in 3-foot or shorter segments. Thus, their height can be 3 feet or 6 feet, and their width can be 3 feet, 6 feet, 9 feet, and so on. You can set 3-foot shelves on a deep desk or table, securing them to a wall. To create an inexpensive counter-height work and storage area, you can wire several shelving units back to back, topping them with a 24- or 30-inch-wide door or plywood sheet. The result? An inexpensive counter-height work and storage area. Since you are likely to relocate your office at least once, the "Tinkertoy" flexibility of this kind of shelving is a big plus. And when disassembled, it's easy to transfer and store.

Poor man's "fireproof" storage

In *Tools of the Writer's Trade*, compiled by the American Society of Journalists and Authors (1990), one writer advised fellow writers not to discard an old refrigerator or small freezer. Instead, he suggested putting it in your basement or storage area. "It may not be as efficient as a costly fireproof safe, but it will protect computer disks and one-of-a-kind manuscripts from flames, smoke, and a considerable amount of heat should you have a fire in your home," says ASJA. Your guests may be disappointed, however, when they open it to find software instead of sodas.

Typewriters

Still handy for addressing envelopes and labels and for filling out forms, typewriters retain a place in many offices. I have to say that the electronic versions do not enchant me—with their slow carriage returns and inscrutable modes and codes that I am always forgetting. I still think the IBM Correcting Selectric II was the best typewriter ever made—and there are other old electric workhorses out there, too, including solid portables that take up little space. Used ones are easy to find.

Telephones

Since you already have a phone in your home, you may tend to overlook typical business options when planning your telephone system. Such options do cost extra, but they can pay for themselves in convenience and the businesslike impression you make when people call you. They range from hold buttons and multiple-line phones to intercommunication systems, the ability to play music or a commercial message while your caller waits, and voice mail (either your own system or an outside one with any number of "mailboxes," depending on your business needs).

If you use the same line for business and personal use, as I do, consider this tip: I equipped all the phone outlets in my home with instruments that have a hold button, so that I can gracefully get to my office to handle a business call no matter where I pick up the phone. Also, when I put in a second phone line for my fax and modem, I bought two two-line phones for my office and ran the fax line to them. I use the second line for outgoing calls when the first line is in use. Having two lines conveniently at hand has proved well worth the investment. If a fax comes in while I'm on the line, the sender receives a busy signal and tries again.

Local phone companies are ecstatic about the home office boom and provide special services, literature, and advice for home-based entrepreneurs, including 800 (toll-free) and 900 (caller-pays) numbers. Check it out—but be sure to learn whether you will be required to pay a higher rate if your number is identified as a business phone.

Cellular phones

Car phones are easy to purchase now—but they are still expensive to use, since you must pay by the minute for every call you make or receive. If you are often on the road and your work involves quick turnaround and fast answers, your clients will definitely appreciate being able to reach you. However, a pager (see below) would do the same job for much less money. Some mobile entrepreneurs even equip their cars with faxes—a most impressive feature—but one that is probably quite dispensible for a writer.

Pagers

More and more small-business people are using pagers to stay in touch with their clients. The small devices clip on your belt or purse and beep or vibrate when you have a message. Most display the number, and sometimes a message, of the caller. At $50 to $100 and up for the unit and under $10 a month for the service, an "electronic leash" might be a good idea—depending on the kind of work you do. Or it might be a bad idea. You may dislike interruptions from people who really don't need immediate attention.

But a pager is something to consider. For a small additional charge, paging firms can provide you with a custom message, voicemail, and other services. When you travel, they may be able to set you up with a temporary paging service out of town.

Answering machines and answering services

As a home-based entrepreneur, you *must* have a convenient and dependable way to receive phone messages. A good answering machine is the usual choice. You can screen calls when you're busy (that is, you can listen to the caller start to leave her message and pick up the receiver if you want to accept her call). When you're away, you can pick up your messages and even change your own outgoing message remotely. Some machines have two or more "voice mailboxes"—handy if you share a home business with a spouse or roommate: *"If you're calling Ted Garcia Copywriting, press 1. If you're calling Annie Garcia Design Service, press 2."*

A friend with a marketing firm clings to her old-fashioned live answering service. She hates machines on principle and thinks it's more prestigious to have a real person answering the phone when she's away. But I fume every time I want to leave a message too detailed for the operator to take down. If you prefer a live answering service, consider one with a voicemail option: *"Bob Okamura is at a trade show today. I can take your number and have him call you—or would you like to leave a message on his voice mail?"* Very professional!

My son, who does computer consulting out of his home, has come up with a slick combination of phone services. Using Delayed Call Forwarding, he has his calls automatically forwarded to his paging number after the third ring. There a message invites callers to leave him a recorded message or to page him by entering their phone number. This seamless system requires callers to keep track of only one number.

Fax machines

A few years ago I thought I could get by without a fax machine. The machines then were $600 or $700, and my nearby fax service (in a stationery store) charged only a dollar a page to send or receive. Then one Friday before a holiday weekend, a good client, the employee communications director for a major bank, called to say she had a rush project—a newsletter that was written but needed to be laid out. Could I do it by Tuesday? "Sure," I said. I was already familiar with the newsletter's format and asked her to fax it to me. Since I was busy all day Friday, I planned to pick up the work on Saturday morning. But when I got there, the stationery store was locked up tight with a sign in the window saying, "Closed for the weekend." On Tuesday, after apologizing to my client for blowing the job, I went out and bought my own fax machine.

Faxes are a basic part of communications today, although business writer Alan Horowitz, profiled in Chapter Four, is an E-mail devotee who called faxes "a gizmo on its way out." With fax-modem software available for your computer, why not join the movement? Personally, I still prefer my stand-alone machine, but if you buy a stand-alone fax, make sure it has the features you need. In addition to a paper cutter and a document feeder, other common features include preprogramming for frequently called numbers, automatic redialing, and the ability to automatically send a transmission (such as a press release) to a list of numbers at a predetermined time (such as at night when rates are lower and faxes are less busy). A machine that uses a paper roll larger than the standard 98-foot roll saves money and the bother of changing rolls, as well as lost faxes when you run out of paper.

Don't be impressed by manufacturers' claims that your fax can serve as a copier. It can, but only in a pinch.

Phone-fax-modem managers

Several of my home-based writer friends manage all their phone-related activities on one line with the help of a phone-fax-modem manager. These devices can detect what kind of call is coming in (voice, fax, or modem) and will direct incoming calls to the proper instrument. At least, they're supposed to. In my experience, some of them give you a fax tone when you want to talk with someone, or put someone on the line when you want to send a fax. If you buy a phone-fax-modem manager, make sure it works!

Copiers and combination units

I am surprised how many writers do not own a copier. When I was short on cash, I managed without one for almost three years, running to the copy shop almost every day. Out of frustration, I began studying the classifieds and finally bought a used copier that turned out to be a nightmare of paper jams, toner smears, and repairs (thank God the seller took it back). Chastened, I bought a new 11x17-inch enlarging and reducing Sharp for almost $2,000. Had I not been doing graphics, a much less expensive one would have sufficed. It was one of the best purchases I ever made! The quality on this machine, properly maintained, is so good that I often paste up its output directly into low-budget layouts. Today I can't imagine life without a copier.

Next time you take off for the copy shop, consider what your time is worth. Personal copiers start at about $500. Take a look at combination fax-copier-printer-scanner units, too. These use plain paper and might meet your needs.

Calculators

No doubt you have a pocket calculator—that's all I use to this day. But a larger printing calculator might be useful. If you work with financial material, it might be essential. If you handle technical material, you may need a scientific calculator.

Postal meters and scales

If you do a lot of mailing, a postal meter is a labor- and money-saving tool, since you can dial in the correct postage instead of hunting for the right stamps. Pitney Bowes leases an inexpensive unit to home entrepreneurs and small businesses. (But consider whether doing a mailing is really a good use of your time—small mailing houses are set up to do it much more efficiently.)

Even if you don't have much outgoing mail, a mechanical postal scale ($20 and up) is a necessity. You certainly don't want your material returned for insufficient postage; nor do you want to waste money on excess postage. An electronic calculating postal scale (more than $100) calculates the necessary postage with the help of a pop-in rate cartridge that can be updated.

Binding machines

Office-supply discount stores and mail-order catalogs provide several bindery options, including plastic-comb-binding machines (about $500), which produce bound documents that will lie open, and various other units that bind documents on the side. I picked up a plastic-comb-binding machine in OK condition at the Salvation Army for $5.00. (They didn't know what it was.) A new or used unit might be a good investment if you often prepare material for presentation—writing proposals, for example. Presenting your own samples in a neatly bound package also makes a dynamite impression. Several other types of binding systems are also available.

Color copiers

Color copiers print from reflective originals or slides and are too costly for most home offices, as prices start at around $14,000. They offer enlargement, reduction, and even some color correction for $1.00 or less a page. The quality is surprisingly good—good enough for design comps to show your clients—and may even be good enough for your own promotional materials.

Tape recorders and transcribers

If you're a writer who does taped interviews, you already have a tape recorder. If not, an inexpensive unit (either standard or microcassette) of any reliable brand will cost from $30 to about $100 and will do just fine. When I'm taping phone interviews from home, my recorder is hooked up to a reliable $20 device from Radio Shack that can turn my remote-controlled tape recorder on automatically as soon as the receiver is lifted and produces good-quality recordings.

Transcribing these interviews is, unfortunately, a time-consuming pain in the neck! You can't bill for it at your normal creative rates, and it's hard to find vendors to do it without losing both time and money—to say nothing of the difficulty getting an accurate transcription. A professional transcribing machine, with a foot pedal and speed control, sells for $200 to $300 new—and anything that makes transcription easier is a bonus in my book.

TOWARD A BUSINESS PLAN

Success Worksheet Thirteen

Buy only the equipment you need.

The funds you have available will determine how extensive your initial setup can be—but remember that as you become established and find your focus, your needs may change.

■ What usable office furniture and equipment do you already have?

_____

_____

_____

■ What additional office furniture and equipment will you need during your first year?

Item	Estimated Cost
__ Furniture, files, shelving	$ _____
__ Typewriter,	$ _____
__ word processors	$ _____
__ Telephones, including cellular phone	$ _____
__ Pager	$ _____
__ Answering machine vs. answering service	$ _____
__ Fax machine (or fax-modem software)	$ _____
__ Copier	$ _____
__ Calculator	$ _____
__ Postal meter	$ _____
__ Binding machine	$ _____
__ Tape recorder, transcriber	$ _____
__ Graphic arts equipment	$ _____
Other?	$ _____

- Can any of this equipment be bought used or obtained through trading or surplus sources? How much can you save?

  _____

  _____

- Can you use a copy center to avoid buying a copier during your first year?

  _____

- What equipment can you wait until your second year to purchase?

  _____

  _____

- What will your total office furniture and equipment costs be during the first year?

  _____

Jan Franck
Frank Communications, West Des Moines, Iowa

Positioning for Profit

After a few years in business, Jan Franck went from calling herself a "free-lance writer" to referring to herself as a "marketing consultant" and everything changed.

With an undergraduate degree in advertising and a master's in mass communications, Franck was "ready to conquer the world" in 1981 with her new degree. But Des Moines was in a recession, and the only job offers she received were to build business for advertising agencies. Since she had minimal financial pressure at the time and two small children to care for, she decided, "I could do that for myself."

Franck began knocking on doors, taking any communications job she could find, from trade-show booths to brochures to press releases, and was profitable within six months. But something was wrong. She was defining her business as a "cottage industry" and found it sounded like "kitchen table" to her mostly male clients. "Freelance writer" sounded like "side income, pin money." And her strategy of "since I'm home-based, I can do it for less" was perceived not as a benefit but as a compromise with quality.

"I erased all that from my presentation," she says, "and came on as a professional, customized service, and things really started to click."

Today, Franck Communications provides a combination of research, marketing plans, and marketing materials. Handling sales, client strategy, and most of the writing herself, she calls on some fifteen subcontractors—research specialists, designers, illustrators, and photographers. "I get the best creative services for the project," she says. "Too many agencies hire a generalist and hope he or she can do whatever comes in the door."

Franck pays her subs and printers and handles all client billing. "I manage the project," she explains, "that makes clients come back to me."

Initially expecting that she would have to lure jobs away from established agencies, Franck says she was surprised to find "how much work is out there." She reports, "I've always been able to find a niche where I can provide something that is too specialized or too small for the client's agency or too expensive to do at agency rates."

Franck has become part of the online revolution but feels it has drawbacks as well as benefits. She works with several Website providers to supply traditional marketing materials that their clients need—and uses the providers to supply Websites for her clients.

"'Welcome! Here we are!' is not cutting it anymore on the Web," she says. "I work with the client and the provider to come up with a statement: 'The purpose of this Website is going to be such-and-such. And to accomplish that, we'll need to include this information and give the user these options. Sometimes I do a lot of reworking to make it a one-idea-to-a-screen design. Most users are not going to scroll down nine pages of text or sit and wait for elaborate graphics to come down."

Looking for improved organization and access to be "the next revolution on the Net," Franck says she would prefer to subcontract with an Internet research expert, rather than spend her own time seeking special information on the ever-more-crowded information superhighway.

Franck also has a bone to pick with those who invade her E-mail. "Your address is out there because you belong to associations and so you get strangers out of the blue E-mailing you and saying, 'Hey, Jan, I understand you're a marketer and I have this question for you. How do you bill?' Or 'Do you advertise?' Or "What is your greatest problem operating a home-based business?' They rarely give any up-front information about themselves. Oftentimes I don't even know what part of the country they're from. You hate to give away information that has value without having some idea of where it's going and how it's going to be used. It could be a competitor from across the street." She would like to see Internet protocol ("netiquette") refined to handle such situations.

Franck has looked into teaming with other marketing specialists to go after larger clients but finds "virtual corporations" to be something of a disappointment. "It can take an awful lot of discussion for an hour of billable time," she warns. "You join with other entrepreneurs and everybody is an entrepreneur largely because they like to be in control."

Franck is involved with such groups as the International Association of Business Communicators and the Marketing Association of America. As a networker, she knows "someone at every agency in town" and privately does an annual rate survey of Des Moines–area advertising agencies. She says that getting "even a ballpark figure" helps her stay both profitable and competitive.

Referrals are an important and cost-effective component to Franck's marketing plan. "At the end of a project, I always say, 'Thanks for the business, and now that we've worked together and you know what I can do, is there anyone else you can refer me to?'"

In another successful marketing activity, Franck teaches free seminars on "how to start your own business" for the Small Business Administration and passes out cards entitling new entrepreneurs to a free hour of consulting. "I'm seeding the field for the future," she says, "and sometimes I hit a business that's ready to grow now."

CHAPTER SIX

COMPUTERS, ONLINE SERVICES, AND ANOTHER LOOK AT START-UP COSTS

SELECTING YOUR COMPUTER

My purpose in this section is not to review the mass of computer-related products flooding today's market but to give you some idea of the kinds of hardware and software you will need to do various kinds of work—and, further, to suggest techniques for shopping smart and obtaining reliable information.

The computing needs of a desktop publisher or Webpage designer are far more extensive than those of a writer, and, even though I encourage you to consider these specialities, I will not try to cover their hardware and software requirements here.

Mac vs. PC

Let it be said: An Apple Macintosh, or one of its clones, and an IBM-compatible personal computer (PC) running Windows 95 are comparable computers.

PCs are more widely available and more widely used in business. Traditionally, they have been a little cheaper. Macintosh still maintains a slight edge on ease of use, and Macs are well established in the graphics world (but not as well established as they used to be). Until recently, Apple has lagged in producing fast computers, but the PowerPC has helped Macintosh catch up. *PowerPC* is a confusing term because it refers not to an IBM-compatible PC but to a Macintosh with a processor different from and faster than that of the venerable 680X0 series. Making the transition from an older Mac to a PowerPC is generally smooth, with a few inconveniences—but 680X0 machines are still a feasible choice for a business writer. This book's being written on one.

If software availability is one of your criteria, it's true that a great deal of software is produced only for the PC. (We Mac types get used to asking routinely, whenever we hear of an interesting software program or peripheral, "Is it available for the Mac?" PC users rarely ask that question.) If you write in a specialty where you must use a PC-only program, your decision will have been made. However, Mac software is available for every normal computer use.

Some writers feel it's desirable to use the kind of computer that the majority of their clients use. This is a factor if you are going to share files, but not if you are simply delivering text, such as an article E-mailed to an editor. For some working relationships, being on the same platform (that is, type of computer operating system) can be convenient. However, in my experience, using a different platform need not put you out of the running. Most files can be converted—and here the Mac does have an advantage, because it can both read PC disks and format disks to be read on a PC. (PC software to do this with Mac disks is also available.)

In the final analysis, the Mac-PC decision is still based on your own familiarity and preference. If you already own a Mac or a PC, by all means use it in your business to save vital cash. If it isn't powerful enough (more about that later), perhaps it can be upgraded. However, if it isn't powerful enough and cannot be upgraded, bite the bullet and get a computer that will meet your needs.

What's ahead for Windows and Mac?

As we all know by now, nothing lasts long in the computer world. In spite of its lavish product launch, many view Windows 95 as a transitional operating system destined to give way to Windows NT, which is more stable and more powerful with major networking advantages. NT runs Windows 95 software but cannot be installed as an upgrade, so if you're already using Windows 95, Windows NT will require reinstallation of everything on your computer. Of course, that may be a small price for greater functionality.

On the Macintosh side, after the major upgrade to System 7.x a few years back, Apple has announced plans to adapt the UNIX-based NEXT operating system as it's replacement for the aging system 7.x, while the industry watches with mixed expectations. The impact this development and the growing use of Windows NT will have on Apple's shrinking market share remains to be seen.

Success Worksheet Fourteen

Determine your computing needs.

Different activities require different levels of computer hardware. This checklist will help you decide what you need.

Check If You Need	Enter Points
_____ Basic word processing (1)	_____
_____ Personal finance or small-business software (1)	_____
_____ Small contact database (1)	_____
_____ Resources on CD–ROMs (2)	_____
_____ Online services, including World Wide Web (3)	_____
_____ Large spreadsheets (3)	_____
_____ Large industry or client databases (3)	_____
_____ Desktop publishing (one- to three-color work) (3)	_____
_____ Desktop publishing (four-color work) (4)	_____
_____ Image editing (for example, Photoshop) (3)	_____
_____ Illustration and paint programs (3)	_____
_____ Multimedia (see below)	_____
TOTAL POINTS	_____

If your total is 3 or under, you can use an old computer such as a 386 PC or a Macintosh ci. If your total is over 6, you need at least a 486 or newer Macintosh 680x0 series. Over 9, you need a fairly fast Pentium or a low-end Macintosh PowerPC. If you do multimedia, you need a fast Pentium or a high-end Mac PowerPC.

How much power do I need?

Before the online revolution, a professional writer could get by with very limited computing power. Most of what he did was simple word processing—one of a computer's easier assignments. Now, to handle online graphics satisfactorily, equip yourself with at least a 486 PC or a 68040 Macintosh. If you're buying a new computer, select the fastest Pentium processor or Mac PowerPC you can afford (speed being measured in megahertz, or MHz) and expect to pay $2,000 and up for a model with a CD–ROM drive and a 28.8K bps (baud-per-second) fax-modem. Monitor and keyboard will be additional. If you find a good buy in a computer that lacks an internal CD–ROM or fax-modem, be aware that you can add these as external peripherals.

Get all the memory (RAM, or random access memory) and all the hard drive storage you can afford. Windows 95 works best with at least 16 megabytes (MB) of RAM, and newer Macs need about the same. With either platform, the more RAM the better. Fortunately, in mid-1996 RAM costs dropped significantly, so make sure the computer you buy accepts RAM upgrades. *Consumer Reports*, in an excellent article on equipment for the home office (September 1996), also stresses that the computer you buy should be upgradeable. CR advises, "You should expect a computer purchased today to work for at least two or three years before it needs to be upgraded." As for hard drives, the typical capacity on new Macs and PCs now exceeds one gigabyte.

Even though I have given you my best advice here, I need to point out that when I interviewed them in mid-1996, two of the successful writers profiled for this book were still working (and making nice profits) on what are by today's standards very old computers. One was using a 286 PC (with access to faster equipment at a client's office); the other, a Macintosh SE-30 (with a large monitor added). What is it they say? "Give a great photographer a box camera, and he'll still get great pictures."

Should I buy a used computer?

Don't be afraid of a used computer, especially if you're buying from a dealer who offers some type of guarantee. I've run my business on used computers for years, and I'm here to tell you that you can save a significant amount of money. If a fairly recent computer runs well, it will probably continue running well because its electronic components are OK and its mechanical parts still have mileage on them. When buying from an individual, ask a computer-savvy friend or pay a consultant to help you look the machine over.

Notebooks and smaller

If your work involves travel, you may need a notebook or laptop computer ($1,000 and up, up, up). If you own a good one, you really don't need a separate desktop computer—unless someone in your office must use it while you are gone. Many notebook computers can be turned into desktop computers by plugging in a full-size keyboard and monitor. In this case, of course, you will need to get a color laptop. Notebook computers that can run a large monitor are great for off-site presentations.

New palm-size computers and "personal digital assistants" ($500 and up) take even less room than notebooks, virtually fitting into your coat pocket. They function as personal organizers and are usually compatible with your full-sized computer. Apple's much ballyhooed Newton MessagePad ($800 and up), which operates with a pen, launched the new category of "digital personal assistants," which have even more computing power.

Caution: If possible, wait to buy supplementary computers. While helpful and fun, they are usually not essential. Conserve cash now.

COMPUTER PERIPHERALS AND ACCESSORIES

Hard drive

A hard drive is a data storage device that looks something like a miniature record player. Your hard drive may be mounted inside your computer or in an external box with its own power supply or you may have both. The hard drive holds your operating system, your applications, and any other data you load on it. Even once-simple word-processing programs now gobble up hard drive space, as do most other programs you will use. Graphics and multimedia also generate very large files. A 1.2GB (gigabyte) hard drive has become the standard in new computers.

Other storage devices

You will need to back up your hard drive. There is no getting around this. Computers crash. Hard drives fail. One day it will happen to you. If you are storing material that your clients depend upon, it could even be legally actionable if you were to lose the material and not have it backed up.

You can, of course, back up your data on 1.2 megabyte (MB) floppy disks, using one of many backup programs available. But with hard drives running more than one gigabyte, backing up on floppies could literally take hours of swapping disks. A better solution is an external storage drive such as the popular Iomega Zip Drive ($150 and up), which uses 100 MB cartridges ($20), or the Syquest EZ-135 ($100 and up), which uses 135 MB cartridges ($25). A DAT tape drive, which can store massive amounts of data on special tape cartridges, is another option.

If you are transmitting large graphics or multimedia files to clients, to desktop publishing or multimedia service bureaus, or to printers, a Syquest or a Zip drive would be the solution. Both are widely used in the graphics industry. If you are into CD-ROM authoring, you may need a recordable CD-ROM unit.

Label printers

Some full-size printers do not handle envelopes well. As a result, small auxiliary label printers ($130 and up) have become popular as a quick way to address envelopes and packages. You must use the manufacturer's proprietary (and expensive) labels in these machines, which makes them uneconomical for long runs. (Their formats are not compatible with commercial label-affixing equipment.)

Ink-jet printers

You will need to produce clear, clean printed copy, and an ink-jet printer is your most economical choice ($250 and up). Some are small enough to fit into a brief-case—vital if you travel. However, a portable ink-jet would probably not be fast or heavy-duty enough for all your daily work.

A wide variety of good ink-jets is available from Hewlett Packard, Epson, Apple, and other manufacturers. Resolution (dots-per-inch) is as good as that of most laser printers. Color ink-jet printers can do a wide range of short-run projects; however, very high-quality ink-jet paper for color graphics can be fifty cents to $1.00 a page. Incidentally, if you're printing your own business cards—quite a feasible thing to do these days—be sure to buy blank card stock for the correct printer. Laser stock will come out as a blur on your ink-jet.

Get as much speed (measured in pages-per-minute, or PPM) as you can afford. Waiting for a document to print out can be agonizing. If you're buying a new computer, you may be able to negotiate an ink-jet printer in the deal at a nice discount. If not, watch for sales. This is a very competitive segment of the industry.

While you're shopping, you might as well buy a color ink-jet—in fact, few are now sold without color capability. Color is handy for sales presentations and charts and, of course, is essential in many graphics uses. Be sure to get a printer that has a permanent place for its color cartridge. The cheapest models require you to swap cartridges back and forth. High-end ink-jets, such as Hewlett-Packard's 1600C ($1,400), are designed for heavier-duty color work by individuals and groups and feature better speed and quality in both black and color.

Laser printers

Laser printers create images in fine-powdered toner that is heat-fused to the page; thus, laser printing cannot smear as can ink-jet pages. Lasers are also faster than ink-jets—typically eight PPM versus a low-end ink-jet's three or five PPM in black and much slower output in color. Laser printers are designed for heavier-duty cycles, measured in pages-per-month. The fine resolution of 600 dots-per-inch (DPI) is standard on most lasers today; this is fine enough to reproduce photographs acceptably for low-end uses, such as an in-house newsletter. However, if you are using only type, the older 300 DPI standard is entirely adequate.

Expect to pay $500 to $1,200 for a laser printer. The more expensive models are PostScript-compatible, meaning that they have advanced graphics capabilities and will not give you jagged images on some artwork, as will non-PostScript printers. Color laser printers, like dye sublimation and wax transfer color printers, are used primarily by high-end graphic shops.

Printer combinations

Hewlett-Packard, Brother, Canon, and other manufacturers offer a "do everything" unit that combines printing, copying, faxing, and scanning ($600 and up). These machines receive your faxes on plain paper and can scan or copy flat sheets at fairly low resolutions. (They can't copy pages from books, because sheets must run through the unit.) They may include optical character recognition (OCR) software, so that you can read and edit scanned text documents on your computer.

If these units really did everything as well as stand-alone units, the market for stand-alones would have dried up. But a "do everything" just might meet your needs. Check it out.

Fax/modems

What else do you need? Today you definitely need a modem. Connected to your computer and to a telephone line, a modem translates digital computer data into telephone signals. At the other end of the line, another modem is needed to receive the transmission and convert it back into computer-speak.

Modems have been gaining speed ever since they were introduced. The present standard is 28.8K bps (baud-per-second) V.34 (both internal and external models run slightly over $100). Slower, 14.4K bps modems are are still available for about $50. Newly introduced are 33.6K bps units—and ever-higher-speed options are available using other technology. Since online activities have become such a vital part of the daily routines of most full-time business writers, I strongly recommend that you buy the fastest modem you can afford. Downloading time is money!

With your modem you will probably receive communications and fax software. Fax software has enabled many writers to use their computers to handle their faxing needs (you may want to look into a better faxing program than the freebie that comes with your modem). This system has two main drawbacks, however. First, documents that are not already in your computer (a printed flyer, a hand-corrected page of copy) must be scanned before they can be faxed. Second, unless you leave your computer on at all times with a dedicated phone line, people who want to fax something to you may have to make contact with you first to establish the connection. Switching units are available that purport to direct the call appropriately after detecting which kind of call is coming in. In my experience, some of these units work better than others.

Large monitors

If I were not a desktop publisher as well as a writer, I would probably never have bought a 19-inch monitor—but now I can't imagine writing without it. Try a large monitor (17 inches and up) in a store or at a training center sometime and see how it feels. This could be something to save for!

Working with a large monitor, you can see one or two full pages at a time. Most applications allow you to open several documents at the same time. You can move them around on the big screen, layering them behind one another and pulling them forward as you need them. You can make corrections in related passages, and copy material from one document to another. Working on this book, with each chapter set up as a separate document, my 19-inch screen has been invaluable! With multitasking, you can also work on documents from more than one application at the same time.

"Portrait" monitors allow you to view one full page. They look like a regular monitor turned on its side, and, in fact, the popular Portrait Display Labs' Pivot one-page monitor can be used either way. Two-page monitors are usually 19, 20, or 21 inches. For a 17-inch color monitor, you'll pay $800 and up. For a 20-inch black-and-white monitor, budget $1,500; for color, $2,000 or more. Used monitors are a less expensive option. You may need an add-on board to drive a larger monitor. Check with your dealer.

One caveat about monitors: *Beware of flicker and distortion.* A poor monitor can cause eyestrain after only a few minutes—to say nothing of staring at it for eight or ten hours. Make sure you can return any monitor you buy—even a used one—if it does not perform satisfactorily with your system! The prices I have quoted are low-end, and you may have to pay more for the monitor you want. But for the sake of your eyes and your productivity, it's worth it.

Keyboards, input devices, and wrist supports

You don't have to stick with the keyboard that came with your computer. A variety of custom keyboards are available ($50 and up). Mice, too, come in a variety of custom models, as do trackballs and digital pens, which many people find more convenient than a mouse. Since you will spend a lot of time at your keyboard, invest in one that suits you.

The accessory section of your computer store will also offer several wrist supports ($10 and up)—or you could make yourself one. I recommended them for avoiding wrist fatigue—and they are vital if you already have wrist problems.

To give myself more desk space, I installed a keyboard drawer, which pulls out from under my worktable and comes with a convenient wrist support. Working on this book made me aware of another benefit of a keyboard drawer. My cat began to resent being ignored and took to walking back and forth in front of my monitor. When I left my worktable, I was able to push the drawer in so he couldn't walk on the keys.

Scanners

As a writer, you will almost certainly find the optical character recognition (OCR) capabilities of scanners useful—although this is a purchase you can defer. (Scanning services are available at service bureaus and large copy centers to meet an occasional need.) With OCR software, a scanner can "read" clean printed or typewritten text—such as your client's manual that needs editing, a long quote from a printed source, or a list of parts for a catalog. Good OCR software can read in several languages. You can create a separate document of the scanned pages, or you may be able to insert the scanned material directly into the document you are working on.

A much more frequent use for scanners is to translate photos, illustrations, and drawings into digital images that can be edited (with still more software) and used in publications and presentations.

Hand-held scanners ($120 and up) read a 4- or 5-inch pass. If one pass does not take in the entire subject, the software allows passes to be combined. These scanners are sold with basic OCR and graphics software. Full-page color flatbed scanners are available for $350 to $2,000 or more for better-quality scans.

Scanning color slides poses a special problem, which is solved by separate color slide scanners and by color slide adapters for flatbed scanners.

Other scanner variants are small business-card scanners and a new category of roll-through scanners about the size of a box of aluminum foil. Examples are the Hewlett-Packard ScanJet 4s ($250) and the Visioneer PaperPort Vx ($300). These machines are designed to sit between your monitor and your keyboard. Supplied with OCR software, they are intended to "handle paper." Any printed material that can be fed through the rollers—from a business card to an 8½ x 30-inch sheet—instantly becomes an electronic document that you can edit, print, transmit to via E-mail, insert into other documents, or file for future use. Such a tool could have many applications for writers.

If the scanner you buy does not provide it, you will need OCR software ($70 for a "light" program; more than $500 for a full-featured one). Shop carefully. OCR can be a great convenience, but the results are sometimes unusable.

CD–ROM drive

Looking like familiar audio CDs, CD–ROM disks have a 600-megabyte capacity, allowing them to carry a vast amount of digital information. And they represent an emerging market for computer-savvy writers and graphic designers, since material must be tailored to this medium's unique capabilities.

CD–ROMs make color visuals, text, and sound quickly and randomly accessible. With an internal or external CD–ROM drive ($125 and up), you can view a growing number of business reference titles, directories, and how-to guides as well as family, cultural, and entertainment resources.

As a writer, you will find a CD–ROM drive a useful addition to your computer system. (In 1996 *Writer's Digest* for the first time introduced a CD–ROM version of its old standby, the 1997 edition of *Writer's Market*—and here's where the new technology's functionality comes into play. The CD version includes software with which users can keep track of all their manuscript submissions.) When you are shopping for a CD–ROM drive, the major specification you will hear about is speed—how fast the drive can access data and how fast it can transfer the data it has located. The measurement of "4X" or "6X" or "8X" means that the drive in question is four times, six times, or eight times faster than the original drives introduced a few years ago.

Photo CD

If you provide your clients with photos, you may already be using the new technology that Kodak has developed for digitizing photographs and putting them on photo CDs. Kodak's entry into the world of CD–ROM provides a needed link between traditional photography and electronic media. Photo CD image scans are inexpensive and of high quality. To process a 24-exposure roll of color film and transfer it to a Photo CD costs about $20.

Here's how Photo CD works: The processor takes your film and scans all photos on the roll at various resolutions (a set of resolutions is called an "image pack"). You receive your slides or negatives (and prints if you wish), along with a Photo CD that can be used to put photos directly into page layout programs, presentations, multimedia, or Websites. One Photo CD can store 100 to 150 images, and additional photos can be added to the CD later. Since you can't erase the images, you may want to have your photos developed first and digitize only selected photos.

Electronic photography

If you write articles—especially for trade journals and smaller magazines—or if you do corporate or organizational newsletters, you may be called upon to provide photos.

For quality color photos, the Photo CD approach, described above, is a solid choice.

A simple, "down-and-dirty" technique that I use for low-budget black-and-white newsletters is to shoot color negatives and scan the color prints in black-and-white on my Hewlett-Packard ScanJet 3c. (Getting color film processed today is far easier and less expensive than black-and-white film, and if you want a proof sheet, Kodak and other processors will supply one in half-size.) I do whatever tonal balance or cleanup is necessary in Adobe Photoshop and drop the photo into the page as I assemble it.

I've taken the same approach to developing Websites. Here color photos are an big plus, but high-quality reproduction is far less important than small files that will download quickly. Starting with a color print that I have taken or received from my client, I scan the print in color, clean it up in Photoshop, and save it as a JPEG or GIF file of the smallest acceptable size.

Both of these methods allow you to use traditional film and your own high-quality still camera with its myriad lenses and options—a technology that is already highly evolved. But here's another way to go.

Buy an electronic still camera ($400 and up, but coming down) that will give you photos comparable to those of a point-and-shoot camera, producing digital images on a reusable cartridge. The image can also be "improved" in Photoshop and placed directly into your document. If turnaround time is a factor, this approach offers a huge advantage: no trip to the photo processor. But since current cartridges hold only a limited number of images, you can't use the "mother-fish approach"—favored by some photojournalists—of laying a thousand eggs to hatch one. Electronic photo filesare huge. Make sure you have plenty of storage space.

Networking

If your office has more than one computer or printer, you will need to network link these devices so that all computers can access all printers. But that's just the beginning. Computers can be linked to share files and send E-mail—even across platforms, from a PC to a Mac or vice versa. Such linking is called a local area network (LAN). Networking takes technical savvy, so check with a consultant.

Power controls

Surge suppressor power strips ($12 and up) are widely sold for use with computer equipment. If your computer is connected to your household power through a surge suppressor, occasional power spikes cannot harm your hardware or your data—at least, that's what most of the country believes. Lightning-conscious Floridians don't trust surge suppressors and unplug during severe storms or when they are away. Some more expensive surge suppressors come with $10,000 (or higher) equipment damage guarantees.

For another kind of protection, units are available to provide a few minutes of reserve power, during which you can save your data in case of a power failure ($180 and up). If your area experiences frequent power outages, such a fail-safe device might be a wise investment.

Accessories

You can add many other accessories to your computer arsenal—including mouse pads, copy holders, dust covers for keyboards and computers, monitor stands, printer stands, CPU stands, computer traveling cases, floppy disk cases and wallets, floppy disk mailers, security devices to prevent computer theft, antiglare monitor filters, reference guides listing commands for specific applications, computer tool and cleaning kits, power converters to plug your notebook computer into your car cigarette lighter, and more and more. A favorite accessory can be a delight and well worth its price. But shop carefully.

TOWARD A BUSINESS PLAN

Success Worksheet Fifteen

Plan your computer system.

Having short-range and long-range objectives for your computer system will increase your functionality and help you grow your business.

- What kind of computer will you use? Can your present computer be upgraded? Will you need to purchase new equipment? If so, what kind?

  _____

  _____

  _____ *Have this equipment now?*

  _____ *Plan to get this equipment (month, year)?* _____

  Estimated cost $_____

- Will you also need a laptop or notebook computer, a palm-size computer, or a personal digital assistant? (Delay purchasing an additional computer if possible.)

  _____

  _____ *Have this equipment now?*

_____ *Plan to get this equipment (month, year)?* _____

Estimated cost $_____

■ What size internal hard drive will you need? Will you need an external hard drive? If so, what size?

_____

_____ *Have this equipment now?*

_____ *Plan to get this equipment (month, year)?* _____

Estimated cost $_____

■ Will you need additional storage devices? If so, what kind?

_____

_____ *Have this equipment now?*

_____ *Plan to get this equipment (month, year)?* _____

Estimated cost $_____

■ What kind of printer will you use?

_____

_____ *Have this equipment now?*

_____ *Plan to get this equipment (month, year)?* _____

Estimated cost $_____

■ Would a combination printer-copier-fax-scanner meet your needs? If so, what kind?

_____

_____ *Have this equipment now?*

_____ *Plan to get this equipment (month, year)?* _____

Estimated cost $_____

■ Will you need an accessory printer, such as a portable printer or a label printer? If so, what kind?

_____

_____ *Have this equipment now?*

_____ *Plan to get this equipment (month, year)?* _____

Estimated cost $_____

- What kind of modem will you use?

_____

_____ *Have this equipment now?*

_____ *Plan to get this equipment (month, year)?* _____

Estimated cost $_____

- Would a larger monitor be an asset to you? If so, what kind?

_____

_____ *Have this equipment now?*

_____ *Plan to get this equipment (month, year)?* _____

Estimated cost $_____

- Will you need a different keyboard or input device(s)? Will you need a wrist support? If so, what kind?

_____

_____ *Have this equipment now?*

_____ *Plan to get this equipment (month, year)?* _____

Estimated cost $_____

- Will you need a scanner? If so, what kind?

_____

_____ *Have this equipment now?*

_____ *Plan to get this equipment (month, year)?* _____

Estimated cost $_____

- Will you need a CD–ROM? If so, what kind?

_____

_____ *Have this equipment now?*

_____ *Plan to get this equipment (month, year)?* _____

Estimated cost $_____

- Will you need a digital camera? If so, what kind?

  _____

  _____ *Have this equipment now?*

  _____ *Plan to get this equipment (month, year)?* _____

  Estimated cost $_____

- What kind of computer networking will you need, if any?

  _____

  _____ *Have this equipment now?*

  _____ *Plan to get this equipment (month, year)?* _____

  Estimated cost $_____

- What kind of power controls will you use?

  _____

  _____ *Have this equipment now?*

  _____ *Plan to get this equipment (month, year)?* _____

  Estimated cost $_____

SOFTWARE FOR WRITERS

Word processing

Most word processors have more features and more power than we users take advantage of—which is our loss. The trend is for word processors to add more page layout features and for page layout programs to add more word-processing features, bringing the two closer together. But they still have their distinct roles to play. Some word-processing programs are favored by certain industries. The legal profession, for example, leans toward WordPerfect. See if this is true in the field you intend to write for.

If you do general business writing, you might save time on certain assignments with special software programs like an employee manual maker, a job description maker, or a company policy maker. If you write about specialized subjects, watch for software designed to serve them. One southern California book author, who includes cats and genealogy among her writing specialties, uses a program that handles pet pedigrees (she noticed that it was used by a national cat registry service), as well as a "family tree" program she learned about in a genealogy magazine. You won't find such specialized software in the big software mail-order catalogs, but tracking them down could be worth your while.

All word-processing programs incorporate at least some of the following features:

Grammar- and spell-checking

Dictionary

Thesaurus

Quotations

Headers and footers

Foreign language support

Bibliography and footnote making

Extensions adding graphics, page layouts, and other features

Resumé making

Outlining

Forms making

Table of contents making

Envelope addressing

Legal and sales letters

Merging (with database files)

Sorting

Optical character recognition scanning and editing

HTML conversion for the World Wide Web

Page layout

Here's a quick rundown of the programs most used by desktop publishers to combine text and graphics. *The Pricing Guide for Desktop Publishing Services* (see Bibliography) lists software used by survey respondents by platform and program, indicating what percentage reported using each program.

Page layout programs include the following:

■ Adobe **PageMaker** (PC, Mac $550)

The leading seller and a very solid program, a good choice if you design for both Macs and PCs or must interface with clients' files, but not the best choice for long documents.

■ Quark **XPress** (PC $570, and Mac $650)

My personal favorite. Very powerful typography control, very stable, efficient use of memory. Offers many useful extensions, including one for Web authoring.

- **CorelDRAW** (PC $430, earlier version $200). A lot for the money.

  The old PC page layout program, Ventura, has been incorporated into this feature-rich graphics program.

- Adobe **FrameMaker** (PC, Mac $590)

  Well suited for long documents.

Web authoring

A category in flux as new techniques are introduced to the World Wide Web. Among the best-known current programs are Adobe PageMill (Mac, $100) and SiteMill (Mac, $300) (Adobe has said programs will be made available for the PC), Corel WEB.GRAPHICS Suite (PC, $200), Claris Home Page (Mac and PC, $100), and Microsoft FrontPage 97 (PC, $135–soon to be available for the Mac). Many other commercial programs are available, along with lots of Web authoring shareware.

Other graphics categories of interest to writers

If you are involved in putting your words in graphic form, you will need to investigate fonts, clip art, stock photos, illustration and paint programs, image editing, presentations, chart making 3-D, and perhaps multimedia.

TOWARD A BUSINESS PLAN

Success Worksheet Sixteen

The right software can make you more productive.

Use this worksheet to form an overview of your software needs for writing and graphics. Check all the categories that apply. If you know which programs you will use, write down the names.

Category	Program	Cost if Not on Hand
_____ Word processing	_____	$ _____
_____ Page layout	_____	$ _____
_____ Web authoring	_____	$ _____
_____ Fonts, clip art	_____	$ _____
_____ Stock photos	_____	$ _____
_____ Illustration, paint	_____	$ _____
_____ Image editing	_____	$ _____

_____ Presentations	_____	$ _____
_____ Chart making	_____	$ _____
_____ 3-D	_____	$ _____
_____ Multimedia	_____	$ _____
TOTAL COST		$ _____

Software is available in the following general categories to help you run your business. Read reviews. Attend formal demonstrations or ask for demonstrations in the store. Talk to colleagues. Which categories fit your needs? Within those categories, which software packages appeal to you?

Communications

_____ Telecommunications (modem operation)

_____ Computer fax

_____ Internet access software

_____ Phone dialer

_____ Remote control for computer

_____ E-mail

_____ Voicemail

_____ Web browser and accessory programs

Financial

_____ Personal and small-business accounting, check writing, payroll

_____ Tax preparation (may be integrated with accounting program)

_____ Time/job recording, client billing

_____ Financial planning, investment management

Organizational

_____ Daily planning, scheduling, calendar making, on-screen reminders

_____ Project managing

_____ Message managing

Utilities

_____ Computer work-space organizer, menu builder

_____ Screen saver (the only fun item on this list!)

_____ Antivirus protection

_____ Security, passwords, file access

_____ File backup

_____ File retrieval and browsing

_____ File managing, cataloging

_____ Reconciling different versions of files

_____ Universal file viewing, such as Adobe Acrobat

_____ High-speed file transfer

_____ Data compression

_____ Data recovery

_____ Diagnostics, file repair

_____ System status check

_____ Memory allocation

_____ Hard disk optimization and reformatting

_____ Utility package (combining several utilities)

Connectivity

_____ Mac–PC file transfer

_____ Networking

Database managers

_____ Large, multipurpose database programs

_____ Contact managers

_____ Other simplified databases

_____ Address, label, and directory making

_____ Bulk mailing

_____ Custom databases

_____ Report creation

Spreadsheets

_____ Financial reporting, analysis, projections

_____ Business modeling

_____ Works (integrated application packages that contain limited
versions of programs for word processing, spreadsheets, database,
drawing, telecommunications, etc.)

Miscellaneous

_____ Brainstorming, outlining, idea generation

_____ Business plan making

_____ Sales and marketing forecasting

_____ Publicity generating

_____ Resumé making

_____ Employee handbook making

_____ Interior designing (for office planning)

_____ Address list sorting and postal coding

_____ Banner making

_____ Training programs specific to applications

_____ Information resources on floppy disks or CD–ROM disks (including marketing databases, atlases, medical references, U.S. history, fact books, Bibles, encyclopedias)

COMPUTER SHOPPING

The most important thing I can tell you about computer shopping is to view all hardware and software as disposable. You will never be completely set up, and you will never be finished buying.

Whenever possible, leapfrog over versions of both hardware and software. Take pride in doing so. If you can jump from Word Hog 3.0 to Word Hog 5.0 without laying out your hard-earned cash for versions 3.01, 4.0, and 4.2—*and* do it without your business suffering—you're ahead of the game. And by the time you buy the upgrade, you will be buying a proven new version.

Don't buy new hardware or software unless there is a vital task you can't perform without it or unless you find it significantly faster or more convenient. When I am tempted to buy something that I really don't need, I think of the $100 I laid out for ThinkTank, an outlining program that I have not used once, and the $109 that I spent for Kensington Turbo Mouse, which I disliked from the start and which now sits in the closet while my old mouse rolls along.

Stay on a single platform as much as possible. Converting files between platforms will cause unnecessary problems.

Look for hardware and software that offer maximum compatibility with what most clients are using and most service bureaus can support.

For desktop publishing buy as much speed, memory, and disk capacity as you can afford and then increase them later. It's like the old saying, "You can never be too rich or too thin."

As I pointed out when discussing computers, don't be afraid to buy used. (This applies to peripherals as well). If the word *used* scares you, remember that dealers who specialize in used computers provide guarantees. Better bargains are available from individuals (check classified ads, recycler publications, user groups, and swap-meets). I am no techno-whiz able to spot a faulty circuit at ten paces, but I have bought many pieces of used hardware from individuals, saving many, many dollars, and never once have I been burned. Companies getting rid of surplus equipment are another source of used bargains, one that is often overlooked.

When you must buy new, compare prices and service. There's a "street" price for almost everything in the computer world. But don't underestimate the value of a live person who will help you solve problems after you get the equipment (or software) home. The big mail-order firms offer discounts, as do the computer superstores. Smaller, older computer retailers compete by advertising sale prices (often in the Saturday sports section of your newspaper). These are the vendors who may lease you what you need, if you qualify.

After a recent trip to the bright, cold, crowded confusion of a major computer discount store, where the clerk I finally lassoed knew nothing and seemed offended at the interruption, I have decided that comparing computer products in the store is hopeless. Mail-order catalogs are the only way. Still, I'm not entirely sure. One competent, friendly clerk could change my mind.

Getting help when you need it—consider a consultant

Wherever you buy, ask if the vendor, manufacturer, or publisher offers follow-up customer assistance (beyond the usual repair or replacement if the product does not work). Some mail-order equipment firms offer twenty-four-hour phone technical support for their systems.

If not, consider using a consultant, preferably one who doesn't have an interest in selling certain products. To find a consultant, check the Yellow Pages, look for consultants' cards posted in computer stores (or ask a store for a referral), check classified newspaper and computer or business journal listings, ask friends and colleagues, or inquire at computer user groups. You'll probably find that your consultant is another home-based entrepreneur—a good person to do business with! Paying for several hours of a consultant's time is a prudent way to get your system set up properly. And you'll know whom to call when your inevitable computer crisis occurs.

Finding reliable information

The secret here is—there is no secret. You just have to do it! Learn to be alert for information about the hardware and software you use or plan to use. Attune yourself to news of bugs, new versions, and discontinuations. The biggest source of this information is computer magazines. Subscribe to one or more, and keep back issues for at least two years. If you take formal computer training, ask the advice of your instructor. Attend free product demonstrations held in computer showrooms and training centers. Join a user group and ask associates what hardware and software they use and why.

One day people will begin calling you—just as some friends and business associates now call me—to ask your advice about a hardware or software purchase. Maybe you won't know everything—I certainly don't. But you may be surprised at how much you do know!

TOWARD A BUSINESS PLAN

Success Worksheet Seventeen

When buying computer hardware and software, buy smart.

View all computer hardware and software as disposable. Leapfrog over versions whenever possible. Buy only what you really need. Stay on a single platform if you can. In general, stay with widely used products. Get as much speed and memory as you can afford. Don't be afraid to buy used. When you must buy new, compare prices and service.

■ Make a list of the usable computer hardware and software you already have.

_____

_____

■ Make a list of the additional hardware and software you will need during your first year. Make notes about manufacturers, models, sources, and prices where you can.

Computer

_____

Hard drive

_____

Other storage devices

_____

Printers

_____

Modem

_____

Monitor

_____

Special keyboards, input devices, wrist supports

_____

Scanners

_____

CD–ROM drive, including use of photo CDs

_____

Networking hardware and software

_____

Data storage devices

_____

Power controls

_____

Accessories

_____

Software in the following categories

    Word processing _____

    Page layout _____

    Web authoring _____

    Graphics, including scanning and image editing _____

    _____

    Multimedia _____

Communications _____

Financial _____

Financial _____

Organizational _____

Utilities _____

Connectivity _____

Database managers _____

Spreadsheets _____

Training programs _____

Miscellaneous, including applications used to write about
special subjects _____

Specialized information on CD–ROMs _____
_____

■ Do you have a general plan covering key hardware and software products you
will need—what to get, when, how much to spend?

_____

_____

_____

■ Can you borrow or rent any hardware or software during your first year? How?

_____

_____

■ Total your expenses for items you must purchase. What will this hardware and
software cost if you buy it new? Can any of it be bought used? How much can
you save?

_____

_____

_____

USING ONLINE SERVICES

If you don't already have an E-mail address, get one before starting your business and familiarize yourself with E-mail procedures (no biggie—just send a few messages to relatives or friends). The easiest way to do this is to sign up for America Online or CompuServe. Other commercial services are available, but these are the most widely used by home-based writers.

Connecting via your modem will involve a local call unless you are in a remote part of the country. To sign up, you'll need software provided by each company on ubiquitous disks sent out constantly to everyone on computer mailing lists and often enclosed with computer magazines. If you don't have one of these disks, check with a computer-savvy friend or computer store or call AOL at (800) 827–6364 or CompuServe at (800) 769–6747.

CompuServe has been serving the business world longer than AOL and is well established in the area of corporate communications. However, both services maintain active forums for many different kinds of writers. Both services are easy to use and provide lots of user assistance. Both offer access to the Internet, although their telephone lines may be clogged, and their Web browsers are not considered the best. Depending on your writing specialties, one or the other may offer better research resources, and either one will give you E-mail service.

Another approach is to sign up with a national or local Internet service provider (ISP). According to Steve Morrill (the computer-savvy writer/editor profiled in Chapter Six, "For the serious writer/researcher an unlimited internet access account is necessary. In fact, those can give you access to some parts of the internet that the online services—for reasons of their own—jdo not grant.

Check http://www.thelist.com to find an ISP serving your area. Internet access software is available commercially for both PC and Mac platforms, or your ISP may provide you with the proper software. Many ISPs offer Internet access for about $20 a month *with unlimited use*. Some offer discounts. For example, my ISP, Florida Online, gives educators, students, and user group members a monthly discount, which more than pays for my annual membership in the Bay Area Macintosh Users Group. If you travel frequently, be aware that national service providers such as Netcom or Earthlink offer local dialup numbers in most major cities. Regional and local providers don't have this benefit, so you will incur long-distance charges to check your E-mail or surf the Web when you're out of town.

Your ISP account, charged monthly to a major credit card, will include E-mail services and sometimes a small personal Website that you can create yourself. You won't have your own domain address, of course. Your URL (uniform resource locator) will read something like http://www.provider.com/users/your_name. Having a separate domain address—http://www.your_name.com—is a good idea if you plan to market yourself seriously on the World Wide Web, but it involves extra costs, discussed in Chapter Seven.

When selecting an ISP, be aware that phone companies and cable companies are getting into the act. Investigate through a computer store, computer-savvy friend, or computer user group to find out what kinds of Internet access are available in your community. Some areas also have low-cost community access offered through a library or other nonprofit agency. Shop around.

In addition to the mind-boggling information and research resources of the Web, the Internet offers newsgroups for professional writers. Try the keywords *writer* and *journalist*. Read the comments to determine which groups will be most helpful to you, then join in the discussions. You'll learn plenty, and you may pick up some business, although some online resources for professional writers are by invitation only.

ANALYZING YOUR START-UP COSTS

Now that you have considered all of the expenditures required to get your business started (as discussed in Chapters Five and Six), you can put your start-up costs into perspective. Read Success Worksheet Eighteen below, and follow the directions for matching expenditures with funds available.

Success Worksheet Eighteen

Conserve cash.

The goal is to be *in* business, not to have a perfect business setting. Your business focus will probably change. Invest only what you actually need to get started.

- Based on the kinds of work you plan to do and the kinds of clients you plan to serve, what kinds of space, office equipment, and computer hardware and software (as analyzed in Worksheets, Thirteen and Seventeen above) will you need during your first year in business?

_____

_____

_____

- Which of these needs can you meet—even temporarily—without spending money? For example, what can you borrow—perhaps a relative's typewriter or the occasional use of an associate's scanner?

_____

_____

_____

- Can you use business services to avoid large capital outlays? Which services?

_____

_____

- Would leasing equipment help you get started quickly? (You probably will not qualify for a business lease for two or three years, but you may be able to arrange a lease based on your consumer credit.) If you lease, will your lease payments apply to a purchase? Explain any leasing plans.

_____

_____

- If you must borrow, which sources will you draw on now and which will you leave in reserve? What is the maximum risk you are willing to take to get started?

_____

_____

Computers, Online Services, and Another Look at Start-Up Costs **135**

START-UP COSTS VS. FUNDS AVAILABLE

By now you have a good idea of what it will take to set yourself up in business. Filling out Worksheet Nineteen will give you a clear picture of your situation in terms of resources. On the first go-around, include under start-up funds your savings (reserving a portion for emergencies), anticipated income from items or property you can sell, securities you can liquidate (other than your retirement funds), and any anticipated surplus from your own full- or part-time income and that of your spouse or significant other during the start-up phase.

Will these funds cover your start-up expenses?

If not, take another look at your costs and pare them where you can. Since small-business loans are difficult to obtain for creative start-ups like ours, a business loan is not a likely option—but to make sure, talk to your mentors, your accountant, your banker, or a Small Business Administration counselor.

To meet your start-up expenses, you may have to turn to other sources of funds, such as personal loans from relatives or friends, borrowing on your home or insurance, and funds from credit cards and signature loans. A gift of up to $10,000 can be given annually from one individual to another without tax consequences to donor or recipient (nice if you can get it!). If you decide to borrow from relatives or friends, financial experts offer these guidelines:

- Determine an interest rate and a repayment schedule, and put the agreement in writing.

- Have a witness sign your loan document.

- If possible, secure the loan with some form of collateral. This can benefit your lender if you default. If your lender attempts to collect the money or the collateral, whether successful or not, the IRS may consider the loan a capital loss for income tax purposes. Discuss this with your accountant.

Success Worksheet Nineteen

Balance your needs against your resources.

ESSENTIAL FIRST-YEAR COSTS

Possible one-time expenses

Item	Estimated Costs
Office furniture and equipment	$ _____
Basic office supplies	$ _____
Office or residential remodeling	$ _____
Computer	$ _____
Computer equipment	$ _____
Software	$ _____
Permit and license fees	$ _____
TOTAL	$ _____

Possible monthly expenses
(or monthly percentage of regularly-recurring expenses)

Item	Estimated Costs
Office supplies	$ _____
Auto expenses (business-related)	$ _____
Utilities (business-related)	$ _____
Lease payments	$ _____
Service _____	$ _____
Service _____	$ _____
Service _____	$ _____

(Mailing, copying, addressing, clerical, consultant, bookkeeping, legal, graphics, Website, other)

Extra telephone	$ _____
Online service fees	$ _____
Equipment insurance	$ _____
Risk insurance	$ _____

Professional membership fees $ _____

Professional meetings $ _____

Publication subscription fees $ _____

Printing $ _____

Postage, shipping $ _____

Advertising $ _____

Travel, meals, entertainment $ _____

Subcontractor payments $ _____

Referral fees $ _____

Occasional labor $ _____

Repairs and maintenance $ _____

Education, training $ _____

Debt service (business-related) $ _____

Owner draw (salary) $ _____

TOTAL $ _____

FIRST-YEAR START-UP FUNDS AND INCOME

Possible Start-up Funds

Revenue Source	For Start-up	Monthly
Savings	$ _____	$ _____
Severance package	$ _____	$ _____
Income from investments	$ _____	$ _____
Your part-time income	$ _____	$ _____
Spouse's or other family income	$ _____	$ _____
Sale of property (real or personal)	$ _____	$ _____
Loans from family/friends	$ _____	$ _____
Loans on home, securities, insurance, or other property	$ _____	$ _____
Credit cards (use carefully!)	$ _____	$ _____
TOTALS	$ _____	$ _____

Computers, Online Services, and Another Look at Start-Up Costs

Business income (monthly planning guide)

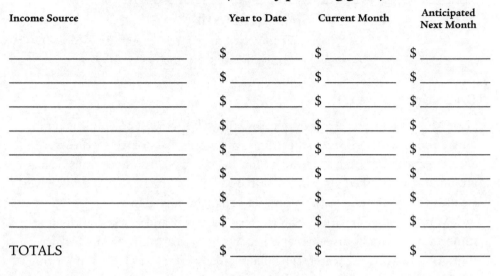

Income Source	Year to Date	Current Month	Anticipated Next Month
_____	$ _____	$ _____	$ _____
_____	$ _____	$ _____	$ _____
_____	$ _____	$ _____	$ _____
_____	$ _____	$ _____	$ _____
_____	$ _____	$ _____	$ _____
_____	$ _____	$ _____	$ _____
_____	$ _____	$ _____	$ _____
_____	$ _____	$ _____	$ _____
TOTALS	$ _____	$ _____	$ _____

How do your numbers look? Are you able to balance start-up costs against funds available, expenses against income? If you can get your business started, grow it, and clarify its goals without maxing out your credit cards or taking on a second mortgage, you'll have those sources of funds in reserve if you ever need them. And by the time you do need a more powerful computer system—perhaps to fulfill a profitable new contract—you may be able to qualify for a regular business loan.

Stephen Morrill
Writing, Editing
Tampa, Florida

Diversifying Pays Off

Steve Morrill, a former Army brat, found himself footloose after his own military service in Vietnam, so he came to Tampa, FL, for the weather. He enrolled at the University of South Florida—one of seven universities he has attended—but flunked out, finding it hard to study after 'Nam. "I don't have a college degree," he says, "let alone a journalism degree."

Morrill got a job with a local tugboat company and worked in the maritime industry for fourteen years, becoming a steamship agent. He never thought of writing as a career. His main writing effort was letters imploring the Coast Guard to relieve his ships of fines. But when he realized that his employer was going bankrupt, he decided he wanted a job where he didn't have to work for someone else—where his salary wouldn't be "dependent on incompetent managers," but only on his own work.

He decided to become a writer.

Staying on as an agent to be vested in his retirement plan, Morrill began writing part-time in 1982 with the encouragement of his wife, an architect. The first thing he wrote, he sold—but not without doing his homework. He read books on writing, did research, and finally called the editor of a local magazine. "I'd like to write for you," he said. "What do I have to do?"

"Write something short," she told him. "Do a profile of some person around town and we'll run it in this column in the front of the book. I'll pay you thirty dollars, five more if you give me a photo."

As an outdoorsman interested in canoeing, Morrill decided to interview "the guy who built my canoe—a nationally famous canoe builder," who conveniently gave the writing novice a photo of himself.

"I spent two weeks on this silly project," Morrill recalls. "I turned it in and got $35. I realized two things. One was that I could be published—that big ego trip. And the other was, I had to be more efficient!"

When Morrill quit his job in 1984 to begin writing full-time, he took a steep cut in pay—but within a year he was back to his former salary. In 1988, following the stock market crash, he was hit hard when several local magazines died. Morrill diversified, wrote ad copy, public relations, press releases—but magazine article writing continues to be his mainstay. He has appeared in such national publications as *Horizon, World Wide Shipper,* the *Robb Report, Vista,* the *New York Times Magazine*, and *Business Age.* After abruptly losing his local magazine market, he makes it a point to serve a variety of clients. "I try not to let any one client have more than one-fourth of me," he says.

When asked how he survives without job security, Morrill laughs. "I can't tell you how many editors have asked me that," he says. "They're all gone now. In fact, I've hired some of them to work for me on various projects." For example, when doing a brochure, he often sells his client "the whole package," hiring an art director, a photographer, and "an editor to edit my copy." He even found one recently fired editor a job with a firm that became so outraged by an article Morrill had written about them that they resolved to hire a public relations person. "Just don't tell them who sent you!" he cautioned. She got the job.

A longtime computer buff, Morrill has been online for many years. "I've tried all the services," he says, "but I've consistently used CompuServe, not only for research, but for the journalists' forum—and now the American Society of Journalists and Authors has a place there. He adds that he has gotten jobs through contacts on both AOL and CompuServe.

Morrill enjoys lecturing and teaching. A few years ago he helped a writer friend, Lary Crews, learn how to go online and inadvertently opened a new chapter in his own teaching career. Crews got involved with America Online and became their novel-writing instructor. Seeking to broaden AOL's offerings, Crews recruited Morrill, who now teaches two classes in nonfiction writing for the online service. He also teaches a short course on marketing directly on the Web.

Morrill has done writing for the World Wide Web, including articles for a nonprofit medical foundation's sites. Assigned to do a piece of 1,500 words, Morrill found the story more complex than expected and wrote 6,000—something he acknowledges no professional writer would ever do for a print client.

"She bought the 6,000 and paid me a little extra," he says. "The advantage and the danger of the Web page is that you don't have to buy paper. Paper is the biggest cost any publisher has. But with the Web, space is essentially free. The danger is that even writers like me, who pride themselves on the quality of their work and expect to get paid for it, may not do our best when we write 6,000 words and don't distill it down. It's a danger to the publisher of getting inferior work and to the writer of getting into bad habits."

In line with his determination to diversify, Morrill has several book projects under way, both fiction and nonfiction. One of them is a handbook on businesslike magazine writing practices. To learn more about this promising text, or find out about Morrill's online classes, E-mail him at writers@gte.com for internet information or stevemorrill@aol.com for AOL details.

CHAPTER SEVEN

MARKETING YOUR SERVICES

MARKETING MAKES THE DIFFERENCE

The thing to remember about marketing is that what you do today pays your bills in three to six months. Even if you *have* business now, if you *seek* no new business now, you will have no business three to six months from now. Marketing is your most important investment in the future.

Years ago I took a marketing workshop from a freelance photographer who began his presentation by scribbling these words on a chalkboard: *If you're there, you'll get your share*. At first I resisted his homely slogan. I found it hard to believe that just by showing up in the marketplace, I would get business. But I have learned that he was right. Nevertheless, most freelancer writers I have talked with worry more about marketing—and fail more often at marketing—than any other aspect of their business.

It's tough to send your ideas to an editor and receive a routine letter of rejection. It's tough to meet with a prospect, build rapport, analyze a job, contribute ideas, develop a good price, outdo yourself presenting your proposal, start counting on that $2,000 to meet upcoming bills—and then, when you phone a week later, to receive a casual, "Oh! Didn't anyone call you? We went with someone else."

But you know what? You can survive that kind of rejection. Within a year, you can learn not to take it personally and to understand that, no matter how solid your foothold seems to be, you may not get the job.

Your idea may have been wrong for the magazine or Website. They may have had a similar article on hand. The editor may be a fool.

In the corporate world you learn by experience that a competitor may underbid you, or conversely, that your price may have appeared too low. Or that the owner stepped in and decided to give the work to his brother-in-law. You learn that the project may be canceled or deferred—or that there may never have been a project, just a little research at your expense. And—painful but true—you learn that some prospects will not like your samples—or your personality. (In which case, you probably wouldn't have liked them either.) Above all, you learn never to *plan* on income without a firm job commitment—and never to *count* on income until the work is done.

If most freelancers can learn these difficult lessons, why does marketing often plague them throughout their careers?

I think there are two problems, and neither of them is insoluble.

First of all, as writers, I think we often expect too much of ourselves. "Just being there" isn't good enough for us as creative types, trying to break out of the competitive clutter. We need something smashing, something unforgettable, the kind of thing that will set a new standard.

If you can come up with such a concept, go to it! Too often, however, the perfect project hangs out of reach in our imaginations, and in the meantime, it's best to do some of the meat-and-potatoes marketing this chapter describes.

The second reason freelancers fail at marketing is simpler, but more frustrating. When we have more work than we can handle, we do the most urgent things first and put our marketing aside.

Again, a meat-and-potatoes approach is the answer. Whatever marketing strategies you adopt, make them as routine as possible. Just as you clean your office, do your filing, pay your bills, so you do your marketing. Every day, every week, and every month. If a killer deadline kept you from paying bills when you had planned to, would you stop paying them for three months? No, but many of us do that with our marketing.

Marketing versus selling

When you're a home-based entrepreneur, you wear every business hat from janitor to CEO—and two of the most important are marketing manager and sales representative. Both of these jobs are concerned with selling your services, but they are different in focus.

Marketing is everything you do to make the sale possible—before your first contact with the prospect. Selling is what you do to make that contact and close the sale. When you identify a professional organization whose members could use your services, you go to their monthly meeting and put your brochures on the literature table, and then stand up and give your name and your ten-word business description, you are marketing. But when you make a point of meeting the communications director of the Ajax Corporation, find some common interests, pocket her card, call her, and make an appointment to discuss her needs, you are selling.

MARKETING MAGAZINE ARTICLES

As I explained in Chapter One, the focus of this book is "the hidden market" for commercial writing, often called the business or corporate market—jobs that are available to beginning professionals in every community. Selling articles to big-name magazines obviously does not fall under this category. However, selling articles to hundreds of smaller, specialized magazines does. Many corporate writers boost their incomes with such assignments.

While I don't do much writing of this type, I have received assignments from *Psychiatric Times*—a national newsjournal for psychiatrists edited in southern California, near where I was living at the time. Some article ideas I proposed; others were assigned to me by the editors. Their per-word payment and my efficiency were sufficient to earn nearly as much for my time as corporate work.

If you have selected an area of specialization—business writing, technical writing, whatever it may be—look at both corporate/organizational clients and magazines as possible sources of work.

Multiple marketing

A great deal is already in print about magazine article writing, query letter writing, and dealing with magazine editors—entire volumes on each topic—but perhaps the most important concept I can share with you here is "multiple marketing." I once heard a successful magazine writer explain this concept in detail at a meeting of the Independent Writers of Southern California. His point was that from one article idea he earned as much as, and sometimes more than a friend of his typically earned from one of the prestigious articles she regularly sold to top women's magazines.

He illustrated his presentation with tables comparing time invested and income received. His secret was multiple marketing—taking the same interviews and research, reslanting and rewriting the story, and selling separate, new articles to several noncompeting magazines. With the exclusivity, extensive rewriting, and high pressure the other writer experienced from her editors, he claimed it took her at least as long to write one well-compensated piece as it did him to write several for smaller payments that could add up to more in the end.

Steve Morrill (the Tampa writer-editor profiled in Chapter Six) explained this approach further.

A Marketing Plan for Magazine Queries

"I don't send out multiple queries," Morrill told me during our interview.

Many magazine writers do indulge in this somewhat controversial practice—approaching, or "querying," several magazines at the same time with the same idea. These writers want to circumvent the slow query-rejection, query-rejection process and operate on the theory that editors may as well compete simultaneously for their ideas.

Morrill does not avoid multiple queries just to be polite, however. Imagine the dilemma of the writer who gets a call from the nation's leading dairy magazine. "We love your milk production idea!" the editor enthuses. "We'll take it for our November cover." To which the writer must reply: "I'm sorry, I've already sold it to our county association journal." Morrill's reasons for not sending multiple queries should be obvious from this example.

Here's what he does instead—a procedure you may want to emulate. (Thank you, Steve!)

"I've submitted multiple queries a few times and gotten burned," Morrill admitted. "What I've learned is that the first editor on the phone is the cheapest one because they know that the only way they ever get writers to write for them is to call before the other editors."

When Morrill has an article idea to sell, he makes up a marketing plan, drawing on his personal database of 400 magazines.

"Here's an idea I'm working on right now," he told me. "It's about Ybor City social clubs."

If you've never visited Tampa, FL, let me explain that Ybor City is a well-preserved and well-loved slice of the city's colorful past, a district that still looks like an exotic foreign town. Here Cubans, Italians, and blacks made up a unique ethnic stew, rolling Tampa's famous cigars in vast factories—a humble but proud craft that has all but disappeared.

"I divide my marketing plans into five types of magazines, only because five happens to fit more easily on the page," Morrill explained. "When I'm done making the marketing plan for this article, I'll have twenty-five magazines—although I notice I'm a little short," he added. "I only have twenty-three.

"The first category is 'history' and the first magazine is *Victoria*. I put it first because it pays $1.50 a word. I don't have any guidelines from them, so the first thing I did was to request guidelines, and I've made a note that I've done that. The next magazine was *American Legion* at $1.00 a word, but I scratched them out because when I looked at their guidelines, they weren't really suitable. The next one down is *Civilization*, put out by the Library of Congress. They pay $1.00 a word. The next one is *Smithsonian*, also $1.00 a word. After that is *American Heritage*, at 52 cents.

"That covers 'history,' and I've done nothing with that category except to request guidelines from *Victoria*; I'm going to hold out for that $1.50 rate," Morrill stated. "I could have sent off queries to *Civilization* and *Smithsonian* right away, but what if one of them accepts me and then *Victoria* comes back and I would rather have written it for them?"

Morrill still had four other categories to explain.

"The next one is 'Florida,'" he said. "Most of these are newspaper inserts—the weekly for the Ft. Lauderdale paper, the weekly for the *Miami Herald,* and a couple of others. They're all low-paying—31 cents down to 24 cents a word. The next category is 'historic preservation.' I've already sent a query off to *Historic Preservation Magazine*, and I've got two more historic preservation magazines waiting in the wings. Next one down is 'ethnic,' and I've not yet sent a query to anyone, but I'll probably start with *Essence*, which is a black magazine that pays $1.00 a word. It's the only ethnic magazine that pays really well. *Black Enterprise* pays 50 cents. The next category is 'travel,' and I've sent a query off to *Car and Travel*, which is a Triple-A publication.

"In theory," Morrill summarized, "I could send out five simultaneous query letters, but I'm not going to send five letters to the history magazines and accept the first one that calls me on the phone. Each query is slanted to a different category of magazines.

"This Ybor City article happens to be a good example," he pointed out. "You can't always get five categories of magazines that don't overlap. Travel often overlaps with in-flight, and in-flight overlaps with business. Women might overlap with health. Things like that. Anyway, the point is, I can have as many queries out as the guy who does the shotgun querying, but I can write an article for every one of them!" (If you'd like to learn more about article writing and marketing, enroll in one of Morrill's online classes. For information, E-mail him at writers@gte.com regarding his Internet classes or stevemoril@aol.com regarding his classes on America Online.)

MARKETING AND SELLING— AN ENTREPRENEURIAL EXAMPLE

Let's turn to corporate writing. The following case study is fictional but based on experience. Whether you are a writer or a writer–desktop publisher, whether you are selling to large clients or small in a city or a rural area–this example shows how each step in the marketing and selling process can lead to the business you want.

Rob is a writer who has decided to make his lifetime interest in athletics a part of "what he does and for whom." A former high school athlete who worked as a sports publicist in college, he would like to be involved with competitive athletics more than as a fan. With this goal in mind, he undertakes a marketing and sales effort composed of twelve parts:

1. Marketing research
2. Marketing strategy
3. Determining and presenting a business image
4. Publicity
5. Advertising
6. Sales prospecting
7. Sales follow-up
8. Sales presentation
9. Close, or . . .
10. Additional follow-up or appropriate disposition of prospects
11. Solicitation of additional business
12. Evaluation

1. Marketing research

Rob's research turns up seventeen high schools, two colleges, and a state university in his region. Many of these schools have a recurring need for game programs and media guides for major sports, along with such recurring collateral material as posters, flyers, and schedules. He collects samples of typical programs and learns by phoning school athletic departments that some are produced by outside vendors. As far as he can tell by questioning prospects and checking the ads of his competitors, no local writer or desktop publisher is specializing in sports programs and team media guides. Rob discusses his ideas with a desktop publisher colleague who is also interested in sports. Both believe they can fit seasonal projects into their work flow.

Rob knows that season programs are usually financed by advertising, so when calling the schools, he inquires about their advertising procedures and finds that a few schools engage outside professionals to sell ads, while others rely on students or parent volunteers to do the selling.

Rob researches ways to reach decision makers and learns that it will be difficult to reach coaches, athletic directors, and sports information directors through local organizations. Luncheons held occasionally for college sports officials and media representatives are not open to him. He discovers, however, that the annual College Sports Information Directors of America will be meeting in his region next year, and he investigates attending as a vendor. He also identifies several professional journals in the field where he might advertise or obtain publicity.

2. Marketing strategy

Rob recognizes that becoming a specialist in sports programs and media guides requires long-range effort, but he believes it will pay off in seasonally recurring work. In addition, working regularly with local coaches could lead to contacts with such potential clients as athletic equipment manufacturers, specialists in sports medicine, professional sports promoters, and summer sports camps. He also sees spin-off work in magazine articles and newspaper features.

Studying the samples he has collected, Rob determines what he and his colleague would have to charge to write, design and produce sports programs and media guides. They decide that they can lower their prices if they are assured of several jobs a year from the same school—a sales benefit to the prospect. Rob also notices that most of the samples could be improved by professional design—another sales benefit.

So far, Rob's research has determined an ongoing need, his strategy has determined what appears to be a fit with his capabilities, and he has thought of several benefits he can sell. Encouraged, he goes on to develop more detailed strategies. What else can he sell? How can he make it easier for clients to deal with him? What could set his service apart from others?

Rob considers buying printing at a discount from trade printers (those dealing only with resellers) and reselling it for more money, but he quickly tables the idea because of the large cash outlay required and the risks involved if a printing job should be unacceptable or if a client should fail to pay. Instead, he and his associate decide to offer production supervision as a compensated part of their service.

Since Rob is interested in having more control of the job as well as in making more money, he considers joint venturing with Amy, a friend who formerly sold newspaper ads and is now eager to make money part-time at home. After discussion, Rob and Amy agree that if she sells program ads for one of Rob's customers, she will give him a percentage of her profits.

Because schools may require photographic services, Rob lines up a reliable photographer with experience in athletics. In this case, he does not propose a percentage fee but looks at the referral as an aid in making the sale. Rob figures that any assignments he directs to the photographer will come back to him in referrals.

3. Determining and presenting a business image

Rob decides to build an athletics capability into his business image by including athletics programs and media guides in his basic list of business services and adding a sentence about his background in athletics to his business resumé. He also creates a new, sports-oriented slogan for his business: *"Win with peak performance."*

4. Publicizing himself and his services

Since he is doing volunteer work as a Little League coach, Rob seeks ways to capitalize on this activity for business publicity. He writes an article for his local chamber of commerce newsletter about volunteer opportunities in youth sports. Although the school coaches, athletics directors, and sports publicists he needs to reach are unlikely to see this article, Rob plans to use reprints of it in his presentation.

Business networking groups also give Rob an opportunity to put his athletic experience and writing-design capabilities in front of potential buyers. His knowledge of athletics begins to impress prospects who share his interests—but he has yet to sign up a school to produce a season program or media guide.

5. Advertising

Rob considers placing his own ad for writing and design in local game programs, but he rejects the idea. Consumer ads will not bring him business. Instead, he decides to take one-line listings in his local business Yellow Pages and in the services directory of a regional business magazine. Even though these listings are too brief to mention his specialty in athletics, Rob believes they enhance his general credibility in the marketplace. Shortly after placing these ads, he receives calls from several new prospects in other fields.

6. Sales prospecting

Moving into the selling phase, Rob begins prospecting, using his research to set up prospect files on his computer. His lists include local high school and college coaches in major sports, as well as directors of athletics and sports information.

All of this effort has taken Rob about six months, involving a few hours of work a week. Now he begins calling his prospects for appointments and finds this to be the most difficult task he has tackled so far. It is hard to find time to make the calls, hard to reach the busy prospects—and really hard to convince them to see him, since most do not perceive an immediate need for his services.

7. Sales follow-up

Rob knows that business people often fail to get the order—even when they have the names of prospects who need and can afford their products—because they fail to follow up. They fail to get an appointment for a presentation. They fail to get a bid request after making a presentation. They fail to get a purchase commitment after bidding. And finally, they fail to solicit repeat orders after completing the initial order.

Determined to work in athletics, Rob brainstorms about ways to break through the resistance he has encountered. He could prepare and mail a flyer about his services. He could try to meet some prospects through professional or social activities. He could call and offer to write and design a small job free as an introduction. He could mark up his sample of the team's current program, showing how he would improve it, and send it to the prospect. Rob is intrigued with the latter idea until he realizes that he might antagonize a prospect by criticizing designs the prospect likes.

Finally, Rob prepares a mailing, offering to show the prospect—in a fifteen-minute interview—five ways that professional writing and design can improve the image of the team and get more media attention, while being cost-effective. Phoning for appointments a week after his mailing, Rob finally lines up some interviews!

8. Sales presentation

Even though none of his previous work is athletics-related, Rob selects the best samples he can find and pulls together an outline of the features and benefits of his services, aiming at what he believes are the needs of the market. Then he adapts his material to a fifteen-minute benefits blast and heads for his interviews. In the back of his mind is an idea for a brochure and maybe a journal article based on his presentation—"five cost-effective ways professional writing and design can improve your team's image."

Sitting down with his prospects, Rob finds that most of them voluntarily extend the brief interview when they begin talking about their own needs. Since athletic needs are seasonal, he takes care to find out when he can check back for upcoming projects—and he gets each prospect's permission to do so. (Months later, when the reminder pops up on his computer tickler file, he can say, "Coach Smith asked me to call him this month regarding the season's program.") Rob also probes to find out who else may be involved in purchasing decisions and later contacts many of these prospects.

Rob makes notes about each interview and modifies his presentation, dropping some points and adding others. He also notes which samples created the best impression or provided the best openings to discuss his strengths.

9. **Close**

Rob makes his biggest inroads at a small liberal arts college where he is asked to bid on media guides and programs in three sports. Knowing that the college is accepting competitive bids, Rob calls the decision makers to ferret out any price problems after he presents his bid. Following some price negotiation, he is able to close the deal. Now he is actually doing the work he has been seeking!

10. **Additional follow-up or appropriate disposition of prospects**

Using news of his assignment at the liberal arts college as an opening wedge, Rob telephones his other prospects. He realizes that most of the high schools cannot afford him and removes them from his active prospect file. Since he has gotten to know several of the high school coaches through phone conversations, he keeps their names in an inactive file. Who knows? Someday he may need to contact one of them.

11. **Solicitation of additional business**

Within a few months, Rob is asked to do a seasonal booster club newsletter for the liberal arts college. He is also selected to produce a basketball program for the state university—and, as he anticipated, side benefits of his marketing campaign start coming in.

Rob is hired to prepare promotional materials for several sports camps. Through a client introduction, he picks up work from a professional soccer team—and does a brochure about the team's work with disadvantaged children. The brochure wins an award, and he sends press releases about the award to local news and business media and receives coverage. Then he mails reprints to his prospect list with a friendly note. As a result, two previously resistant prospects agree to meet with him. With his growing credibility in this specialized field, Rob calls on a local athletic equipment manufacturer and receives a lucrative assignment when the marketing director, in frustration, pulls a catalog away from the company's high-priced ad agency.

12. **Evaluating and updating his marketing plan**

Where Rob goes with this new business will be up to him. As he compares the profitability of various jobs, he may put less effort into college and university work and more into assignments from professional teams or sports promoters. Realizing that catalog writing can be a lucrative specialty, he may go after athletic equipment manufacturers in other states. Distance shouldn't be a problem, using E-mail. With his increased cash flow, Rob may start bidding on printing—adding a profitable sideline. To handle more business, he may hire an assistant or subcontract work to other home-based professionals.

On the other hand, Rob could decide to move away from "behind the scenes" writing such as team press kits and sports camp brochures. He might use his knowledge and contacts in the field to write magazine articles or books on athletics—even though a new marketing task will confront him as he begins researching editors and publishers.

Any and all of this is possible—if Rob continues to make marketing a regular part of his business routine!

WHAT CAN MARKETING RESEARCH DO FOR YOU?

"Marketing research" sounds intimidating. It has overtones of focus groups, surveys, and statistical analysis. But business decisions cannot be made without answering such simple questions as "Is there a market for it?" "What features do clients like or dislike?" "What should I charge?" And in point of fact, an informal focus group is easy to arrange. Just buy a pizza for a few clients or prospective clients, throw out some provocative marketing questions, and listen to the enlightening replies!

When I was selling printing for a local, family-owned firm and thinking about starting my own business, I noticed that most of our business came from a relatively small group of repeat clients in our own geographic area.

While you never want all of your work to come from one or two clients (a good rule of thumb is to make sure no single client accounts for more than 20 to 25 percent of your work), you, too, are likely to be doing most of your work for a small number of clients in your own geographic region. Even if you serve many nonrepeating clients—running a resumé service, for example—the bulk of your business will come from a few key sources. Even if you serve clients nationwide—perhaps doing specialized technical writing—a few networks will provide your business contacts. Thus, your marketing research need not be massive. One or two weeks of serious, full-time study—or its equivalent—can provide the planning data you need as you begin your writing business.

WHERE AND HOW TO GET MARKETING INFORMATION

What you're looking for

Basically, you are looking for client categories and names of potential clients, along with any information you can find out about them—their products or services, sales volume, number of employees, branch locations, affiliated companies, and prospects for stability or growth. You also want to know who is serving these clients now for their outside writing and desktop publishing, presentation, or Website needs, what these competitors charge, and how crowded the field is.

If you are writing articles, you want to know which magazines serve your field, what they buy, what they pay, and who edits them. Check writers' publications and libraries for directories of magazines; then write for guidelines and sample copies.

Standard reference sources

Some easy sources of such information include your own previous employers and business associates, professional organizations, and "leads" clubs, where business people gather to share leads. Another possible source is the sophisticated and usually expensive databases available from computerized list companies. But most home-based entrepreneurs begin their serious marketing research with directories—telephone books, industry directories, and other compilations available in most libraries. Today many of these directories are available on CD–ROMs, making it much easier to capture and use the data. Seminars in "desktop marketing" are cropping up to help you use new resources.

Before you leave your home office to do outside research, see what you can learn from the Internet and other online services. So many businesses have Websites now that it's easy to gather information about them—but getting the names of the right businesses or the right persons to contact may require additional research.

Your reference librarian will be helpful. So will your chamber of commerce. Chambers often sell local business directories—printed or on disk. College and university libraries may have good business resources. Online databases can connect you with huge amounts of information but may have limited ability to provide you with details specific to your region.

Looking for potential clients by name? Perhaps they belong to a trade association. Most chambers of commerce maintain lists of local organizations. Your library will have a national directory of associations, whose national offices can provide information about local chapters.

Association membership lists are often available only to members, but joining may be worth it if the organization includes many potential clients. Or a guerrilla marketer might borrow the directory from a member friend.

Your daily newspaper's business pages are a gold mine, as are local business periodicals and trade journals. These inexpensive resources are often insufficiently appreciated by home-based entrepreneurs. Read them carefully and save clippings. The information adds up.

Set up an information retrieval system

To retrieve the information you are collecting, set up a filing system, using a computer database program, file folders, loose-leaf notebooks, 3-x-5 cards—whatever works for you. You may be using this information for a long time, so be aware that computerizing your data can pay off many times in ease of use.

Test the waters with a phone survey

As you gather information about potential clients, make a dozen or so calls—to buyers by name or to job titles. Explain that you are doing marketing research for a start-up business and draft two or three brief questions to find out whether and how they use the services you plan to provide. If the answers are discouraging, take another look. You may be offering the wrong service or going after the wrong clientele. If they do use the services you provide, ask whom they use and whether they have trouble finding good writers. If you establish really positive rapport, you might ask about prices for typical jobs, but many buyers will refuse to share such information.

Will you need to create a market?

You may find that you want to provide a service for which a market must be created. An example would be custom-written and desktop-published family histories. This service is not as well accepted as is the group photograph that many families arrange for on a regular basis. Families must to be told about this new service and convinced that they need and can afford it. Customized storybooks for children with the child's name, hometown, school, or pets worked into the story pose a similar challenge. If your service falls into this category, plan on extra marketing with heavy emphasis on publicity that will explain the need you plan to fill.

Research the competition

While you have your information resources in hand, make a separate search for names and any details you can find about your competition. Additional sources of information about competitors are creative services directories, clients, and professional associations. Find out what you can about your competitors' specialties and reputations and how long they have been in business.

Economic and demographic projections

To gather information on the economic and demographic outlook for an industry or region, turn again to the Internet or your library or chamber of commerce. Government census and business data as well as regional economic reports will reveal trends that can affect your business plans. Business publications also provide such information—both by region and by industry.

Creditworthiness

For creditworthiness, you must evaluate each client individually, but industry statistics (and common sense) will suggest which types of clients are more reliable, which are less. You need not pass up clients with shaky or unknown credit. But you should insist on a big down payment, and the balance on delivery.

The guerrilla marketer takes over

At this point, you have enough information to begin learning, in depth, what kinds of writing the clients you are concerned with buy, from whom they buy it, and what they are paying. Gathering this information will be less straightforward, and the distinction between marketing and sales will become blurred. In every sales contact, for example, you will be trying to collect these valuable nuggets—from your initial call for an appointment, during your sales presentation, and in all the rest of your encounters with that client. Even though many firms have policies against revealing exactly what they paid for a job, questions about price ranges may bring you an answer.

Vendors such as Website providers may also provide information—especially about who is doing what for whom. And, of course, there are your competitors themselves. It might be crude to ask, "How much did you charge for that job?" But you might find out. Or a friend or family member with a writing project might solicit bids from some of your competitors.

Marketing research tells you who's buying what. It also gets you into the ballpark on price. In Chapter Nine you will learn about pricing issues in detail.

MARKETING STRATEGIES AND POSITIONING

Developing strategies gives you an edge over the competition and helps you position yourself.

That was what Rob, the writer, did when he decided to present himself as a specialist in sports materials and to go after sports-related accounts. That was what I did when I decided to pare away some of my less profitable, nonrepeating business and began concentrating on newsletter jobs.

If you are in the early stages of establishing your business, don't worry if the words *strategy* and *positioning* create a mental blur. You need some marketplace experience in order to form strategies. You need to find out which jobs are profitable and professionally satisfying and which are not. And finally, you need to discover how clients perceive you, versus how you want to be perceived.

TOWARD A BUSINESS PLAN

Success Worksheet Twenty

Understand your market and position yourself strategically.

To answer the questions below, do the research first, then use creativity techniques such as brainstorming (coming up with as many solutions to a problem as possible within a limited time—no evaluations or judgments allowed). Do free-associational right-brain thinking. Float over the situation mentally, looking for new patterns and approaches.

- What sources will you use to obtain marketing information?

  _____

  _____

- Who are the actual clients in the industries you plan to serve?

  _____

  _____

- What specific writing services are these clients buying now?

  _____

  _____

- What are the best ways to reach your potential clients and sell to them?

  _____

  _____

- What are the going rates of payment—high, low, average? Where do you fit in?

  _____

  _____

- How creditworthy are your prospects?

  _____

  _____

- Who are your competitors? What are their qualifications? How long have they been in business?

  _____

  _____

- What niches are not currently being filled?

  _____

  _____

- Examine the general economic and demographic outlook for the industries you want to serve. What are the market trends and opportunities? Can the industries you have selected accommodate more vendors?

  _____

  _____

- Do you plan to offer a service for which a new market will have to be created? List what you will do.

  _____

  _____

- In addition to your skills, experience, and equipment, your personality, personal history, age, and other unique characteristics can help you carve out a market position that is credible and appealing. List your strengths.

  _____

  _____

- Involve others. Seek feedback from clients and associates. Who can help you?

  _____

  _____

- Consider using a marketing consultant. Independent marketers are available at an hourly rate or by assignment. Give any consultant you hire a full and open hearing, and follow his or her advice when you feel comfortable with it at gut level. How might you locate a consultant? What can you afford to pay?

_____

_____

DETERMINING AND PRESENTING YOUR IMAGE

Since you work at home, clients may never come to your office. In most cases, the image your business presents will be based on your business name; your logo, letterhead, and business card; your marketing materials; your Website, if you decide to use one; and, of course, your own personal appearance and demeanor and your professional reputation.

Your business name

While magazine writers normally write under their own names, many commercial writers use a business name. This name is a very important part of your business image. If you find, after a period of time, that the name you selected and licensed yourself under does not describe what you are selling as effectively as another name would, go ahead and make a change. You can do this either gradually, with a minor change in emphasis and the same or similar graphics on your business materials. Or—if you think the situation warrants a new identity—make a total change with a completely new name and new graphics. Either way, it's wise to make sure your business is registered under the correct business name, even if it involves additional fees.

Designing your logo

I believe logos are very important—and not just because I used to design them. Throughout my independent writing and designing career, I have used a pen-and-ink portrait of myself. (Fortunately a drawing doesn't age as fast as a photo.) When I first put the drawing on my letterhead and stationery, I thought it might seem pushy or conceited, but I have received nothing but positive responses. People see my logo, remember it, and often comment on it. I have even gotten business solely on the basis of my card!

But don't delay starting your business until you have the perfect logo. A real entrepreneur goes to the instant print shop and gets something, anything, printed in order to get started right away and then develops a good logo within the first six months. Or if you have the design skills, print your own card on your ink-jet or laser printer.

Your logo can be registered as a trademark or service mark with your state or the federal government. (See the Source Directory.) For most of us—especially if our own name is part of our business name—obtaining a registered service mark is probably not necessary. But for certain names in certain markets (the trademark-sensitive computer industry, for example), it could be a wise move. Having to reprint all of your materials and redo your business licenses because someone has already registered the name you chose would take time and money, while damaging the image you have established.

Your image on your printed materials

The printed or online images that represent you are very important and should have a graphic unity that grows from, or is compatible with, your logo design. This includes your business card, letterhead, envelopes, labels, fax cover sheet, forms, invoices, brochures—whatever bears your business name and message.

Everything does not have to match precisely, but as you develop each piece, lay your materials side by side and make sure they work together. Having a unified graphic theme makes your business more memorable—and it suggests good planning and organization.

Your personal appearance

You thought you were getting away from business dress codes by starting your own home business! Well, yes and no. In your office, of course, you can wear what you like. One designer told me she makes it a point to get dressed every day—as opposed, apparently, to working in robe and pajamas. It never occurred to me not to get dressed before going into my home office. In fact, a for-profit outfit has recently been hawking its "business opportunity" wares to home business hopefuls with an ad that I find quite offensive. It shows a grinning family standing around in their bathrobes! That's not my idea of a home-based entrepreneur.

However, I often do battle with myself about what is the least "dressed" I can be when I zap over to a client's office. I'm talking about just picking up some copy or dropping off a proof—not making a sales call. For a sales call or serious business conference, I always dress to fit the marketplace. And you should do the same.

A corporate editor I have worked for recalls referring a writer friend, a newly minted freelancer, to a colleague in her firm. To my client's dismay, the writer arrived for her first appointment in sweats, carrying her baby. "She'll never get another referral from me!" said the editor. Corporate people have to wear collars and ties or heels and hose all day, every day (except for an occasional "dress-down Friday"), and they expect you to be equally professional. Clients in other environments have their own distinctive dress codes or guidelines, and you should observe them. It shows awareness and respect.

Your phone and office image

Make sure that your phone is answered professionally during business hours and that messages are taken reliably when you are out. Your promptness (or the lack of it) in returning calls also forms an image in the minds of callers. If clients or vendors come to your home office, make sure that public areas are presentable, and have a table and chairs available to go over materials comfortably.

PUBLICIZING YOURSELF AND YOUR SERVICES

Many marketing people look on publicity as "free advertising." On the plus side, having someone else talk about you builds credibility (as opposed to talking about yourself). On the minus side, you can't be sure you will get coverage, and you can't control what will be said. And, of course, you have to provide something worth saying.

Maximum return for minimum cost

In spite of being difficult to control, publicity in all its forms is a very good way to market a home-based writing business. It can provide maximum return for minimum cost. The impact of publicity is cumulative; over time, having your name associated with your industry in a positive way establishes you as an authority and an industry leader. On the sales side, including reprints of selected clippings can strengthen your business biography or sales presentation. Reprints of a significant article (say, your views on writing effective business letters) can form the basis of an inexpensive, friendly, yet authoritative special mailing to solicit new business.

Getting it done

The main problem with publicity is doing it—planning where you will send business news about yourself, making sure your media names and addresses are current, tailoring releases to each outlet, getting a supply of good quality photos (if appropriate), and sending everything out while the item is still news. If doing publicity is part of your client services, doing publicity about yourself should be easy. An established writer might find it worthwhile to buy services from a home-based associate who specializes in publicity. Just starting out, you'll probably have to do it for yourself.

Remember that the rule about marketing in general applies to publicity as well—make it part of your routine, and do it on a regular basis.

Two types of media publicity

Media publicity falls into two general categories: The first is the simple release that announces some news about you or your business. You send it out and hope it will be used. After mailing, faxing, or E-mailing a release to newspapers, magazines, radio and TV stations, and news services, many publicists phone them all to try to ensure coverage. But this procedure may annoy, rather than ingratiate. Call only if you have a reason for calling. For example: "If you think you might use the story, I can supply pictures." "If you're planning to attend my lecture, I can arrange free parking for you."

The second publicity category is engineered coverage—something set up in advance with the cooperation of editors or reporters. Engineered coverage might be a newspaper profile of you as a successful home entrepreneur; it might be an article written by you in a trade journal; it might be you participating in a radio or TV business show, discussing ways to improve business communication. If business reporters are aware of you from receiving useful press releases in the past, they may call on you for a quote relating to another story. Always be available. It pays off.

Preparing and submitting news releases

Media releases are often sent by fax these days. They should be double-spaced and error-free. If mailed or hand-delivered, they should be in black ink on white 8½ x 11 paper. Multiple pages should be stapled. Photos must have captions attached and will not be returned. A cover letter is not necessary. If you are E-mailing your release, you can attach a scanned photo, but be sure it meets the medium's technical requirements.

Releases are usually written in journalistic style, covering "who, what, when, where, why, and how." A brief headline may be used above the text to summarize the story. Keep copy as short as possible. If detailed additional information is relevant, include it as a separate fact sheet on which the editor may draw.

A release should include a heading that identifies its source, the name and phone number of someone to contact for more information, an origination date, and the words "RELEASE AFTER (DATE)" or "FOR IMMEDIATE RELEASE." The end of the release should be marked with some designation, such as ###. If the information runs more than one page, write "MORE" at the bottom of each continuing page, and make sure every page is clearly numbered and identified. When sending a release to broadcast media, it is best to rewrite it in a briefer form, designed to be read aloud. Broadcast material is often typed in capital letters for the convenience of announcers.

"Media kits" are used by professional publicists to generate interest in celebrities and major events. A media kit consists of a folder containing one or more releases, biographical information, photos, reprints of clippings, and any other pertinent material. When might *you* need a media kit? Perhaps before doing a series of lectures, after publishing a book—or when spearheading a group in some significant community effort. The start of a new business could be an occasion for a media kit, but most home-based freelancers start on too small a scale to warrant major media attention. A news release announcing your start-up would be more appropriate.

A Website offers an elegant (and cheap) way to deliver a "media kit" with all the material downloadable—including photos scanned in several formats. The problem here is getting editors or meeting planners who might use you as a speaker to go to the site.

More important than any wording or form of presentation is selecting media that might be interested in your release—media that you know carry the type of information you are supplying. Next in importance to selecting the right media is getting the material to them at the right time—neither too early nor too late. For daily and weekly publications and local broadcast media, allow two weeks. For monthly publications, lead time varies widely, so check with editors.

What's worthy of publicity?

Activities that can bring you publicity include winning an award, landing a major new client, adding a new business service or a new associate, taking an office on the board of a professional organization, publishing a business-related article or book, serving on a business-related committee, teaching a class or seminar, giving a lecture, or serving on a panel on a business-related topic.

Network and volunteer to help

Here is a more subtle way to gain publicity, while doing some good at the same time: Network in professional and community organizations and volunteer to help in a way that will draw the attention of prospective clients to your business—and then make sure you get credit for your services.

Producing materials for a charity event supported by the local business community would be an ideal example. Be on the lookout for service opportunities that fit both your business goals and your charitable interests. But beware of doing too many free projects in hopes of gaining attention! A designer friend volunteered for our United Way's communications committee—a select group that included many potential clients—but so overcommitted himself with free work that he could barely serve the clients he already had. Be selective!

Selectivity also applies to the professional organizations you participate in. If you are not meeting prospective clients, gaining referrals, or learning things you need to know, the group is probably not worth your time.

Where will your publicity be used?

Major outlets for business publicity are local daily and weekly newspapers; local and regional business publications; local, regional, and national trade publications that deal with communications or an industry you serve; and—very important—the newsletters, magazines, and Websites published by your networking organizations. Other media possibilities include talk shows and community calendars on local radio and TV (including cable TV). Business-related computer bulletin boards and ongoing computer network discussions are another outlet.

Finally, don't overlook the value of listings. Being listed as an officer in a professional association puts you in good company. Being listed by a local community college as the instructor for a course on writing speeches puts your name in front of thousands of people who might not take your class but are nevertheless potential customers for your speechwriting service. Of course, those who take your class are all potential clients.

Selecting media

Aim your publicity efforts at media that can reach potential clients or individuals who may give you referrals. Just by thinking about it, you can come up with the names of several media that potential clients may see, but racking your brains won't do the whole job. Lists of media, including the names of reporters and editors specializing in various topics, are provided in annual media directories. Several standard media guides are listed in the Bibliography. These directories are costly, but current editions may be available in your library.

Your most useful guide, however, will probably be the one covering your local media. Most communities have local media directories. If you don't know whether yours has one, check with your library or inquire in the public relations office of a local corporation, college, or hospital.

If you receive good coverage that will not be seen by potential clients or by individuals who may give you referrals (for example, an out-of-town newspaper report on a seminar you presented at a conference), incorporate clippings or transcripts of this coverage in your promotional materials to help create interest in your business.

Do some of the work in advance

Busy writers often miss out on publicity opportunities because getting a release out can be time-consuming. To circumvent this problem, have your supplies ready.

TOWARD A BUSINESS PLAN

Success Worksheet Twenty-One

Build your own publicity toolkit and keep it current.

Here is what your toolkit should contain:

- An updated biography of yourself in narrative format, typewritten and double-spaced, drafted in at least two versions (one no more than half a page, the other no more than two pages). Be sure to mention any prestigious clients.

  ___ I have this now   ___ I will produce this by (date)_____

- A good, professionally photographed business portrait of yourself. (Either color or black-and-white will be acceptable.)

  ___ I have this now   ___ I will produce this by (date)_____

- A basic description of your business, perhaps in brochure format.

  ___ I have this now   ___ I will produce this by (date)_____

- A current list of local and other pertinent news media on a computer database or on labels.

  ___ I have this now   ___ I will produce this by (date)_____

- A planning calendar.

  ___ I have this now   ___ I will produce this by (date)_____

ADVERTISING YOUR SERVICES

Advertising costs money, and home-based freelancers must be cautious about commitments that may produce limited results. Make it standard procedure to find out how every inquiry from a new prospect as well as every referral came about so that you will know which marketing efforts are paying off.

Forms of advertising you might consider include display advertising, broadcast time, classified advertising, cooperative advertising, Yellow Pages, other directories, direct mail, newsletters, and imprinted novelty gifts. One form of advertising that is free is posting your business card in copy shops, art and office supply stores, and other locations. Check to see if a bulletin board is supplied for that purpose—and use it if it fits your type of service.

Display advertising

Display ads make sense for you only in low-cost publications that reach a very targeted audience. Normally, a small ad repeated on a regular basis will be more effective than a single large ad. Rates come down when ads are repeated, so negotiate.

Broadcast time

Radio or TV time is not a cost-effective buy for you unless an extremely targeted, low-cost slot is available. Try instead to be a resource interviewed occasionally by a business talk-show host, if this fits your specialty.

Classified advertising

Local and regional business publications often carry classified service directories in their back pages. Your daily newspaper's business section may do so as well. If you can afford it, test such an ad, and repeat periodically if it pulls.

Cooperative advertising

Normally, *cooperative advertising* refers to ads jointly promoting manufacturers and retailers, but you may be able to arrange your own co-op ads, exchanging some business service for a mention in a display ad paid for by another advertiser. It's worth considering.

Yellow Pages

Never underestimate the power of the Yellow Pages. Some enterprises derive virtually all their business from them. These ads, ranging from simple one-line listings to large display ads, are billed every month and cannot be stopped until the following year, so consider the commitment carefully. Since both consumer and business-to-business Yellow Pages may carry listings for writers, consider which directories will be most profitable for you, including suburban directories if you're in a large urban region. Consider various category listings, such as "advertising," "marketing consultants," and "public relations."

It's vital to place your ad before the deadline or you will miss a whole year's exposure. Companies that publish several commercial phone directories stagger their deadlines. If you plan this kind of advertising, check the deadlines immediately!

Other directories

In general, being in directories that reach potential clients or referral sources is a very cost-effective strategy. Some large communities have creative directories designed for clients in advertising, public relations, and marketing. Professional associations to which you belong may sell display ads in their annual directories. Buy what you can afford and track the results.

Direct mail

Here is another technique that makes sense for home-based writers. Even though postage and printing costs continue to climb, you can target your mailing precisely and spread costs over several months by mailing to one small segment of your list at a time—the number that you can follow up with phone calls within the next week or ten days. Be careful about faxing or E-mailing unsolicited material. Many areas prohibit this practice for faxing, and recipients of an unwelcome E-mail may jam your own E-mail box with garbage in revenge. If you want to send to members of a group, for example, make your message useful and find a way to tie it in officially with the group.

Telephone canvassing can also find prospects for you. This topic is covered more fully in Chapter Eight.

Newsletter

No other form of advertising is more appropriate for a writer or a desktop publisher than a newsletter. While introducing you as an authority, showcasing your abilities, and conveying some sense of your personality, a newsletter provides your clients and prospects with useful information about your specialty. People pass good newsletters around and keep them on file—ensuring that your name and number will be handy when a writer or desktop publisher is needed! One continuous source of high-interest newsletter copy is client profiles, wherein you show how a client has profited from projects you have done for them. A four-page newsletter is plenty long. Two pages will do. And quarterly is a good plan for publication—often enough to make an impact, but infrequent enough for you to produce and pay for it.

Many newsletters are faxed or sent by E-mail these days, but make sure your recipient requests these methods of distribution.

Imprinted novelty gifts

An imprinted novelty gift, especially one that will sit on a desk or win some other lasting spot in the work environment, is a great idea and well worth the money. An imprinted gift can get you in the door to see a prospect—and it can build loyalty in a regular client. If you can tie in some play on words or symbolism relating to your company name or business specialty, so much the better. Keep you eyes open for truly distinctive items. Advertising novelty firms offer many excellent ideas, but since imprinting can be purchased separately, you are not limited to their selections. Buy what you can afford, and keep the gifts on hand for times when you believe they will make an impact.

Marketing message on your phone

Having a custom marketing message played while callers are on hold is not for all writers, but it might be a good move for some. It suggests size and professionalism at surprisingly low cost. You can have a message made and installed commercially—or devices are available to play a tape you make yourself.

TOWARD A BUSINESS PLAN

Success Worksheet Twenty-two

Advertise your services for maximum impact.

Targeting, repetition, and testing are three keys to successful advertising. Decide what you can spend, no matter how little, and develop a plan, perhaps on an annual basis, that will maximize your efforts. To reach more prospects, consider using several media. If possible, include online resources. Keep track of where your business comes from to see which ads are working.

■ Check the traditional advertising media you think could bring you business.

_____ Display advertising. Which publications will you use? Can you also get publicity in these publications?

_____

_____ Broadcast time. Which stations will you use? Can you get airtime via a talk show that would accomplish the same thing?

_____

_____ Classified advertising. Which publications will you use?

_____

_____ Cooperative advertising. How can this be arranged?

_____

_____ Yellow Pages. Which communities do you want to reach? If your community has separate business and consumer directories, which will you choose?

_____

_____ Other directories. Which publications will you use?

_____

_____ Direct-mail, fax, or phone solicitations. Describe your target audience. How will you get the list? What will your mailing package consist of? Will you include a special offer? How will you follow up?

_____

_____ Newsletter. Describe your target audience. How will you get the list? With what service will your newsletter provide these readers? Describe your newsletter—number of pages, contents, design, frequency of publication, production method, production costs.

_____

_____ Imprinted novelty gifts. Describe the gifts. How will you use them? How much will they cost?

_____

_____ Marketing message on your phone. What message will you use? What production services and equipment will be required? What will the cost be?

_____

MARKETING YOURSELF ONLINE

This is currently such a hot topic that books are being written about it, courses are being offered, and consultants galore are hanging out their shingles. In preparing this revised edition, I asked all of the successful writers profiled what online marketing activities they were involved in—if any.

Only two, Joy Meiko White and Judith Broadhurst, were planning Websites—Joy's to market her technical writing/design brokerage firm, InfoTeam, Inc.; Judith's to market the writers' newsletter, _Freelance Success_, which he founded and recently sold in print and via E-mail. Several of the commercial/corporate writers expressed doubts about the ability of a Website to reach users who might become their clients—although this is possibly not typical. Many freelance writers in this category have established Websites. None of the magazine or book writers had plans to use a site to market their work. However, most of the writers in both categories were finding that participation in writers' forums and newsgroups was producing business.

From this overview, one message seems clear: It pays to get online and communicate with people in your area of specialization and with other writers. You'll gain professional knowledge, and you may capture referrals and assignments.

I look forward to the day when online marketing, networking, publicity, and advertising will be integrated with traditional media—even as the online revolution affects these media in ways we cannot fully imagine. Will printed directories and catalogs be a memory in fifteen years? Will our entertainment be delivered on demand? What will newspapers be like? Don't think the *New York Times* and the *Wall Street Journal* created their impressive Web presences just to be nice to information surfers. If that's where the consumers of the future are going to get their news, that's where these powerhouses have to be—even though no one yet knows exactly how online information can best be paid for.

According to the *Times* online for the weekend of August 10–11, 1996 (there's no fat Sunday cyber-edition yet!), the search service Lycos has "catalogued more than 55 million of an estimated 80 million Web pages available free to the public." Since 1994, says the *Times*, this number has increased tenfold each year! This article places its estimate of Web users at sixteen million and says the number is "doubling every year," but because estimates vary, I think this figure may be low.

The business writer's perspective

Brian Konradt, publisher of the new Oradell, NJ-based magazine for writers, *Today's $85,000 Freelancer*, offers tips for online marketing under the title "Clients Are Surfing Cyberspace to Seek Freelance Talents." The article appeared in Vol. 1, No. 3 of his *Today's Freelancer*, a newsletter precursor to the magazine.

"Imagine your entire portfolio—samples of brochures, sales letters, publicity campaigns, promotional material, and so forth . . . displayed in vivid color . . . right in front of the prospect's eyes," says the article. "If the prospect finds your samples impressive and wants you for an upcoming project, all he has to do is click on a button to send you E-mail."

For a good example of such a Website, check http://www.aaow.com .wordshapers/. Martin R. Smith of Lawrenceville, GA, an experienced freelance writer with eleven books to his credit, has fashioned a persuasive message for potential business clients. Try search engines under "writer," "copywriter," or "technical writer" to see others and critique them for yourself. Some are effective, some less so. Websites are an especially important form of marketing if you serve high-tech clients or provide high-tech services—including Website authoring. With faxes and E-mail, clients can be thousands of miles away. In fact, a client in one location may be surfing the Web precisely to find a writer in a distant city where she does business.

The article writer's perspective

Judith Broadhurst, author of *The Woman's Guide to Online Services* (McGraw-Hill 1995), who is profiled in Chapter Nine, takes a very cautious of putting samples of her magazine article work online. "I don't know any professional writer who would do that," she told me. "I want to withhold my copyrights for resale." And in point of fact, the Web itself brims with pleas for free or minimally compensated writing—pleas that you, as a beginning commercial writer, should ignore unless you can be certain the work will bring you to the attention of potential customers. Pros write for pay.

In spite of copy right caution, however, many magazine and book writers have Websites, not only to promote their writing, but their teaching, lecturing, and any information products they may offer.

Getting online

Brian Konradt, the publisher of *Today's $85,000 Freelancer*, offers several ways to get yourself on the Web, from creating your own Website to being listed in online job banks and directories, such as OASYS Network (http://www.oasysnet.com), Freelance Online (http://www.haven.ios.com/~freelans/) and The Reporters Network (http://www.reporters.net/). He points out, however, that "the disadvantage to using . . . any . . . online directory is the clutter of competition."

On the Internet and other online services, clutter is indeed a problem—and that's one of the baffling and challenging characteristics of this new medium. Marketing and selling are usually about going to the prospect, not about waiting for the prospect to come to you. But online, the user makes a choice. With the exception of Website ads, prospects in cyberspace can't be *forced* to view your message; they must be *attracted* to it.

Katie Lachance, a young entrepreneur in Clearwater, FL, is an independent writer and marketer who has made a specialty of helping businesses use the Internet. (Check her Website at http://www.netbis.com.) The publisher of instructional booklets and a newsletter called *Online Marketing Times*, Lachance does consulting and offers some tips for home-based writers.

"I think of the Internet as a huge cocktail party where everybody is talking back and forth," she says. "It's very friendly—a low-pressure and low-cost environment."

Below are some of her suggestions, combined with some of mine.

An online planning checklist

1. If you decide to create your own Website, you will need a "site provider" (unless you know how to set up a server and really want to do it yourself). Your current Internet service provider may give you a free "home page" that may accept messages and forms E-mailed to you by users. However, if you require other services, such as sending out messages via an autoresponder, collecting data about those who visit your page, or handling credit card billing, you may need to use a firm that specializes in Website providing. This service won't be free, but for what you get, Web marketing can be extremely cost-effective.

2. Should you build (create) your own site? Maybe, maybe not. Website authoring software such as Adobe PageMill, Claris Home Page, and Microsoft Front-Page has simplified the job of creating Web pages, especially for those already familiar with page layout graphics. But accept the fact that this new craft will take time to learn! If you don't want to invest the effort, use a professional designer.

3. Operate your Website in an interesting, changing manner that keeps people coming back. In my view, creating a Website to market your business is very much like publishing a marketing newsletter. It will be effective only insofar as it is in some way helpful or at least interesting to a carefully targeted audience. If your site provides useful information related to the kind of writing you do, and if it is adequately publicized, it stands a good chance of bringing you business.

4. Keep it brief! Web surfers are a restless lot. To take the opposite view, the World Wide Web is also turning out to be a place where newspapers and magazines can offer the full texts of speeches and technical reports—and even the research notes of reporters to back up controversial stories. This may be a very significant journalistic development! Web publication is cheaper and far more readily available than paper, so if including a long source document on your site makes sense for you, consider doing it. It may lend you authority and be the very thing that brings potential clients to your page.

5. The Internet is an interactive medium. Make your Website as interactive as possible, giving users choices of information to select and one or more ways to respond. Beware, however, of offering links to other sites before users have had a chance to view your message. They may click away and not come back.

6. Consider getting your own domain name. This will ensure better, more memorable access. Your Web address would then be http://www.hotwriter.com, rather than http://www.netprovider.com /hotwriter (or some similar sub-address under your provider's domain name). The setup fee and annual charge will vary with your provider's surcharge, but the cost is not prohibitive.

7. Get your site listed on as many search engines as possible under carefully chosen keywords. (This service is available online for a reasonable fee.)

8. Participate in selected newsgroups. Direct advertising is not considered good "netiquette" here, so tread lightly. It's better to contribute and help others and, in so doing, mention your Website.

9. Find like or related sites and get your site cross-linked—with the site operator's permission ("netiquette" again).

10. Consider using an E-mail "autoresponder" to send information to users on request. Lachance, the Florida Internet marketing consultant, says this technique frees her to work with prospects who are really interested, rather than handling individual E-mail inquiries herself.

11. Use E-mail for marketing and marketing research. Unsolicited E-mail is even more unwelcome than the unsolicited "snail" mail. Nevertheless, you can use E-mail to do marketing research, as well as to seek out clients. E-mail addresses are easy to obtain through Web directories and other sources. When making a cold approach, identify yourself and explain your purpose and what you are asking the recipient to do. If you share any common ground with the recipient, such as membership in an organization or the same kind of work, point this out. Describe any benefits to the recipient—particularly if you are seeking his business. If there is a service you could provide in return for the information you have requested, offer it. And if a recipient helps you, E-mail a word of thanks.

12. If you are serving a very targeted market, consider running an ad on a Website that serves your clientele—if the price is right.

13. Check out Web directory listings such as those suggested above by Brian Konradt, publisher of *Today's $85,000 Freelancer*. But check carefully. Listing yourself among wannabes and nonprofessionals won't improve your image.

14. Don't overlook the venerable computer bulletin boards in your community. They may put you in touch with certain kinds of clients, through a directory listing or as a participant.

15. Incorporate your online marketing activities with your regular marketing program—and be sure to include your Website and E-mail addresses in your traditional ads and printed materials.

TOWARD A BUSINESS PLAN

Success Worksheet Twenty-Three

Include online marketing in your plan.

Online advertising and promotion are still new and being developed. Don't fall behind. Be part of this revolution and make plans to use some form(s) of online marketing—then continually test and evaluate your results.

■ Check the online techniques you think could bring you business.

_____ Website. Discuss how you will develop your Website and for whom. Will you get your own domain name? How will you publicize your site? How will you keep it interesting and up-to-date? How will you make it interactive? Will you use an E-mail autoresponder? Do you have items to sell on your site?

_____

_____ World Wide Web directories. Which directories will you use?

_____

_____ Internet and other online service newsgroups. Which newsgroups will you participate in? What will be your objectives in participating?

_____

_____ E-mail for marketing and marketing research. What request(s) will you make? To whom? How will you get their E-mail addresses? How will you present yourself and justify your request(s)?

_____

_____ Web advertising. Which site(s) will you use? How much will it cost? How will you focus your message? Can you measure response? How?

_____

_____ Local bulletin boards. Which boards will you use and how?

_____

KEEPING RECORDS TO EVALUATE AND UPDATE YOUR MARKETING PLAN

Marketing is a process, and as such it is always evolving. Keep a record of where your inquiries and new clients come from. These data—when correlated with management data on the amount and the profitability of business from each client—will tell you what works best for the least effort and expense, what brings you the most desirable clients, and what brings you no business at all. Adapt your efforts, based on what you learn. Some programs, like publicity and newsletters, will take a year or more to have an effect, so allow time for such marketing to work.

When a brochure, an ad, a directory listing, or any other marketing effort brings you profitable business, keep using it until results start to diminish. When an effort doesn't work, try something else.

TOWARD A BUSINESS PLAN

Success Worksheet Twenty-Four

Evaluate your marketing plan regularly.

It's important to have a written marketing plan and to *do* your marketing regularly—but you won't get maximum benefit unless you *evaluate* it regularly as well.

- Skim back over this chapter and list the marketing activities your plan will include. Put dates beside each item (for instance, annually on March 1, weekly, monthly). Include online marketing.

MARKETING ACTIVITY	DATE(S)
_____	_____
_____	_____
_____	_____
_____	_____
_____	_____
_____	_____
_____	_____

■ How will you capture information about where your business is coming from?

_____

_____

■ How will you analyze your business source data?

_____

_____

■ How will you correlate your business source data with data on marketing activities and job profitability? Some marketing activities may bring in little or no work, while others bring in a lot. Two activities may produce equal amounts of work, but those attracting marginal jobs are of less value than those attracting profitable ones. How often will you make such an analysis?

_____

_____

_____

■ How will you revise your marketing plan to eliminate unproductive efforts and increase efforts that bring in profitable business?

_____

_____

Ilene A. Schneider
Schneider the Writer, Irvine, California

Combining Business and Family

Ilene A. Schneider had always thought of "freelancing" in terms of staying home to be a mom. It took a terrifying medical experience to show her how much she really wanted to be a home-based writer.

After college, Schneider had worked as an editor for *TV Guide* in Cleveland, then spent six years with a Cleveland trade magazine, where she learned technical writing. Moving to California with her husband, she went to work as a public relations representative for Beckman Instruments, a large medical and scientific equipment firm.

Schneider enjoyed her work and stayed at Beckman for seven years, but she and her husband were becoming concerned about starting their family.

"I went in for surgery in December of 1984 to find out why I wasn't getting pregnant," Schneider recalls, "and for a time we thought I had a life-threatening condition. I asked myself what I wanted to do with my life and got motivated to make changes."

Her experience prompted her to act quickly, and she decided to leave Beckman in 1985, after a second necessary operation.

While recuperating, she says, "from bed I was contacting future clients so I could make money from Day One." She dubbed her firm Schneider the Writer. Nine months and one week from the day she started her business, Schneider's daughter was born—and Schneider has never used day care.

Schneider's initial idea was to find "a lot of little Beckmans" that would not have in-house public relations capabilities. Today her clients include large corporations, growing high-technology companies, and nonprofit organizations. She especially enjoys "the dual challenge of high-tech PR—being technically accurate while making the concept interesting to a wide range of people."

Networking, especially through Women in Communications, Inc. (she's a chapter past-president), helps Schneider gain clients. Her introduction to TRW as a client, for example, came through a WICI friend she had known in Cleveland twenty years ago.

Schneider's services range from press releases, articles, and newsletters to full-blown public relations programs and trade shows. She often works fourteen-hour days and frequently asks for—and gets—50 percent payment up front.

"You have to draw a fine line between your working hours and your other hours" Schneider says, "or you start being a computer potato at some point, instead of a couch potato." During the past few years, her hard work has paid off in significantly increased income. "I've raised my rates somewhat," she reports, "but you don't want to go higher than the traffic will bear. I'd rather charge slightly less and get the work. I also want to keep enjoying my work and my relationships with clients."

Another concern for a solo writer like Schneider is times when "everybody wants something." As she explains it, "At the moment I have nine clients, and there was a weekend when six had projects going!" To help even the load, she's looking into working with a student intern and possibly subcontracting with other writers. Her previous subcontracting has been for services out of her specialty, such as graphic design.

Schneider says she has found the Internet invaluable for worldwide research, especially in biomedical writing and grant proposal work. "It's the quickest way to find out exactly what's out there up to the minute," she observes.

Motherhood has been a constant theme in Schneider's home-based business. "My daughter and the business have kind of grown up at the same time," she says, "and it's really been great to be able to raise her while making a living. Now that she needs me a little less, with all her activities, it's easier to spend more hours working."

One landmark, both in her daughter's and her business's growth, came in 1992, when her daughter entered first grade. "At that point I began calling myself a consultant, rather than a freelance writer," Schneider explains, "and it's made a real difference in how people view me."

Asked about new directions, Schneider says, "I'm trying to grow without compromising the quality of my work, while still being intimately involved with all my clients. It's a challenge."

CHAPTER EIGHT

SELLING YOUR SERVICES

PROSPECTS ARE JUST PEOPLE

Selling is everything you do to make direct contact with prospects and close sales. And the most important thing to remember about selling is that even a Fortune 500 corporation is just people solving problems and meeting deadlines. The same goes for the rest of your prospects—they're men and women you might meet at a chamber of commerce breakfast or on a telephone prospecting call—people with hobbies and families, priorities and preferences. Above all, they're people with emotions—because, no matter why they *think* they buy, people base buying decisions on what they *feel*.

As a salesperson, it's your job to identify these people and find out what they need and how you can help them. If you are offering competent help, a certain percentage of these people will want to know about it. Actually, it's their job to know about it! And this is just as true of editors as it is of corporate buyers. They will keep your card, résumé, or brochure. They will listen to your presentation. And of that group, a certain percentage will buy your services.

Cross my heart. Trust me. It's true!

It's often been said that nothing happens until somebody sells something. Salespeople like this saying, and they like to think of themselves as the most important people in the business cycle. Incomes tend to bear this out, because some top salespeople earn more than their CEOs.

"But selling can't be as important as producing a product," you protest. "The product or service is what matters. Salespeople just inflate their egos to make up for the rejection they have to face."

I don't think so.

I love the writing and designing process, and I enjoy sitting at my computer being creative. But that moment when a deal is set, when an enthusiastic client says "yes!" and starts to anticipate the job I am going to do, is matched only by the moment when I deliver a good, creative job—on schedule and within budget—to a happy, satisfied client. Those are the times when I feel really great about my life as a freelance writer and graphic designer. And those are times when selling is taking place. They are sales opportunities—because the very best time to solicit more business is when your client is happy with the work you have already done!

THE BENEFITS OF SELLING—AND OF SALES TRAINING

Fortunately for us, the same basic methods used in selling most products and services are also appropriate for selling writing to prospects in business firms, retail stores, professional groups, hospitals, government agencies, and universities, among others.

We may not think of ourselves as fortunate to have to sell our services over and over, compared with a novelist or screenwriter who is represented by an agent and doesn't have to pound on the doors of her publishers or producers. But remember that at least 15 percent of everything she earns goes to that agent, who may or may not be worth it.

We, on the other hand, are mastering our own survival skills, learning every day to keep our fingers on the market pulse. And to help us, we have a vast storehouse of motivational and technical sales training—offered in virtually every city and town—along with enough books and tapes on selling to keep us closing deals for the rest of our lives and then some.

When I was working in higher education, I tended to scorn what I thought of as the "rah-rah" self-motivation and self-improvement of the marketplace. From Napoleon Hill to Anthony Robbins, I thought it was corny and commercial. But that was before I became an outside salesperson living solely on commission! I became humble in a hurry when I found that listening to a tape in my car before a difficult sales call gave me the confidence to sail through my presentation and an evening spent in a training seminar would translate into more calls, more proposals, and more sales.

I even changed my mind about the "positive thinking" so central to sales training when I saw what a few days of negative thinking could do to my sales performance. I no longer derided it as superficial. In fact, I realized that attitude lies at the very core of meaning and survival in our lives.

In his book *Successful Cold Call Selling* (1983), sales trainer Lee Boyan reminds his readers of the work of Viktor Frankl, the renowned Austrian psychiatrist who survived the Nazi concentration camps and described his experiences in his famous book, *Man's Search for Meaning* (English translation, 1959). According to Boyan,

Frankl "observed that everything can be taken away from human beings except what he called the last of the human freedoms. And that is freedom to choose one's attitude in any given situation."

We are not faced with the life-and-death circumstances of a concentration camp, but as Boyan points out, we are "faced with situations where . . . inner decisions will determine our circumstances, our relationships with other people, and how we're going to feel."

So be glad your work requires you to sell—and to choose the positive way.

When you offer your services, it's true that you will meet rejection. But what is rejection? Isn't it getting past those who currently have no need or interest? Much rejection is no more than that—the prospect doesn't need your services *at this point in time*. He may buy later, or he may not. Either way, if you stay focused on the benefits of your services and your desire to help your clients, you will start connecting with people who do want what you have to offer.

The material presented in this chapter is just a taste of the resources available to help you sell. Among the many nonbillable activities required to run your business, I urge you to devote time to sales motivation and sales techniques. Unfortunately, reading one book or attending one class won't be enough. You need to keep reading books and articles, listening to tapes, and attending lectures and seminars—frequently at first, and later on an occasional repeating basis. You'll be able to measure the results!

THE VALUE OF A PROSPECT LIST

Your good prospects and eventually your buyers will emerge out of your prospect list. I had an object lesson in the value of such a list a few years ago, working with the Direct Marketing Association of Orange County, for whom I was producing a newsletter. Ever since its founding, this organization had wanted to build a relationship with the higher education community, but they had made virtually no progress. I knew why, having worked for colleges and universities for years. That environment is hard to penetrate if you don't know your way around.

Then one day, shortly before a major West Coast direct-marketing conference, a two-year-old list of marketing educators fell into the hands of the new education committee. Now they knew what to do! Giving a direct marketer a list is like giving a case of lobster to a chef. Never mind that the list was old and didn't include every school in the region. The committee mailed out letters offering several free (magic direct-marketing word) admissions to the conference.

Instant response! Faculty were vying for the privilege of attending. As a result, one instructor developed a new course in direct marketing. Others invited profes-

PROSPECT INFORMATION FORM

Prospect rating A_____ B_____ C_____

Company/organization_____

Name of Prospect_____

Title_____

Address_____

City_____ State_____ Zip code_____

Phone (_____)_____ Ext._____ Fax (_____)_____

E-mail, pager, other _____

Is this person the decision maker? Yes_____ No_____

If not, who is? Name(s), title(s) _____

_____

Source of referral_____

Referral thanks (if appropriate) Date _____

PERSONAL/PROFESSIONAL INFO (prospect's interests, background, birthday, etc.)

TYPE OF SERVICES PURCHASED

Probability of repeat business   High_____ Avg_____ Low_____

Probability of reliable payment High_____ Avg_____ Low_____

Current suppliers (if known)_____

_____

SALES ANGLES (upcoming needs, problems with current suppliers, special interests)

FOLLOW-UP

Date_____ Contact: Phone____ In person____ Other_____

COMMENTS

Outcome_____

Continue following? Yes____ No____ Scheduled follow-up date_____

Date_____ Contact: Phone____ In person____ Other_____

COMMENTS

Outcome_____

Continue following? Yes____ No____ Scheduled follow-up date_____

Date_____ Contact: Phone____ In person____ Other_____

COMMENTS

Outcome_____

Continue following? Yes____ No____ Scheduled follow-up date_____

FOLLOW-UP

Date_____ Contact: Phone_____ In person_____ Other_____

COMMENTS

Outcome_____

Continue following? Yes_____ No_____ Scheduled follow-up date_____

Date_____ Contact: Phone_____ In person_____ Other_____

COMMENTS

Outcome_____

Continue following? Yes_____ No_____ Scheduled follow-up date_____

Date_____ Contact: Phone_____ In person_____ Other_____

COMMENTS

Outcome_____

Continue following? Yes_____ No_____ Scheduled follow-up date_____ sionals to address their classes. Students began coming to the group's monthly meetings as the guests of member firms. Later a major university developed a direct-marketing certificate program with club members as advisors.

What can we learn from this in terms of building our own businesses? If your list has even a few names that fit your client profile, start calling. Refine your list as you go. Don't wait for the complete and perfect list or you'll be out of business before you finish assembling it.

QUALIFYING PROSPECTS

Your marketing research helps you develop an initial list of people likely to buy your services, but once you are in business, you will continue adding to your prospect list. As you gather names, don't clutter your list with those you have no intention of following up on. Instead, develop a quick test for qualifying your prospects, based on what you do and for whom. Here are some questions to ask:

- Do they have an ongoing need for my services? (One-time clients are much less profitable than repeat clients.)
- Can they afford my services?
- Is their credit reliable?
- Will I be credible to them in terms of the quality of my work and my experience?
- Who makes the buying decisions, and how can I get to that person?
- Do I want to work with this client?

For some prospects, your general knowledge will provide most of the answers. In other cases, you will have to phone the prospect or do some library or online research. Always look for the names and titles of those who do the buying. Qualifying a prospect includes not only finding out if there is a fit but also finding out who makes the purchasing decisions. One of the most frustrating mistakes in sales is to spend time selling a "prospect" who just loves your service but turns out not to have the authority to buy.

SOURCES OF PROSPECTS

In addition to the kinds of online and library marketing research covered in Chapter Seven, here are some ongoing sources of prospect names.

Media

Since your marketing research has identified the categories of clients you are looking for, make it a habit to watch for prospects as you read newspapers and business journals. Pick up names from news media. Watch for news of appointments, business start-ups, and reorganizations as well as new contracts and projects. Clip articles, make notes, and add the names to your database.

Networking

One of the oldest sayings in sales is that people buy from people they know. And it's true. Meeting people at business organizations has brought me at least 75 percent of my freelance clients. I enjoy meeting people and learning about their interests—and, of course, I collect their business cards. I concentrate on communications organizations, such as the International Association of Business Communicators, Women in Communications, Inc., and the Society for Technical Communication. You should research the groups available in your community and see what works for you, based on the services you offer and the clients you are seeking.

Sales authorities will tell you that without a referral or previous contact, it can take five to ten sales approaches (such as a mailing or a phone call) to get a face-to-face meeting with a buyer, even when that buyer has a potential need for what you're selling. I find that having had lunch with a buyer in a friendly environment can get me an appointment with just one or two phone calls. Of course, the buyer must have been favorably impressed at our initial meeting and have some need for my services.

Another way to use networking as a prospecting tool is to keep track of awards given by advertising, public relations, and other communications and marketing groups in your community. Collect the names of winning clients and those who did the creative work and the production. Then select for follow-up those who appear to fit your services. In some cases, this may be a two-step process. For example, you might want to use an award-winning printer or photographer for some of your own projects, or you might refer them some business. The printer or photographer, in turn, might become a source of referrals for you. And, of course, you may want to start calling on the award-winning client with some creative ideas of your own.

My personal view about networking is this: *Don't be a tourist!* Pick a few organizations you care about and work for them. Be a contributor. Of course, you can visit other groups occasionally—perhaps to hear a special speaker, or just to check them out. But the business butterfly flitting through a premeeting reception, scattering and collecting business cards, often makes a negative impression.

Experts on networking suggest that you do the following:

- Set a few goals before the meeting.

- Have a supply of business cards conveniently at hand.

- Put out samples or brochures if appropriate.

- Prepare a short description of your business in case public introductions are called for. Be sure to include something listeners will remember.

- Avoid talking or sitting only with people you know.

- Spend enough time with each person you meet to learn something about that individual.

- Follow up on good prospects within a week.

While you may get more direct assignments for writing through networking in business, industry, or professional groups, don't overlook your own trade groups—organizations for writers. In addition to current information about your craft, you'll have a chance to learn about local rates of payment and business customs and build a network of referrals for jobs. For example, it was by serving on the board of the Independent Writers of Southern California that I met the editor who asked me to write this book.

Referrals

Asking for referrals is one of the very best ways to obtain prospects. Yet few of us do it often enough or consistently enough. Clients are usually your best sources of referrals. When you are serving a large firm, a client referral may be to another department within the same organization. For example, if you're already doing a good job for human resources, the marketing department is more likely to be interested in your services than if you had never served the firm. Salespeople call this "penetrating" an account.

Other important sources of referrals are business associates (including vendors) and personal associates. If you belong to a social organization such as a country club or tennis club, take advantage of it and make your personal contacts extra productive.

The value of a referral is that it gets you in the door. You can say, "Joe Smith suggested I call you." If you know Joe well enough, ask him to pave the way by telling the prospect you will be calling. That's even more persuasive—and it forces you into following up. You don't want to hear Joe say, "Hey, my friend at the ad agency said you never called her."

Make it a habit to ask for and follow up on referrals.

Inquiry tracking

Whenever you get an inquiry, make it a point to ask how the prospect heard about you. This is essential information if you are to evaluate the effectiveness of your marketing and sales efforts. I suspect that most writers keep this kind of information in their heads, but I urge you to set up a tracking device for your leads—if no more than a computer document or a sheet of paper listing inquiries chronologically and indicating the source of each lead. In six months or a year, you will have a clear idea of where your new business is coming from.

Referral courtesies

When you receive a referral from an associate, it's an important point of business etiquette to thank that person. This is just common courtesy, but it also keeps the wheels of your marketing operation turning smoothly. A note or phone call is the usual method. Sometimes your thanks can be more elaborate, taking the form of a luncheon or a small gift—or even a referral fee.

Referral fees fall close to some ethically gray areas. When does a referral fee become a kickback? When I was selling printing, a local public relations man asked us to build in a referral fee of 10 percent whenever he requested a quote for his client. The client never knew about this fee. When the bill was paid, my firm sent the public relations man a check. This practice is not illegal and may be very common in certain industries, but I was never especially comfortable with it. On the other hand, if the public relations man had handled payment for the printing, he would naturally be expected to mark up the bill when passing it on to his client.

Use your networking contacts to find out whether referral fees are accepted (or even expected) in your community and the industries you serve.

Advertising and public relations

These topics were discussed under marketing techniques in the previous chapter. For our purposes here, I'm lumping together all of your efforts to put your name in front of prospective buyers—whether it's through a display or classified ad, a Website, a direct-mail campaign, a directory listing, an ad in a postcard deck, your card on a bulletin board, your name in the paper for having won an award or on a committee for a community event, your face on a business talk show, a display of your work, or you in person, giving a lecture or teaching a class. The result is the same: A prospective buyer learns about and contacts you.

What do you do? Of course, you fulfill any specific request promptly, whether the prospect has requested a copy of an article you wrote or asked to see your samples and brochure. After that, if the prospect is qualified, you add his or her name to your database for further cultivation. If the prospect doesn't need or can't afford your type of services but is impressed with your work, ask for some referrals.

Trade shows and conferences

I met my oldest and one of my best clients through a trade show. I swapped some writing services for a booth in a desktop publishing exhibition, and through that event I was introduced to a client whose newsletter I produced for many years. Large trade shows will be too costly for you to exhibit in, but if an event is targeted and affordable, put together an interesting display and give it a try. Make sure you have a good device for capturing names while you're busy talking to other visitors in your booth. Collecting business cards for a drawing is a tried-and-true method.

Even without being an exhibitor, a trade show or conference provides a good opportunity to meet prospects, since many people with similar interests are gathered in one place. Be aware, too, that conference planners sometimes designate an area where attendees can display their literature. To be on the safe side, bring a supply of literature along.

Take-one boxes

Putting a box of your literature in a place where prospects are likely to see it is a technique that might be suitable for certain writing specialties, such as a resumé writer. If you work with a quick printer, for example, ask if you can put your literature on the counter.

Seizing the moment

People who are extremely difficult to reach will usually talk with you when they are on public view—when they are giving a lecture, teaching a class, or attending a trade show or other public event. Your goal is to get a card and an invitation to call—or a referral to the appropriate person in the VIP's organization. (Then you can legitimately say, "I met Mr. VIP when he spoke at our trade association recently, and he suggested I call you.") But don't push too hard. Crude use of this technique can backfire. I watched a promoter trap an internationally known communications mogul in a hotel elevator once. The famous man had to listen, since the promoter was holding the door open—but I'm not sure he appreciated it.

Success Worksheet Twenty-Five

Keep building your prospect list.

Your prospect list is one of your essential business assets. Keep developing it. Make it as current as possible. Capture useful details. Discard those who don't qualify. Above all, *make contact*! An uncontacted prospect is as useless to you as an unqualified one.

- ■ Check the prospect sources that sound most productive to you and briefly note how you will use them to build and refine your prospect list.

_____ Media

_____

_____ Networking

_____

_____ Referrals

_____

_____ Inquiry tracking

_____

_____ Advertising and public relations

_____

_____ Trade shows and conferences

_____

_____ Take-one boxes

_____

_____ Other

_____

_____

TELEMARKETING, E-MAILING, AND MAILING

Telemarketing involves calling lists of people with a standardized message and objective. This is a vast topic and one that is becoming increasingly important in the business world. As the cost of making in-person sales calls rises, phone selling grows ever more attractive—and that is just as true for you and me as it is for a multibillion-dollar corporation.

Telemarketing will be useful for the following:

- Qualifying prospects—and seeking an appointment or a chance to bid.

- Follow-up—again seeking an appointment or a chance to bid.

- Soliciting business from past clients.

Unsolicited faxing or E-mailing can serve the same purposes and can encounter as much, if not more, resistance. However, as I explained in Chapter Seven under Marketing Yourself Online, a carefully prepared fax or E-mail message can get past a prospect's initial resistance.

What I am defining as telemarketing is what we freelancers congenitally put off whenever we possibly can: the time when we must sit down to call a list of names—be they new prospects, old prospects, those in a certain industry, or past clients we haven't heard from recently.

Telemarketing can help you identify new prospects who might use your type of service, let existing prospects know about a new service you have added, or see if prospects or clients have any jobs available.

A few years ago I heard a presentation on telephone selling by a smart young sales trainer named John Klymshyn of Palmdale, CA. With his permission, I'm going to share some of his ideas—what he calls the Klymshyn Method. At the same time, let me stress that his approach is just one of many.

Klymshyn advises making calls in twenty-call bursts. Making twenty calls at a time keeps you focused, he says. Since not all calls will be completed, you must follow up later. Start the call by identifying yourself, your company, and the purpose of your call. Note that this is also the correct way to begin an unsolicited E-mail message. Don't play games letting your recipient guess who has written and why. That "delete" button is very easy to hit.

Once you have explained, "What I do is . . ." follow that with such open-ended questions as "Who makes decisions about this type of service?" "How familiar are you with this type of service?" Avoid any that can be answered with a yes or no. Know what you want to accomplish with the call and stay on track.

Since many people consider a phone call an intrusion, Klymshyn tells his students, "Go in with the idea that what you are presenting has value." (Equally true for E-mail.) You have information that can benefit the person you're calling. As the caller responds, take notes for your database. Next time you call, you can bring up specifics and the prospect will be impressed by your interest and knowledge of his firm.

In Klymshyn's view, for any kind of selling, you must identify a need, create interest, and get out. "Don't bang your head against the wall," he says. "Most salespeople don't know when to shut up."

Is the prospect away from her desk? Leave a message. Klymshyn views voicemail as a sales opportunity. Your message can create interest by suggesting a benefit and can show you're proud of the service you provide.

But even with the best technique, no telemarketer completes all of his or her calls. How many times should you work through a list, trying to reach those you previously missed? "You want to try a minimum of three times to get to the decision maker," says Klymshyn. "After that, it's a judgment call based on what you feel is worthwhile. Valuable information can be gained by treating the decision maker's secretary as an equal. If you don't feel you have a shot, move on."

TOWARD A BUSINESS PLAN

Success Worksheet Twenty-Six

Make every prospecting contact effective.

The Klymshyn Method identifies eight requirements for effective telemarketing. I believe these requirements can be applied to unsolicited E-mail and regular mail prospecting as well.

> When you review the points below, imagine that you are prospecting by phone, E-mail, or regular mail to sell a specific writing service to one of your target markets. Note briefly how you would apply each requirement to this situation.
>
> _____ *Imagination.* Says Klymshyn: "People buy on the basis of emotion. Imagine your customer enjoying the benefits of your product or service."
>
> _____
>
> _____ *Organization.* Says Klymshyn: "Who are you going to call? What result do you want? Why should the prospect buy?"
>
> _____

_____ *Discipline*. Says Klymshyn: "Don't make fewer than twenty calls at a time. At about the seventh call, you'll start to make the contacts you need. It will begin to feel natural for you to be on the phone." Discipline also applies to E-mail and regular mail solicitations. Send a specific number of messages on a specific date to a list that is as current and correct as possible.

_____ *Perspective*. Says Klymshyn: "If your calls go well, it's great! If your calls go badly, the phone seems like a monster. Step back from both good and bad calls. Remember, it's persistent effort that pays off." Similarly, if you receive no response to your E-mail or regular mail—or, perhaps worse, if you get "flamed" by an irate E-mail recipient—put it in perspective. Reword your message to make it more persuasive and stay on schedule with periodic solicitations.

_____ *Enthusiasm*. Says Klymshyn: "Enthusiasm is contagious. Do you know what IASM means? It means, 'I Am Sold Myself.'"

_____ *Strong communication skills*. Says Klymshyn: "It's the old eighty-twenty rule. Eighty percent of our job is to shut up and listen. If you can get the customer to talk, you stay in control. There's only one issue in a sales call—the customer. And the customer is interested in WIIFM—"What's In It For Me?'" Similarly, in written communication emphasize "you" not "I." The point is not how wonderful your service is but *how the prospect will benefit*!

_____ *Product knowledge*. Says Klymshyn: "Without this, our entire presentation can fail. Buyers lose confidence if a salesperson can't answer their questions." You have an advantage here, since you're selling yourself.

_____ *Clear objectives*. Says Klymshyn: "Every sales call should have five objectives: (1) to sell, (2) to gather information, (3) to share information, (4) to establish a relationship, (5) to maintain a relationship." Written communications can also accomplish these objectives.

ORGANIZING YOUR DATABASE
AND MANAGING YOUR CONTACTS

It's essential that you put information about your prospects in some unified and accessible form. A card file or pages in a loose-leaf notebook will work, and many salespeople still use these simple tools. But since you are already computer-based, why not take advantage of one of the many contact management–mailing list programs available? Such programs are not difficult to learn and can boost your productivity enormously!

If you could produce a set of labels for, say, all the real estate brokers on your prospect list by simply hitting a few keys on your computer, guess what? You might send out a quick postcard promotion that would bring you in some nice flier or newsletter business. But if you had to go through all your prospect files, including folders stuffed with newspaper clippings and boxes full of business cards, to pick out the real estate brokers, and then if you had to type up several dozen individual envelopes, would you do it?

Incidentally, the work of building and maintaining your database can be shared by family members or occasional paid workers. It will get done if you line up others to do it. Sure, you may be interrupted to answer questions as the data are entered, but consider the alternatives—doing it yourself or not doing it at all.

Contact management–address programs usually allow you to record the prospect's full name, title, company, department, address, phone, fax, even birthday. Categories for grouping and sorting can be assigned to each record—client, top prospect, secondary prospect, prospect in a specific industry, and so on. You determine the categories. Most programs provide a free-form field for background information, such as the prospect's needs, interests, tastes, and current suppliers. Data can usually be formatted and printed out in various ways, such as on mailing labels, in an address book to carry with you, or on a flat list. The program may also be able to dial the phone for you.

The goal of a contact management program is to keep track of each contact you have with a prospect as well as the outcome of that contact. You make a plan for your next contact and remind yourself with a tickler method, such as a computer calendar, a pocket calendar, or monthly file folders. This may be built into your contact database program, as it is in Symantec's popular ACT!

Usually you are the one who must decide what and when the next contact will be. For example, you might want to call an editor on the first of the month because he told you that was when he normally assigns articles. To a list of fifteen instant printers you got from a business directory, you might decide to send a series of three mailings, one every other month, followed by phone calls. For a restaurant that occasionally requires menu design, you might decide to call the owner every six months.

Sometimes it is the prospect who establishes a contact date. "I don't need anything now," she may say. "Call me next month." Or, "I may need a proposal written in September. Call me then." Such an invitation from a prospect is very valuable! Treat it with respect and follow up religiously. Be sure to remind the prospect that he or she asked you to call back. Being able to say that Ms. Jones asked you to call is also useful in getting past her secretary.

As long as you see evidence that the prospect needs and can afford your services, it's not unusual for a writer or desktop publisher to make such follow-up contacts for months or even years before making a sale. Veteran sales reps will tell you that such dogged persistence pays off. It builds confidence and respect. The prospect is convinced that you are interested and that you keep your word.

FOLLOW-UP TECHNIQUES

The purpose of the follow-up phase is to get to know the prospect and increase the prospect's interest. While this section has been written for corporate writers, parts of it can be adapted by magazine writers attempting to break into new markets. Stay focused on benefits to the client and on the sales progression you need to make—

- A presentation
- An invitation to bid
- Awarding of a job
- Awarding of future jobs

Somehow, gathering the names of prospects seems to be a lot more appealing than following up on those names. As a result, many of us have files bulging with names we haven't gotten around to calling. Not to mention the piles of cards from people we don't call because we're embarrassed to say, "Hi, I'm Bob Stone, the writer you met at the advertising luncheon a year ago. I said I'd call you." I think the solution to this dilemma is to gather fewer names or separate the names we gather into "real" prospects and "whenever" prospects. Such preliminary sorting will make your data manageable.

Follow-up, also euphemistically described as "cultivation," can be a long process, but it is your best form of business insurance. We're all tempted to forget prospecting and drop everything for the wonder client who appears out of nowhere and gives us a series of profitable jobs. But that client can disappear just as suddenly—and then what? A solid prospecting base with a number of good potential clients who are aware of your work can always be counted on to produce some new jobs.

This chapter has already suggested several types of follow-up. Here's a quick overview.

Networking contacts

For your initial follow-up on a networking contact (such as a referral or someone you met at a professional event), send a note and then make a phone call. Or just make a call. Try to learn more about the prospect's role in the professional group, as well as about his need for your kind of services. If possible, offer some useful information, along with some background about what you do. If the prospect seems interested, suggest a meeting. If not, schedule him for follow-up. Appearing too pushy when contacting a buyer you have been referred to or met at a professional meeting will be resented. Buyers from high-profile organizations have told me horror stories about vampire vendors descending on them the day after the meeting.

Phone calls

One of your most basic selling techniques, already covered, thanks to trainer John Klymshyn.

Sales letters

This is another huge field about which much has been written and said. If you're a writer who can craft successful sales letters, you can make very, very good money! If you're seeking to interest prospects with your own sales letter, here are some tips.

Open with something that will arouse interest in your service. It could be an example of how another client has benefited or a way for the reader to solve a problem or save money. Stay in the "you" viewpoint. When you're finished writing, count the number of times "you" has been used, versus "I" or "we." If necessary, rewrite to put the focus on "you." In the case of E-mail, be sure to identify yourself clearly at the start and be brief. Your detailed message might be handled as an attachment or printed below your basic introduction.

In the body of the letter, present your most powerful selling point, emphasizing how it benefits the reader. Provide evidence to support your claims. Avoid "stoppers"—anything the reader might find confusing or disagree with. A poorly worded sentence can be a stopper. So can words that may unwittingly offend, such as "mailman" (substitute "mail carrier").

In closing, state the action you want the reader to take. Provide an incentive for responding (such as a free informational brochure or a free consultation). Make it easy to respond, by including a business reply card, phone number, or fax number. (E-mail has a clear advantage here).

Sales letters have no fixed length. In fact, they can be quite long if they are well written and brimming with benefits. Finally, research shows that a post script (P.S.) scores high readership, so include one. It's your last chance to motivate action.

Try your sales letter out on test readers representative of your intended audience, and study their responses. If you are doing a large mailing and want your marketing to be effective, you must record and measure the response you receive. Studying responses allows you to learn from both success and failure. Consider testing your mail package by varying one element (usually the letter itself or the offer) for part of your list. Measure and compare the response.

If a sales letter pulls, use it again.

Samples

Samples are your most important sales tool. Be sure to keep samples of every job. Organize your samples in a way that will protect them, make them easy to find, and assure you of an adequate supply. If you are using your last copy of a clipping, make more copies now—not a month from now when you're in a hurry and can't remember why you can't find the blankety-blank clipping.

Why do you need many different kinds of samples? Why not just keep copies of your very best work? Because of a human quirk that every experienced salesperson has learned to anticipate. No matter how good the writing or how elegant the design, buyers will respond much more strongly to samples (and also to lists of clients) in fields related to their own.

Testimonials

Testimonials are effective because a third-party endorsement is automatically more convincing than what you say about yourself. Keep copies of complimentary letters from clients. If a client praises you in a significant way, don't hesitate to ask him or her to put it in writing, and explain why. If you want to establish your expertise in a certain area, request that a client write a "to whom it may concern" testimonial letter about a job you have done. Make sure all such letters are on your client's letterhead. I keep original testimonial letters in my client files, but I keep extra copies with my samples, where I can find and use them as needed.

Other sales literature

Your sales literature may include one or more brochures about your services; your resumé, client list, and business cards; a custom Rolodex card with your name and sales message; your own newsletter, articles you have written, and reprints of articles about you; and custom presentation folders. When preparing client lists, be sure you have your customers' permission to use their names. Keep your sales literature organized, accessible, and current. If you run out of an item, update it if necessary. Then reorder promptly. If you can't easily locate what you need when you need it, you will be tempted to put off following up on requests for information and presentations. And that's death!

Keeping samples and sales literature organized and up-to-date represents an area where a family member or occasional worker can make an enormous contribution. It's an investment that will pay for itself many times over.

Specialty items

Advertising specialty catalogs are full of clever and useful items that can be imprinted with your name and business message. Such items may be a good investment. They're ice breakers and can often get you an appointment. For example, Claudia Miller, a California-based desktop publisher, swears by her "cookie."

"If you're going to do a mailing in the creative business, you'd better be creative," Miller says. "I have this cookie notepad. It looks like an Oreo cookie 6 inches in diameter, and inside is a round notepad. On the inside of the lid is my message—telling what a sharp cookie I am! I send my cookie in a box, and people wonder what it is. They're curious and they have to open it. Then it sits on a desk, where others see it. When they open the lid, they read my message, and I reach even more people that way."

Miller often sends the cookie as her first contact with a good prospect, following it up with a phone call. "My cookie," she says, "almost always gets me in the door!"

Getting past purchasing departments

When you sell creative services to large organizations, your actual buyer is usually not the purchasing department—but don't offend these folks by trying to go around them if company policy says they must be in the loop. The purchasing director may be happy to pass you along to the communications director once he has qualified you as a vendor. Or maybe he won't. If you have also built a relationship with the person who will actually use your writing—most likely someone in marketing, or corporate communications, or human resources—then that person may tell purchasing you're the vendor he or she wants.

Making friends with the prospect's staff

View whoever works with your prospects—assistants, secretaries, receptionists, security guards—as your allies. Ask and remember their names. Take time to learn something about them. Be friendly—but also show that you respect their bosses' time. It's amazing how well this tactic works! You'll hear (music to your ears!), "Oh, I think he can find time to see *you*." Another benefit to this approach (aside from its obvious human kindness) is that your prospect may leave and his assistant (already your friend) may be promoted. Or your prospect may leave and the receptionist (still your friend) may tell his replacement what a great person you are.

Getting around a turndown

"We're happy with the freelancers we're using." When you hear this, a good answer is, "I respect your loyalty. I'm loyal to the people I work with, too. But if you ever have an overload or a crisis project when your regular people can't help you, please give me a call." Usually this response will have a calming effect, and the prospect may accept your literature. Although such a client is currently a poor prospect, don't delete her. If she uses freelancers, many things could change. A freelancer could mess up a job, leave the area, or be unable to meet a deadline. Or company staff members could change, creating a whole new ballgame.

Following up at meetings and events

When I see prospects at professional meetings or other events, I make it a point to speak with them and exchange news. Often I learn about bidding opportunities that way. ("The vice president wants me to start a newsletter for our dealers in the fall. I don't know how I'm going to find time for another publication!") It also gives me a chance to share something of interest about my own recent work. Having spoken with the prospect, of course, provides yet another contact opportunity. When I send a note or call her, saying how good it was to see her, I can add, "If you need help writing or designing your dealer newsletter, I've had a lot of experience with that kind of publication. I think we could work something out that would be cost-effective."

Do an "incomparable"

Years ago, I took my first class in printing sales from a tough veteran saleswoman. Her advice for dealing with prospects and clients surprised me. "Do an 'incomparable,'" she told us. "Do something they don't expect, something they appreciate, something no one else would do." Claudia Miller's oversized Oreo cookie is a good example. For my part, I try to listen carefully to the special interests of prospects and clients and provide them with information when I can—nothing expensive, perhaps a newspaper clipping or a magazine article—just a thoughtful gesture that makes me stand out from the crowd. I can't tell you what your "incomparable" would be. But look for it.

Gifts and entertainment

As freelancers, we don't have much money to spend on gifts and entertainment, and in my experience it's not really expected. If the topic is of interest, you might bring a prospect or client to a professional meeting as your guest. Or you might suggest lunch to discuss a project and pick up the tab. In December I deliver small gifts, such as dried fruit, to my clients and their staffs to wish them holiday cheer. (I stopped bringing boxes of chocolate creams when an overweight client received my chocolates with painful groans of obvious dismay. For the same reason, I never give alcohol as a gift.) Be aware that in many business settings, accepting even token gifts or entertainment is prohibited. If you're not sure, ask what the policy is.

TOWARD A BUSINESS PLAN

Success Worksheet Twenty-Seven

Good follow-up techniques turn prospects into clients.

My guess is that more sales are lost from failure to follow up than from any other cause. Consistency and organization are the keys.

Which of these follow-up techniques fits your business and personality? Which will you really carry out? How soon or how frequently? Will you need any special materials?

_____ Prompt initial response to networking contacts

ACTION_____

TIME FRAME _____

MATERIALS, COMMENTS _____

_____ Telephone contacts

ACTION_____

TIME FRAME _____

MATERIALS,COMMENTS _____

Sales letters—either E-mail or regular mail

ACTION_____

TIME FRAME _____

MATERIALS, COMMENTS_____

_____ Samples

ACTION_____

TIME FRAME _____

MATERIALS, COMMENTS_____

_____ Testimonials

ACTION_____

TIME FRAME _____

MATERIALS, COMMENTS_____

_____ Other sales literature

ACTION_____

TIME FRAME _____

MATERIALS, COMMENTS_____

_____ Specialty items

ACTION_____

TIME FRAME _____

MATERIALS, COMMENTS_____

_____ Getting past purchasing departments

ACTION_____

TIME FRAME _____

MATERIALS, COMMENTS_____

_____ Making friends with the prospect's staff

ACTION_____

TIME FRAME _____

MATERIALS, COMMENTS_____

_____ Getting around a turndown

ACTION_____

TIME FRAME _____

MATERIALS, COMMENTS_____

_____ Following up at meetings and events

ACTION_____

TIME FRAME _____

MATERIALS, COMMENTS_____

_____ Doing an "incomparable"

ACTION_____

TIME FRAME _____

MATERIALS, COMMENTS_____

_____ Gifts and entertainment

ACTION_____

TIME FRAME _____

MATERIALS, COMMENTS_____

THE STEPS TOWARD BUYING

Classic sales theory holds that a prospect follows a simple progression toward becoming a buyer:

- Attention
- Interest
- Conviction
- Desire

You cannot rush these steps, and you cannot take them out of order. For example, offering a deeply discounted price to a buyer who has never heard of you will probably not produce a sale—and it may tarnish your reputation.

Until you have the prospect's *attention,* selling cannot take place. Until the prospect is *interested,* has the idea that your services may be useful to him, he will not sit still to learn about their features and benefits.

Now it gets more complicated. The process of *conviction* begins as the prospect learns about the benefits of using your services. (And remember that features and benefits are not the same thing. A feature of your service is that you meet your deadlines. The benefit, however, is that the buyer will have peace of mind.) Until the prospect has seen some proof, both features and benefits remain merely claims. Let's say you show him several testimonial letters from other clients, thanking you for meeting deadlines so efficiently. With proof, the prospect becomes *convinced*.

Even when a prospect is convinced that you can do the job, he may not buy from you. Since he can hire any number of qualified writers, he must have a *desire* to choose you. Perhaps he visualizes how much easier his work will be with your help or how much credit he will get when your materials produce results. Perhaps he begins to like and trust you and to think of how much he would enjoy working with you. Perhaps he fears his competitors and believes that the brochure you have suggested will strengthen his position in the market. Now he feels he must have that brochure!

Now he is ready to buy.

MAKING A SALES PRESENTATION

The presentation, with its numerous methods for overcoming objections and equally numerous techniques for closing the sale, has been the subject of many seminars, books, and tapes. Don't let that scare you. Read up and take some training when you can—and in the meantime, apply these basic pointers to your selling experiences.

I should point out that in the classic sales scenario, the salesperson makes his or her presentation, asks for the order, and closes or fails to close the sale in a single session. In our kind of selling, that's not likely to happen. Your first presentation will probably be quite smooth, as you show your best samples and describe the best features of your services. Your "close" will be to ask for a job to quote, but you may not get one right away. When you are given a request for a proposal, you may go in again to discuss the job requirements. At yet another meeting, either in person or on the phone, you will discuss your proposal. If you're lucky, you'll get a simple go-ahead. Otherwise, you may have to answer objections and negotiate specific issues.

A presentation may not be necessary

If the client starts talking about her project from the moment you arrive, she may already be sold on you. Keep her talking! Forget the presentation you practiced and the samples you prepared, and find out how you can help her.

Use samples to shape your presentation

Your presentations will usually be structured by the samples you have brought. You talk your way through your samples, bringing out features and benefits. Select samples appropriate to the prospect, and arrange them according to the points you want to make, based on your understanding of the prospect's needs. Include appropriate testimonials and copies of your own sales literature. It may seem overwhelming to think of custom-tailoring each and every presentation, but soon you will do it automatically.

Bring material for the prospect's files

Be sure to bring something you can leave with the prospect—usually your brochure, resumé, and client list, along with your business card and some samples (or copies of samples if you can't leave the originals). Putting these in an imprinted folder—or just in a plain file folder with your name already lettered on the tab—is a nice touch. The folder encourages your prospect to put your material in the vertical file—rather than the round one.

Avoid "stoppers"

"Stoppers" during a sales presentation are points the prospect may disagree with, be offended by, or not understand. I'll never forget the artist who called on me when I was a university publications director during the antiwar seventies. He attacked the military with every other word and obviously had not taken the trouble to learn that our institution depended heavily on military students. He did not get my business, even though I agreed with some of his sentiments.

You may be a person with strong opinions, but why risk offending with controversial political and social views? You can also offend by attacking a writing or design style the prospect happens to like or speaking in computer jargon that the prospect doesn't understand. People make up their minds about others very, very quickly.

Never bad-mouth a competitor

It just isn't professional to attack or criticize a competitor—you will come out the loser. On the other hand, you can attack unspecified competitors by noting, "Very few writers have the background to do this job." Or you might say, "My price is a little higher because my quality is, quite frankly, above average." (Then go on to explain what you do to provide better quality.)

But if you are asked directly about a competitor, be either noncommittal or vaguely complimentary. "Mary Williams is a good technical writer," you might say, "and I'm sure she could do the job, but [again bring in a benefit of your services]."

Assume the sale

From the beginning, take a "we" attitude that implies you are part of the prospect's team, a helpful and dependable resource. Convey that you are interested in the prospect's goals and concerned with his success. This is a good position to take, because it's true. You can naturally assume that the prospect will do business with you. But use good judgment. Assuming the sale too aggressively or too soon can backfire and you'll hear, "Now wait just a minute! We're talking to several writers about this manual. We haven't made a decision."

Present features in terms of advantages and benefits

I suggest you do some writing to prepare this part of your presentation, even though it should appear to be extemporaneous to the prospect. List the features of your service. For every feature, identify the advantages it represents and the benefits the client will experience. Be sure to define benefits in terms of feelings and emotions. For example—

- Feature: "I work with several Website providers and designers."

- Advantages: "I have already checked them out and know they are reliable. I can handle the instructions and billing so you will deal with only one vendor."

- Benefits: "You can relax. Everything will be taken care of."

When you make each presentation, you will be able to choose from the prepared material in your head the appropriate features and benefits to address.

Have proof to back up your claims

For every feature of your service, be prepared to offer some proof. Often you will not need to present it, but in some situations testimonial letters, price comparisons, industry statistics, and the like can turn doubt to conviction so that you can get on with the sale.

Handling objections

Veteran sales trainers will tell you that the best way to handle objections is to anticipate them. As you work with prospects, you will begin to recognize areas where objections may arise. Stressing points like "at no extra cost," "with your approval," and "at your convenience" assure prospects that they will be in control and have no unpleasant surprises. But since no presentation is perfect, you will encounter objections. To handle them, here are some tips:

- When the prospect presents an objection, keep him talking to find out what he is really objecting to. Since objections are generally emotional in nature, look for hidden feelings, especially factors that might cause the client to feel worried, overburdened, or vulnerable to criticism.

- Don't contradict a prospect even if her objection reveals misunderstanding or lack of information. If the prospect says, "Our policy manual is too complex for an outside writer to grasp," a good response would begin, "I can understand how you might think that, but . . . " Contradictions are "stoppers" because the client feels he is under attack and must defend himself.

- Don't try to suppress objections, because unanswered objections create more objections. Instead, answer the objection promptly. An objection is like a loop that takes you back into your presentation to cover a point more fully. "It's true that I haven't written financial material before, but I will bring a fresh perspective to the project because of my other experience."

- What appears to be an objection may only be a stall, meaning that the prospect's desire to buy is not yet strong enough.

- Price objections show lack of perceived value. Build more value into the project. (More about that in the next chapter.)

- If possible, convert objections into questions. Suppose the client says, "Four weeks is too long to produce this newsletter." Assuming the sale, you answer the prospect's implied question about timing: "How can we plan the job differently to get it out faster?" But suppose you encounter an even more difficult objection when the prospect announces, "We got a very similar price from your competitor, and she says she can do the job in three weeks." Now you segue to the question, "What are the steps involved in producing a really good newsletter?" And without bad-mouthing your competitor, you try to plant seeds of doubt about a fast job, while showing that your approach will produce a quality product, one that will accomplish its objectives. And so it goes. Some you win. And some you don't.

- If an objection is real and unavoidable, try the "other than that" approach. Often it will clarify key points and reopen negotiations. For example: "I like your writing style, but we have to have a writer who can also shoot photos." "If photos were not an issue," you reply, "would you want me to write this monthly column?" "Yes, but we must have photos. That's why we pay a higher rate for this column." "How many photos do you need?" you ask. "We need at least three photos of the topic store each month—an exterior, an interior, and a close-up of the manager in action."

"What if I guarantee to provide you with professional photos at the same price?" you ask. You're gambling on several things—that a photographer you sometimes work with will help you out for a few months while you improve your photo skills and that each store profiled will buy prints of what he shoots, helping to cover costs while you make up the difference. Later that day you check with the photographer, and the next morning you close the deal. The worst that can happen, if you can't get your photography up to par, is that you continue to accept a lesser fee or resign the account. Either option represents a strong incentive to succeed. After all, we're risk takers or we wouldn't be in this business.

The trial close

Closing scares many salespeople because it is the moment when they may be told "no." But closing is actually a continuous part of the sales process. You do it all along as you assume the sale through simple comments like "When can I get the information from you?" or "Would you like me to proofread the copy, or will someone on your staff do it?" You are getting the prospect on the same wavelength with you, assuming you will work together. From this position, it's a small step to a "trial close."

A trial close is a question that contains an implied purchasing decision, such as, "Shall I start interviewing your people next week, or would two weeks from now be better?" Or you might ask, "Is that price within your budget?" A trial close can be used to flush out hidden objections. It also makes it easier for you to ask for the order. This is something you must eventually do, although, believe it or not, some salespeople are so afraid of being told "no" that they never really ask that crucial question. Instead, they allow the purchasing decision to be deferred to another day, greatly weakening their position.

Remember, no sale is closed until you have the order in hand—establishing full agreement on services, terms, and timing. Some sales trainers use the memory device "ABC"—Always Be Closing—to help salespeople make full use of closing as a powerful sales tool.

Silence

Don't be afraid to be silent after you have presented your proposal or asked for the order. Salespeople often think they must fill an important moment like that with rapid chatter. Wrong. Silence can be a greater pressure on the prospect than words. It keeps you in control.

KEEPING YOUR PROSPECT/CLIENT LIST ACTIVE

If you have not yet been invited to bid, or if you have presented one or several bids and been rejected, you would normally continue to follow a prospect—if you believe business is there for you—until you begin making sales. But just how long you follow each prospect is a judgment call.

Some salespeople will question a prospect on this point, especially if they feel they are being used to provide comparative bids with no real chance of being selected. The approach would be friendly, but concerned: "I've been calling on the Mid-City Corporation for X months now, and I've given you prices on several jobs. You've seen the kind of work I do, and I know my prices are competitive. I'd very much like to work with you here at Mid-City. Do I have a chance of getting an assignment?" You may or may not get a straight answer, but the move is a professional one and will be respected. It could even produce some jobs.

More typically, you will get a clear message when your calls are not returned and you are never asked to bid. Unless you can find another point of entry, there's no business here.

When a client stops buying

A similar, but more serious close-out can occur when you stop getting jobs. Don't ignore this situation. A frank conversation with the buyer may reveal a problem that can be solved. If the client has decided to take the work in-house, use someone else, or discontinue the project, put your efforts elsewhere.

Disposition of prospects

The final step in a contact management program is to dispose of the names of unproductive or inactive prospects and clients. If a name is in your active file, you should be contacting that individual or organization periodically with the expectation of getting work. That's what *active* means. If you do not feel further contacts will be productive, the name should be moved to an inactive file or deleted.

SOLICITING ADDITIONAL BUSINESS

Once you have served a client, having a good contact management program will help you stay in touch to obtain additional assignments. Don't expect the client to call you, even though he may have been delighted with the work you did last month or last year. Many clients give new jobs or bidding opportunities to any qualified vendor who phones or walks in the door. They're not disloyal customers exactly, just busy ones. Work hard to develop repeat business. All studies show that serving existing clients is much more cost-effective than developing new ones—though both kinds of business are necessary, since old clients will eventually drop away.

Sylvia McNair
Travel Writer, Evanston, Illinois

Building on Experience

Travel author Sylvia McNair dreamed of being a writer when she was in the fourth grade, but didn't turn her dream into reality until she was 57 and a widow with four grown children. Downsized from a quality control job with a hotel company, she sold her house, rented an apartment, and launched her freelance career. Fifteen years later, at 72, McNair is the author of fourteen books with commitments for more and she happily spends a quarter of her time in writing-related travel.

A success miracle? Yes—and no.

McNair's success and her courage are an inspiration. But the "miracle" came from planning, networking, tenacity, and building on experience.

Born in Korea to missionary parents, McNair grew up in Vermont, earned an A.B. in economics from Oberlin College, and held a variety of jobs, including one as a magazine production editor. Later, married and caring for children, she did freelance editing at home. "I copy-edited books for a small publisher on subjects I knew nothing about—but at least I knew grammar and punctuation," she says.

Returning to work fulltime, McNair spent ten years with Rand McNally, ending up as a senior editor of travel guides.

"When I left Rand McNally, I thought I would try freelancing," recalls the small, bright-eyed writer. "But I was living in a bedroom community and it was just too lonesome. After being in offices all my life, I just couldn't take it."

So she went to work doing hotel quality inspections, similar to her travel guide research. Two years later, she was laid off and took the freelance plunge.

Already active in travel-writing circles, McNair turned to a friend who was opening a publishing house and snared a contract for two guidebooks. "That was really the big push to get me started," she says. She sold her house and used some of the proceeds for living expenses over the next four years.

"Actually, it was pretty slow," McNair admits. "I got a few magazine assignments. I registered as a temporary office worker and worked in places like Jewish Family Service and the Engineering Department at Northwestern University. I'd work for two or three weeks while somebody was on vacation or having a baby and that kept food on the table, along with slowly taking my money out of the bank. Then, I guess I really got started about 1985."

Around that time, McNair made two leaps forward. She got a contract from Rand McNally to do *Vacation Places Rated*— "a huge job which took me a couple of years"—and through networking, she met an editor at Children's Press, resulting in a contract for a children's social studies book. She has since written ten more seventh- to-ninth-grade books on individual countries and states for this publisher, using her travel-writing skills to research and describe such topics as geography, history, and culture.

"I've just completed books on two countries and have a commitment to do eleven more," the septuagenarian enthuses. "I'm planning to do three books a year over the next four years."

Most of this work involves library research McNair explains, adding, "I try to get a trip to each place for a week or two to get local color. In the case of states, I go to the capitol and the state libraries and see what I can find. A lot of the travel I do is covered," she reveals, "but I would spend money on travel with my last dime anyway."

In addition to her books, McNair has been travel correspondent for *Elks Magazine* for nine years, providing nine feature-length articles a year, usually on domestic travel. "It's been a wonderful relationship," she says.

McNair was formerly on the national board of the American Society of Journalists and Authors (ASJA), is the immediate past president of the Travel Journalists Guild, and a past national board member of the Society of American Travel Writers. As such, she's adamant about networking.

"It's just invaluable! I can't understand freelancers who say, 'Oh, I can't afford it. The dues are too high.' Or, 'It takes too much time.' They don't get it—what the returns are!"

When aspiring writers ask for advice, McNair often quotes Bernie Asbell speaking at an ASJA convention: "Asbell told us he doesn't believe in writing about what you know. He said, 'It's more important to write about what you *don't* know and are dying to find out.' That's it! Write about something you are enthusiastic about." She also stresses the importance of "being willing to cut your losses if you get started on something and it isn't working."

Equipped with a Macintosh computer and an inkjet printer, McNair uses a nearby copy shop for faxing and copying and handles her E-mail through America Online. To home-based writers, she offers one more tip:

"I found out when I first started that I want to be able to look at something nice from an office. When I bought this co-op I picked the room that had the best view. I'm on the seventh floor and I watch the chipmunks going up and down and occasional pigeons on the windowsill. The change of seasons and all of that really makes a difference."

CHAPTER NINE

HOW TO CHARGE AND HOW TO COLLECT

DECIDING WHAT TO CHARGE

"What shall I charge?" is the question I am most frequently asked by would-be or fledgling freelancers. Arriving at the right answers is complicated but essential to your business success. In this chapter, we will examine rates and payment from several different perspectives:

- What others charge
- How to arrive at your own rates
- Determining what work is profitable for your business—your profit zone
- The psychology of setting a price
- The bidding and negotiating process
- Terms of payment and credit approval
- Additional job expenses and the final bill
- Getting paid

WHAT DO OTHERS CHARGE?

Research pertaining to this question falls under two categories—industrywide pricing and local or industry-specific pricing. You should study both, although the second category is the most important in helping you win assignments.

National or regional surveys are a good place to begin your own research. These surveys publish averages or bottom—top ranges for various kinds of writing. You can buy most of this information in book form or borrow it from libraries (see below). But in some cases, you must belong to the organization or subscribe to the publication that conducted the survey to read the results. Since new surveys come out periodically, keep this information current if you are using it in pricing.

Your second source of information is your own ongoing research about what clients like yours are paying writers in your community (or in whatever market you serve).

Collect all the industrywide information you can. Start asking speakers at lectures and seminars how much the jobs under discussion cost and how much time it should take to do each phase of the job. Talk over issues relating to costs and time with your mentors. Consult with colleagues at professional meetings. Discuss pricing with vendors.

Numerous books and trade journals provide information on *how* to do different kinds of jobs, but rarely do they tell us *how long* each phase of the work should take or how much was paid for the project under discussion. We should start asking trade journal editors to include time factors as part of their "how-to" coverage, along with more information on pricing.

National and regional rate studies for writers

Books. Each year, the *Writer's Market* (see Bibliography) includes a section listing current rates for various kinds of writing, along with advice on how to arrive at an hourly rate. The 1997 edition offers thirteen tightly packed pages listing rates for jobs in the following categories: advertising, copywriting, and public relations; audiovisual and electronic communications; book publishing; business; computer, scientific, and technical; editorial/design packages; educational and literary services; magazines and trade journals; newspapers; and miscellaneous.

Here are some sample rates:

Book review:	$35–$200 for larger publications
Research:	$20–$40 per hour
Newsletter writing:	$25–$45 per hour; 25 cents to $1 per word; $25–$300 per page; $35–$2,500 per story; or $375–$2,500 per issue.
Sales letters:	$350–$1,000 for one or two pages
Website design:	$50–$100 per page

Many writers buy a copy of *Writer's Market* annually or at least every few years. But my guess is that few really take time to discover what a treasure-house of information this venerable resource really is! It offers advice on such topics as research, manuscript formats, contracts, and copyright, as well as more than nine hundred pages listing book publishers, magazines (including the trade, technical, and professional journals dealt with in this book), script writing contacts, syndicates, greeting card and gift companies, and writing contests and awards.

Writer's Market is mainly addressed to writers who want to sell fiction or nonfiction to book publishers and magazines, but in the section on what to charge, the editors give a knowing nod to the hidden market for writers who want to make a dependable living at their craft. This is the meat-and-potatoes market we have been discussing throughout this book. Going through the rate listings will give you many ideas for practical jobs you can do in your own community. It's as though the editors were saying under their breaths, "Look, we're devoting this book to the glamorous side of writing, but if you really want to survive, go after jobs like these."

In his popular book, *Secrets of A Freelance Writer: How to Make $85,000 A Year*, Robert W. Bly lists a few "typical fees for commercial freelance writing projects," including an hourly rate for freelance writers of $35–$150 and up (see Bibliography). Bly's is one of the few writing guides to provide any actual figures. The reason, I am sure, is that fees vary widely according to the region, industry, writer's expertise, and type of writing involved. Fees also vary with the condition of the local economy.

Magazines. When writers' magazines such as *The Writer* and *The Writer's Digest* (see Bibliography) report on markets (usually that means magazines) they normally list rates of payment. This can be useful information, but not always for the obvious reasons.

I was feeling noble, accepting an hourly rate far below what I am paid by corporations to write for a regional religious publication (even though I greatly enjoyed the assignment), when a friend told me she was assigned to contribute to a cover story for *People Magazine* at a dollar less per hour than the denominational tabloid was paying me! See what I mean about glamour? Unless you have a name that can command big bucks, even altruism pays better.

Organizations. Some writers' organizations conduct periodic rate surveys. One example is the Independent Writers of Southern California. IWOSC does a rate survey each year, mailing results to members only. Check with your local writers groups. A list of writers' organizations is provided in the Source Directory.

Incidentally, you'll find that writers' organizations fall into several categories, including amateur or professional and literary or commercial. You'll get more help in setting fees from a group that is concerned with giving writers business advice.

Getting local price information

Determining local prices paid by the kinds of clients you want to serve for the kinds of services you want to provide is part of your marketing research (see Chapter Seven). By the time you are actually pricing jobs, you should have some good local guidelines, but a single research effort will not be enough to keep your prices on target for long. Writer/marketing consultant Jan Franck of West Des Moines, IA, profiled in Chapter Five, does a private survey each year of local ad agency rates.

Make it a habit to gather price information whenever you have the chance. Whenever a client, a prospect, or a colleague discusses a job with you, ask about the price. Some people won't divulge price information, but many others will. Or at least you can get a range, such as "over $2,500" or "between $300 and $500."

When a competitor is selected for a job you have bid on, always try to find out why, probing for price among other factors. Some buyers are prohibited by organizational policy from divulging such information, but many will share it if you make it clear that you understand your competitor has been selected for the job and you have no problem with this. You are not trying to persuade the client to change anything; you simply want some guidance for your future marketing efforts. What were the deciding factors that made your competitor's proposal more attractive?

Vendors such as service bureaus and printers are another good source of price information if you provide desktop publishing services. Or call an advertising or public relations firm to see what they charge for what you do. (The figure will probably reflect their high overhead costs.) You might even have a friend obtain bids on a real or bogus job.

DECIDING HOW TO PRICE YOUR SERVICES

Setting your prices is an important process. It determines your personal income. It is a factor in establishing your image in the marketplace. And it helps to decide whether or not you get a specific job and whether your business will survive.

From the client's point of view, the *way* you present your price is also important. Here are some options:

- By the hour: a very common approach for many jobs.

- By the full or half day: usually for on-site work, especially consulting.

- By the head: one way to charge for training or presentations.

- By the word: typical of magazines and newspapers.

- By use: typical of illustrators and some writers. Price depends on how widely or how often work will be used.

- By the project: popular with clients because they feel secure knowing costs in advance.

- Flat rate: the same charge for a repeating job.

- Retainer fee: an agreement that the client will buy X hours of your time each month, frequently used by PR and marketing consultants.

Hourly rates

Regardless of how you present your price to the client, the hourly rate is your real yardstick. I like getting agreement up front with the client that my time is worth, say, $50 or $60 an hour. It's surprising how readily clients will nod in agreement when you tell them your hourly rate. You are establishing yourself as a valued professional—and you are also flushing out clients who can't possibly afford you. This saves time and misunderstandings. Once your rate has been agreed upon, you need only show that each part of the job will take so many hours.

Rarely, however, does a new client agree to an open-ended purchasing decision, authorizing you to work for an unlimited number of hours for a certain hourly fee. Normally, you will be asked to estimate how many hours the job (or each phase of the job) will take. To give yourself latitude, you might say, "This job will take me 10–14 hours at $X per hour."

Some writers use the marketing strategy of offering lower rates for nonprofit clients or for jobs that automatically repeat. As a marketing strategy, there's nothing wrong with this—as long as the numbers work out. In other words, your gross income must be sufficient to meet your expenses and produce a profit. If you get more work at the lower rates, you may be able to keep your numbers up—but beware! You may also end up working sixty- and seventy-hour weeks to turn out low-profit or no-profit jobs.

Different hourly rates for different tasks

Since the marketplace rewards creative and managerial work at higher rates than, say, proofreading, transcribing a tape-recorded interview, or keying in text, you will need to estimate your own time—or that of your employees or subcontractors—at different rates, depending on the job. Furthermore, one creative worker commands a higher rate per hour than another, depending on his or her experience and reputation. Your client may be willing to pay more when you are doing the writing than when it is handled by your assistant. You may be able to sidestep this issue by assuring your clients that all creative work is done under your supervision.

A common trap for creative workers is to start charging less when they themselves are doing less skilled work. Let me illustrate this trap with an example from my own experience.

As a writer, I formerly tape-recorded all interviews for my corporate clients, transcribing them myself. This tedious work took me hours, but when I finished the transcription, I was in a good place mentally to write the article—if I wasn't too exhausted. I invested $250 in a transcription machine, which helped a little, but the job was still tedious. I could not charge $50 or $60 an hour for transcribing tapes, and it was a moot point whether I could charge for transcriptions at all, since my clients usually did not instruct me to tape record their interviews.

Initially I handled the problem by overcharging slightly on my writing hours and not mentioning transcription in my bills. In other words, I was working for less. I have now developed a technique of taking abbreviated notes on my computer, either on my desktop at home, when I am interviewing by phone, or using my laptop in the field. With this method, I have close to a verbatim account of each interview printed out clearly and instantly ready for me to start writing—though some of the spelling is bizarre! This is a much more satisfactory arrangement for many interviews, and while it slows them down a little, I can legitimately charge for that. Furthermore, subjects seem to like knowing I am doing my best to quote them correctly.

What can you learn from this example? The lesson is *don't work for less.* It's a bad business practice, since all you have to sell is your time. Find a way out! If you can get away with it, you might raise your hourly rates enough to cover the time you're doing low-skilled work. You might use a subcontractor and bill for his or her time at a lower rate, plus your markup, of course. Or you might change your procedures, as I did, in order to avoid doing low-paid work.

Charging by the full or half day

Corporations and government agencies are used to this approach—typical of consulting and training services. Figure your rate on a seven- or eight-hour day with a premium for overtime. If preparation time is required prior to your visit, be sure to include it in your estimate.

Charging by the head

Teaching a seminar or a class involving several meetings is often compensated by the head—the number of students who enroll or attend. To protect yourself, you should specify a minimum number of enrollments required for you to teach the class—or a minimum fee you will accept. If attracting the public is a factor in enrollment, you may want permission to do your own publicity since a school district or local college or agency may not do enough promotion to attract the crowd you need.

By the word

This time-honored approach is very familiar to writers who write for national and regional magazines—but is less familiar to those of us who do corporate writing. I received my first payment-by-the-word assignment in eight years of freelancing from a national medical news publication. At 50 cents a word, I was pleased to find the compensation comparable to my corporate projects. Writer colleagues tell me that editors will often negotiate with you for payment above the publication's stated rates if you can show why you're worth it.

By use

Most of the writing discussed in this book is custom-tailored to a client's specific needs, so the issue of "use" rarely comes up. Unless you specify otherwise, your business clients will assume that they are buying all rights to the work you agree to do. Some large firms require work-for-hire agreements stating that you are selling all rights to the creative work done under the agreement.

Some illustrators, photographers, and writers stand their ground, however, insisting that the work belongs to them and that the use made of the work should determine its worth to the client. Widespread or repeated use should be compensated at a higher rate, they maintain. Writers believe they should be compensated for reprint rights when their work is reused in a new context.

Issues surrounding the rights to intellectual property are very complex, regulations are difficult to establish and enforce, and infractions are hard to police. Electronic data transmission especially on the Internet—as well as the ever-growing use of quality, high-speed duplicating equipment have added to the problem, which is certainly beyond the scope of this book.

- Stay informed on accepted rates for various uses and on copyright laws. A good, brief discussion of copyright is given in the *Writer's Market*.

- Work with your industry organizations. Many of them are doing battle on your behalf to establish industry codes and legislation that will provide creative workers with fair compensation, particularly with regard to placing material in electronic databases and on the Internet.

- If your name is to appear on your work, establish with your client in advance your right to approve cuts or alterations. You can back off from this if a client is adamant, or if relinquishing your right to approve alterations becomes a point in price negotiations. But it is important to protect your reputation. Of course, as in all business, earned trust and a reasonable understanding between respected colleagues is the basis for most of what happens.

- Help your clients see your point of view—and listen to theirs. I once hired an artist to do a simple, one-color illustration for a newsletter I produced for a corporate client. The project turned into a nightmare. The client was furious at the artist's rate, which was high because the artist understood the newsletter received national distribution. Furthermore, my client wanted the right to use the illustration again if he chose to, while the artist specified one-time use only and demanded that his original art be returned. We finally dropped the artist and found another one who was easier to get along with.

By the project

This method is popular with clients because they know what they are committing themselves to. Writers like it when they feel the price is advantageous to them since they need not disclose how they arrived at the amount nor how many hours they actually put in. Project pricing also forces you to be efficient—to find ways of doing good work for minimum effort—and to keep track of your time and costs so that you will be on target with future estimates. Project pricing allows you to tailor your work to the project budget. If you quote $1,000 for a brochure, for example, and the client tells you he has a maximum of $800 to spend, you can negotiate what you will provide for that amount. Finally, with project pricing it's easier to charge more when you know you will be dealing with a difficult client and less when you expect smooth sailing.

Charging a flat rate

A flat rate can be advantageous for both you and the client on projects that repeat, such as newsletters, flyers such as those describing real estate properties, or press releases for repeating events. The flat rate makes it easy for the client to plan his budget. It may give you an edge in getting the business, and it contributes to your "nut"—that portion of your monthly gross income that you can count on to cover your costs. If arrived at fairly, a flat rate will average out, with more work one time and less work the next, so that you receive profitable compensation. You may or may not have a formal agreement with the client to do, say, a year's newsletters for $X per issue. Get an agreement if you can.

Charging a retainer fee

Here's another opportunity to increase the monthly income you can plan on. Public relations services are often contracted for on the basis of a retainer fee—usually monthly. Since there is no limit to the amount of promotion that could be done for the client, you agree to set aside a certain number of hours each month and do what can be done within that time frame. It's vital that you plan the work, clear appropriate time for it, and keep the client informed, so that he feels he is getting his money's worth. Otherwise, your retainer might be an easy item to trim off a tight budget.

If a major project, such as a special event, requires more than the allotted time, discuss with the client whether you will bill extra that month or work fewer hours for the next few months. Try to sell your client on the former, since public relations efforts are cumulative: The same amount of work brings a better response when done consistently than when done occasionally.

Is an estimate always required?

Once you have established a relationship with a client, you may not be expected to estimate every job. This is how I work with a regional publication for which I do a variety of tasks, including research, writing, photography, editing, and occasional page design and production. I bill these services at the same rate and the editor and I both know approximately how long various tasks will take. If, for example, a story should run into many more interviews than anticipated, I would call the editor to discuss the mounting charges and consider alternative ways of handling the story.

In my experience, corporate assignments often take this semi-open-ended form—and for me it has been a very profitable approach. For example, I might be asked to write an article of 1,500 words on the launching of a new monitoring device at $50 an hour, not to exceed $700.

HOW TO ARRIVE AT YOUR BASIC HOURLY RATE

First of all, you need to know how much money you must bring in to survive. This means the monthly costs of operating your business—such costs as the portion of your housing expenses, including utilities and maintenance, that you charge to your business; taxes; insurance; equipment depreciation; supplies; services; memberships; subscriptions; and money paid to any employees or contractors. It also means your profits—the money you pay yourself to cover monthly family expenses, including insurance, savings for retirement, and Social Security and income taxes, as well as the surplus income that will enable you to grow your business and eventually improve your family's lifestyle. From these figures you can arrive at your monthly and annual gross income goal.

EXAMPLE	
Monthly cost of business operation	$1,100
Monthly family expenses	3,100
Business surplus	500
Total	$4,700

$4,700 x 12 = $56,400—your annual gross income goal

Basing your hourly rate on your gross income goal

Your annual gross income goal will help you establish your hourly rate, recognizing that only a certain percentage of your working hours are billable. One authority suggests you figure five billable hours a day for yourself and six for any employees. In his *Pricing Guide for Desktop Publishing,* writer and publisher Bob Brenner, profiled in Chapter Ten, proposes a 30-60-10 rule, which states that typical desktop publishers spend 30 percent of their time marketing, 60 percent performing the work, and 10 percent handling administrative details. The same guide would apply to many business writers. Since 60 percent of eight hours a day is four hours and forty-eight minutes, this correlates well with the previous estimate.

Let's work this out using weekly figures. Give yourself two weeks' vacation (you'll need it, though you may not wind up taking it!). Now you have

EXAMPLE
50 weeks x 25 billable hours per week
= 1,250 billable hours a year
$56,400 annual gross income required ÷ 1,250 billable hours a year
= $45.12 per hour

There's a temptation to use the salary you received when you were employed to arrive at your hourly rate. Resist it, or you'll start out thinking too low. If your salary before you opened your business was the amount you now feel you need to survive—$3,100 a month, or $37,200 a year—dividing that by 2,000 hours (40 hours a week x 50) gives you an hourly rate of $18.60.

Basing your hourly rate on the salaries paid to others

But suppose salaried people who do the kind of work your business provides actually earn about what you were earning on your last job—$18.60 an hour. A formula suggested by The National Writers Club in their book, *The Professional Writers Guide* (1990), instructs you to double the typical hourly wage to cover your direct and overhead costs as an entrepreneur. This gives you what the editors call a "gross hourly rate," which, they advise, you must increase by 25 percent "to cover overhead time." The final rate they describe as your "billing rate."

EXAMPLE

$18.60 per hour x 2 = $37.20 gross hourly rate

$37.20 gross hourly rate x 1.25 (a 25 percent increase)

= $46.50 per hour

—very close to the $45.12 arrived at by the previous formula!

Once you have an hourly rate you are confident of—say $50 an hour—the rest of the calculations become fairly simple. Will the proposal take ten hours to write? Then you need to charge $500. How much for a day of your time? Seven hours x $50 = $350—plus preparation time. Will you be paid $15 each for ten students enrolled in a seminar that takes you three hours to prepare and three hours to teach? No way! You'll earn only $150. But you could teach the same seminar profitably with twenty students bringing you $300.

As has been pointed out, you may not be able to bill $50 an hour for every service you provide, such as proofreading or transcribing. In that case, you will need to build in some other costs or increase the total hours to come up with the $50 an hour that you need to make. But what if padding your estimate prices you out of the market? That could happen. If you do a lot of jobs that involve less skilled work, you would be better off hiring someone at $10 or $15 an hour to do work that you can bill out at $20 or $25 an hour. Or you would be better off not doing the job. Finally, some jobs that require special skills, fast turn-around or dealing with difficult situations will justify charging more than your normal hourly rate. Don't hesitate to do so!

FINDING YOUR PROFIT ZONE

As you analyze your price structure and gather data on prices charged by others, you will discover that some types of work are not profitable for you. This may be obvious as soon as you hear what the going rates are. Or you may have to do several jobs and run time/profit analysis on them before a pattern begins to emerge.

Perhaps your quality standards make your price prohibitive, but when you drop your price to get such jobs, you put in long, unpaid hours. Be aware that certain work is better done by writers who are willing and organized to just "knock it out." Perhaps you are unfamiliar with the material you are writing and your client is not willing to compensate you for the time you must spend to complete an assignment. Perhaps you lack capabilities such as photography or desktop publishing, and must buy out part of a job, while competitors can do the whole job in-house. Whatever the reasons may be, search for your own profit zone—the jobs you do well at prices that allow you to make money. Then look for more of those jobs.

Remember, one of the rewards of being in business for yourself is the option of declining jobs you don't want to do.

THE PSYCHOLOGY OF SETTING A PRICE

As necessary as an hourly rate is to your estimating process, don't become fixed on it, or you will stay at or below that rate for the rest of your freelance career. If that happens, you will lose many opportunities for personal and professional growth. What we're about to discuss here is something you won't be able to master until you have some experience as an entrepreneur—the psychology of setting a price.

Joy Mieko White's firm, InfoTeam, in Lake Forest, CA, sets up partnering agreements with writers and desktop publishers to produce technical materials for industry and government. (White is profiled in Chapter Two.) Her experience in pricing psychology makes the point better than I could.

"I follow the marketing strategy established by Gerry Foster, a marketing consultant who works with service-based, rather than product-based businesses," says White. "It's difficult to sell something as intangible as writing and design, and that's what Gerry specializes in—intangibles. I ran into him in 1990 and quickly latched onto his ideas."

White was attending a conference put on by the City of Long Beach on how to do business with the city, and Foster gave a workshop on finding the real prospects in your prospect list. Foster conducts his business, Foster Marketing Resources, out of his home in Laguna Beach, CA.

"Through attending Gerry's workshops and seminars, I learned that I was approaching marketing like a used-car salesman," White says. "I was going after price. In a recession, I was trying to hawk our low prices because we didn't have a high overhead. A lot of clients got turned off on that. They thought the product must be cheap if the price was cheap.

"Through Gerry I learned how to remarket myself and to provide added value," White continues. "In fact, I finally understood what 'added value' is. I learned that prospects will buy your service—even if you have the highest price—if they feel that they will get something spectacular for their money. I learned to walk away from those prospects who only want the best price, and I learned to feel sorry for those who take them on."

White concludes: "We had a prospect who had haggled over price come back to us recently and say, 'You were right. Let's start over!'"

Set a high value on your services

Scrambling to cut corners and save pennies for your client is a self-defeating trap. Your service appears to be worth little, and your client—far from appreciating a bargain—may even be unhappy with the budget price you have agreed to, while you toil resentfully, doing less than your best because "that's all this cheapskate deserves."

You may not always get the price you want, but if you think of yourself as a valuable, high-quality supplier, you will be treated that way!

Bring a strategy to the pricing situation

To get an idea of what I mean, consider buying "How to Get Paid What You Are Worth," a videotape by Maria Piscopo, a California-based creative services consultant. It is one of four marketing videotapes Piscopo has produced for those who sell their own creative services (see Source Directory).

Since creative types find it difficult to talk about themselves and about money at the same time, Piscopo suggests techniques for "taking yourself out of the pricing picture." For example, instead of talking about "what you charge," she advises you to talk about "what it costs." She also offers techniques for creating a win—win pricing situation, "where you get what you want and the client gets what they want." If this intrigues you, buy and study Piscopo's tape. For now, I'll just summarize a few points.

- As your business grows and your prices rise, accept the fact that you may not be able to take old clients with you. You will need to find new ones.

- Think of your work as your property. As Piscopo puts it, "You own it and someone wants to use it." (This strategy does not apply to a "work for hire" situation.)

- When someone asks "What do you charge?" turn that around and ask what they need. Answers to several key questions give you the information you need to price strategically.

- Piscopo suggests a two-step bidding process. First you offer a verbal estimate to get a sense of the budget and other factors. "Writing a policy manual of that type," you tell the prospect, "would probably cost $3,000 to $4,000." If the prospect says, "Oh, we can't possibly pay that much!" you have not automatically lost the job, but can discuss what price range the client can afford and what you can do for that price. The verbal estimate is followed by a detailed written proposal complete with your sales materials. For most business writers, a two-step bidding process would be especially applicable to major jobs or new clients.

- "If the client wants to pay less," says Piscopo, "either you should get more or you should provide less." Be prepared to negotiate—and have your negotiating chips ready in advance. You could get more time to do the job, more sample copies, or a credit line. You could get the guarantee of a series of similar jobs. (You can expect to be more efficient as you become familiar with the work. You will also save time by not having to sell the subsequent projects. Both of these cost-saving factors can be passed on to the client, while you still make money.) If you can't get more, try providing less—perhaps the client will scale back the job, calling for less copy or fewer people to be interviewed.

TOWARD A BUSINESS PLAN

Success Worksheet Twenty-Eight

Know what your basic hourly rate must be and earn it five hours a day.

Your prices must be based on research, both outside and inside your business. While you may use various pricing strategies, setting and getting your basic hourly rate will be the key to your success as a home-based writer. Approximately 60 percent of your time should be billable.

- What research will you do to help you answer the question, "What shall I charge"?

  ____ National or regional rate studies available through books, periodicals, and organizations

_____ Local pricing information

_____ Other_____

- How will you charge for various services? What is your rationale for selecting certain methods of payment?

  _____ By the hour

  _____ By the full or half day

  _____ By the head

  _____ By the word

  _____ By use

  _____ By the project

  _____ Flat rate

  _____ Retainer fee

  _____ Other_____

- How will you avoid the trap of working for less than your normal rates—either in doing low-skill jobs or cut-rate jobs?

  _____

  _____

- Since the laws and customs surrounding intellectual property in your specialties may have an impact on you, how will you inform yourself and stay current on such topics as

  Work for hire _____

  _____

  One-time or multiple use of intellectual property _____

  _____

  Copyright laws_____

  _____

  What rights you retain_____

  _____

Issues surrounding electronic data _____

_____

Right to approve alterations in your work_____

_____

■ How much must your business gross each month?

Monthly cost of business operation $_____

Monthly family expenses   _____

Business surplus   _____

TOTAL $_____

■ To determine how much you must charge to earn the above, how will you establish your basic hourly rate?

_____ Five billable hours a day

_____ The "30-60-10" rule (30% marketing, 60% billable work, 10% administration)

_____ Double the typical hourly wage for your type of work plus 25% overhead

($_____ x 2 = $_____ x 1.25 = $_____)

_____ Other _____

■ What will you start with as your basic hourly rate? $_____

■ What systems will you use to gather information about time and costs on jobs?

_____

■ How will you compare this information with income from jobs?

_____

■ How will you analyze the results to help you price jobs accurately?

_____

■ How will you use this information to find your profit zone—those jobs that are most profitable for you?

_____

- How will you apply the psychology of setting a price?

_____Setting a high value on your services

_____Bringing a strategy to each pricing situation

_____Losing some clients and replacing them with others as your
      business grows

_____ Other _____

THE BIDDING AND NEGOTIATING PROCESS

Establishing your basic hourly rate takes you a long way toward successfully pricing your work. But it's far from the whole story. Here are some additional points on bidding and negotiating.

Taking specifications

Take accurate specifications when you are asked to bid. If possible, meet personally with the prospect. For example, does the client want a newsletter? If so, what is the budget? What is the audience? If readers are older, is type size a factor? What impression does the client want to make? How many pages are they thinking about? What page size? How much copy? How many photos? Any drawings or charts? How many colors? Is there an existing design, or must a new nameplate and format be developed? Is there a company logo or "corporate look" the newsletter must relate to? What materials will the newsletter be used with? How will it be mailed? Will it be folded?

Suppose you are not responsible for the whole project, but only for the writing. Writers, too, collect "specs," though they may not use that term.

A company or trade magazine editor asks you to write an article. What is the topic? How many words? When is the piece due? Who are the readers? What is their reading level? What slant or focus does the editor want? What is the budget and how much research will it cover? Can the editor provide you with background material? Interview suggestions? Any individuals who must be interviewed? Their names and numbers? Will photos be needed? Does the editor want photo ideas? Who will provide the photos? Will you need to write captions? If the material lends itself to sidebars, should you handle it that way? How should the article be delivered—hard copy, E-mail, disk, fax? If rewrites are needed, do you and the editor agree on time and costs? (One set of revisions is usual for many kinds of writing.)

Discussing the job in detail accomplishes several things. First of all, you will know that you are basing your price on what the prospect really wants. Your probing may also reveal client "hot buttons" that will help you sell the job, such as a very tight deadline, or a desire to win an award. Knowing these concerns will help you shape your proposal and your presentation. Even though you will not be using all the information called for to estimate every job, Form Two, the Estimating Form provided later in this chapter, is a good place to start. With such a form, no important information will be overlooked.

Deal with the decision maker

When you gather information about the job, make sure you are getting it from an authoritative source, preferably the final decision maker. If you sense confusion about specifications—perhaps from a very inexperienced buyer—offer to help the buyer put the specifications in writing. This will help assure that you and your competitors will be bidding on the same thing. But don't suggest that the buyer obtain competitive bids. Inexperienced buyers often accept an initial price without negotiations or comparisons—if they feel comfortable with the vendor. Experienced buyers will also appreciate your efforts to get accurate information about the job. That way they know they are comparing apples with apples when they evaluate the bids.

Determine time required for the work you do

Good estimating requires data—not only an accurate description of the job to be done, but a clear idea of the time required to do various jobs. As you develop this information, your estimating and your billing will go hand-in-hand. Keep track of your time spent on each part of each job for billing purposes. Then find a way to summarize this data so that you can analyze it and build your own rate structure.

If you are currently employed doing work similar to what you plan to do as a home-based writer, start keeping track now of how long various tasks take. Ask yourself how much you would be willing to pay an outside vendor to do these tasks. Compare the time you take to do various jobs with the information you have collected on typical job prices. As an entrepreneur, you will view efficiency with more urgency than you do as an employee, and you may find that you need to become more efficient at certain tasks. If you are asked to bid on work you have never done before, try to equate it with jobs you have done previously and consult colleagues for advice.

Direct costs

In addition to the time the job will require, you need to know what other costs you will incur to do the job. Such costs include consumable supplies needed for the job and regular employees or contractors you will have to pay to work on the job. Direct costs also include "buy-outs," such as equipment you will have to lease or rent, consultants or other professionals you will have to hire, service bureau or Website provider costs, photo processing, off-site duplicating, and printing. When you prepare your estimate, put a markup on all buy-outs. This could range from 15 percent up to whatever the traffic will bear. It's one of the areas where you can "sharpen your pencil" when it comes to negotiating the price, but be aware that if you put no markup on a buy-out, you are losing money because it costs you something to handle every purchase.

Reimbursable expenses

Normally, expenses incurred in doing a job, such as phone and fax costs, postage, mileage, meals (especially if related to an interview), and parking are reimbursable. You keep track of these expenses (with documentation) and include them as separate items in your final bill. However, reimbursable expenses may figure in the estimating process if your prospect asks what you think these costs will total. In another possible scenario, your prospect may not be willing to cover these costs, in which case you will need to make sure that they are built into your price.

Hidden costs

Many business writers consider "it took me longer than I thought it would" to be a hidden cost. In a way, it is—but you could also call it "poor estimating." Watch out for unanticipated time spent in client meetings. Watch travel time. What should take one hour will take two in heavy traffic. Getting material for a job in small batches instead of all at once wastes time. So do interruptions. You may encounter unexpected costs in doing research. Checking printing jobs on the press may be unexpectedly time-consuming. If you're late in delivering a job, sending a messenger across town will be an unanticipated cost. Build a contingency fee into your estimate, if you can. Remember that if you do not have your seller's permit on file with your vendors, you pay sales tax on your buy-outs. Long-term storage may also represent a hidden cost on certain jobs.

Many hidden costs fall under Murphy's Law: If anything can go wrong, it will. Over time, you do get better at anticipating problems and faster at solving them. But if an unavoidable disaster skyrockets costs on a job, discuss it with your client. You shouldn't have to "eat" it all.

In my experience, the biggest hidden cost is probably the difficult client. After you've completed your research and started writing the brochure, this client calls to say she needs a new feature of her business covered and tells you to call her partner for details—but, of course, she still needs the copy by Friday and is already paying you "more than your competitor would have charged" so she can't afford to pay you more. Difficult clients usually don't know what they want, but they do know what they don't want. For example, you may have planned to show one set of proofs on an employee handbook, but the client makes repeated changes, demanding three more sets of proofs—which you must take to his office personally, since he wants to discuss them. Loaded for bear when you bring up extra costs, he does not want to pay you for any of this, since you "couldn't get it right."

You can fight to get paid for these extras and risk losing the client, but another approach is to build an "x-plus factor" into subsequent prices—by adding time to each step or by marking up the total. If the client objects to your estimate, the simple fact is, you probably can't afford to serve this client.

Special job requirements

In order to do the job, you may need to purchase a special piece of equipment or software, a specific publication, or some other resource. How you should cover such costs is debatable. If you are likely to use the item for future clients, you probably cannot charge it to the job. Such a purchase is part of your cost of doing business. However, if the item is specific to the client (a detailed electronic database search, for example), you should discuss the matter with the client. Possible arrangements include the client lending you the needed item or the client reimbursing you for the needed item—either paying the full cost at one time or paying for it through markups on several jobs. In the latter case, the client might own the item but let you house it in order to do future jobs for them, or you might own the item.

Develop one or more estimating forms

Develop a form to help you produce estimates quickly and accurately. If you do several kinds of work that are significantly different, you may need more than one form. (See sample estimating form on pages 246–47). If you don't want to develop an actual form with spaces to fill in data and numbers, at least develop a check-list for yourself to make sure you are covering everything. Here's what your worksheet or form should include.

- Labor

  List the steps involved in producing and delivering the job. Estimate the time required for each step and multiply by your hourly rate (or the rate you charge for that task).

- Materials

  List the materials you think will be required. Estimate the costs of materials, including your markup.

- Buy-outs

  Estimate any outside labor costs from subcontractors who work with you—desktop publishers, artists, photographers, or others—and include your markup. You will probably have to contact them to get this information and must allow time for that step in your estimating process. Estimate the cost of other buy-outs, including your markup (for example—research services, special clip art, Website services, printing). Again, it may take extra time to get these prices.

- Shipping or delivery costs, if applicable.

- Out-of-pocket costs

  (Needed only if the client has asked for an estimate.) List the out-of-pocket expenses you think will be required, such as phone, postage, mileage, and parking.

- Other costs

  Storage comes to mind as a billable charge that occasionally comes up. Watch for others that may be unique to the job.

The truth is, you probably will not do such detailed estimating on most jobs after you are established in business. You will develop a "feel" for the work, and you will be doing repeat jobs for which you have a financial track record. But never let yourself get too far from ground zero, where you predict what a job will cost and then compare what you made on the job with what it actually did cost, including any expenses entailed in collecting the money. Losing sight of this central business reality has meant the difference between success and failure for many, many entrepreneurs.

Your presentation

Presenting your price to a client could be as informal as a phone call in which you say, "Hello. Harry? That flyer we discussed will run about $200. Is that OK?" Or it might be a package containing your detailed written estimate along with your resumé, client list, samples of your work, and even testimonials from clients—presented by you, and possibly your associates, at a meeting with the client's entire project group. For each presentation, you should analyze what it will take to get the assignment. Don't invest more than necessary. Overkill could be counterproductive. But don't shortchange yourself or appear too casual. Clients need to know that you take their work seriously, that you are bidding on correct specifications, that this is a fair price, that you are ready to start work and can deliver on time, and that you want to do the job.

Negotiating

You should have your negotiating chips ready when you present a price. One key chip is the lowest price you are willing to accept. When I was selling printing, a firm I represented gave its salespeople a range of prices to present to clients—from the desired price to the lowest acceptable price. And our commission rate was structured to keep us from immediately offering the lowest price, since we made a much higher commission on the profit portion than on the basic costs of the job.

When you're willing to cut your price to get a job, conveying this willingness can be a delicate matter—because you don't want to hear an exasperated prospect demanding, "Why didn't you give me that price to start with? Are you trying to cheat me?"

One technique is to use the salesperson's tried and true phrase for handling objections—"Other than that . . ." (See Chapter Eight.) Suppose your prospect says, "I like your approach to this Website, but we can't afford $2,000."

"Other than that," you reply, "if price were not an issue, would you want me to do the job?" "I think so," says the prospect (a major victory for you!) "but price *is* an issue." "What were you thinking of spending on the Website?" you ask innocently. "We're budgeted for $1,500 maximum," the prospect replies.

Now you have a new negotiating position. You can cut your price, risking a loss of credibility if the cut is large—in this case 25 percent. Or you can offer a smaller cut and see if the prospect will split the difference. If you do drop your price significantly, justify it. For example, "I recently had a big job fall through, so I have some extra time." Or, "I'm trying to get more clients in your industry." Avoid admitting that you are simply lowballing the prospect to get his business. Such an admission puts a client on guard against a big jump in your prices next time around.

Another approach is to tell the prospect what you can do for $1,500 and try to get the project redefined. Or you might offer to include some extra services in order to get your price. Or perhaps you could do the job for less if the client gave you more time, using the work to fill in slow spots. There are many negotiating positions that keep both you and the prospect in a win-win position.

But what if your bid will be examined and the decision made when you are not present? Here's a technique that may keep the door open. Call the prospect to make

ESTIMATING FORM

Estimate #_____ **Estimate due on**_____

Client_____ Phone_____

Job name_____ Date_____

Date Project is due_____ Production time available_____

Rush Job? Yes_____ No_____ Will client pay rush charges? Yes_____ No_____

Client budget (if known) $_____

PROJECT DESCRIPTION

Design this space to fit your needs. Writers might want blanks for sections, length, number of interviews, research requirements, photos, tables, reader level. If you are also handling the desktop publishing, you might want blanks for number of pages, dimensions, amount of copy, photos, illustrations,
charts, scanning and imaging requirements, paper type and color, ink colors, bindery instructions.

In designing a Website, things you will need to know include the overall purpose, approximate
number of pages, text type and length, graphics needed, forms, links, E-mail capabilities, hit-counting
requirements, and multimedia features.

Special instructions _____

Is this a repeat job? Yes_____ No_____ Are related jobs available? Yes_____ No_____

LABOR (including preliminary proposals, client meetings, travel)

Task_____

No. of hours_____ @Hourly rate $_____ $_____

Task_____

No. of hours_____ @Hourly rate $_____ $_____

Task_____

No. of hours_____ @Hourly rate $_____ $_____

MATERIALS

Item_____

Quantity_____ Price each $_____ $_____

Item_____

Quantity_____ Price each $_____ $_____

Item_____

Quantity_____ Price each $_____ $_____

BUY OUTS (labor/materials)

Task_____

    Vendor_____

    No. of hours_____   @Hourly rate $_____

    Estimated cost $_____ x _____ % markup $_____

Item_____

    Vendor_____

    Quantity_____   @Cost each $_____

    Estimated cost $_____ x _____ % markup $_____

Shipping/delivery (describe)_____

    Method_____

    Estimated cost $_____ x _____ % markup $_____

OUT-OF-POCKET COSTS (omit if billable to client later)

Item_____

    Quantity_____   Cost each $_____ $_____

Item_____

    Quantity_____   Cost each $_____ $_____

                                    SUBTOTAL $_____

Subtotal $_____x ____ % overhead/profit $_____

                Rush charge (if applicable) $_____

                TOTAL PROJECT COST $_____

OPTIONS FOR NEGOTIATION

    Lowest acceptable price as described $_____

Possible changes to job descriptions or delivery schedule

_____ Est. saving $_____

_____ Est. saving $_____

sure he has received your estimate. Offer to answer any questions, and tell him, "I feel $2,000 is a fair price for this job, but I'm willing to discuss it. I think (mention a key benefit of your services) would be very helpful to you on this job, so if price is a problem, call me before you make a decision. Will you do that?" If the client says, "No, that's against company policy," you can reduce your price now, on the phone, or take your chances in the bidding process.

In the last analysis, you don't want to do jobs you can't make money on. So if the prospect will not pay your bottom price, let the job go and look for other business.

GETTING PAID

Terms of payment and credit approval

It's important to remember that you, the seller, are entitled to set the terms of payment—though you should make sure your client agrees to your terms—and you are also entitled to check a client's credit record before extending credit. This is normal business procedure. You state your terms on your invoice. If you have any doubt about getting paid, you should state them in your estimate or proposal as well and ask for credit references prior to starting the job.

You may think that appearing to doubt your client's creditworthiness will seem rude and be resented, but a vendor's cautiousness about credit and payment is not something experienced business people take personally. I remember doing a small rush desktop publishing job for an international corporation. The printer I selected because of his good prices and fast turnaround demanded payment in advance from all new clients. Period. It was a bother for me to arrange to have the check cut in advance and run to corporate headquarters to pick it up and take it to the printer, so I built those extra steps into my bill. But nobody resented the printer's policy.

Credit checks

By "credit" I mean the period of time you have to wait for your money after you have done the work. While you wait, you are extending credit.

When dealing with large corporations, government offices, and large nonprofit agencies over the years, I have not checked the client's credit or asked for partial payment in advance unless the job was of long duration. And I have never been stiffed by such clients. If you have any doubts, large credit services, such as Dun and Bradstreet, can check your client's credit quickly for a fee. For a small businessperson dealing with other small businesses or organizations, a more typical way of checking credit would be to ask for three credit references—firms that have recently extended credit to your client. You then send a standard credit reference form (available from stationers) to the firms whose names your client has supplied. Such a form asks how much credit the firm has extended to your client, how recently, and how promptly your client paid. Often you will have to call to get this information after mailing or faxing the form, but in most cases you will get it. Small businesses are used to helping each other in this way.

Terms of payment options

The standard for payment in most business and nonprofit settings is thirty days from date of invoice. Here are some other options you may prefer, depending on the situation

- Payment on delivery.

- Payment due on receipt of invoice.

- Payment due in seven days or fourteen days from date of invoice.

- Discount of 2 percent or so for payment in ten or fifteen days.

- Charge of _____ percent added for payment after thirty days. This might vary with the industry. Find out what is customary, bearing in mind that a slow-paying client may or may not pay your late-payment fee, and you may make enemies if you try to collect it.

- Payment due one-half in advance and one-half on delivery—or one-third in advance, one-third halfway through, and one-third on delivery (or in thirty days). A wide variety of arrangements is possible. The point is to get something up front to protect yourself with an unfamiliar client, or when the job is likely to take several months to complete. When you have confidence in the client, you will probably drop the advance payment request unless you need it to even out your cash flow over an extended period. Insisting on payment in advance or at least prior to delivery is wise, however, when dealing with a financially questionable client, no matter how often you have served them.

In general, finding out what is customary is a good idea when establishing your payment terms. You do not have to follow the local or industry customs, though. Your terms are an individual matter, and if you do good work at good prices, your clients will probably accept them. Clients who refuse to make advance payments or require ninety days to pay may just have to find another vendor.

Billing policies and methods

Recording your time, and the ethics of hourly billing. As in all other dealings with your clients, you must be ethical in billing. To do this, you and your staff or associates must keep good records on a daily basis. There are many ways to keep such records—from computer programs that help you charge time to various clients at various rates, to mechanical timekeeping devices sometimes used in ad agencies, to simple paper-based timekeepers, such as the popular Daytimer system. Be sure that whatever system you use will allow you to extract the information for periodic use in analyzing your pricing strategies and your productivity.

Additional job expenses. When, as a college publications director, I was a buyer of graphic services, I really hated being nickel-and-dimed. I would agree with a vendor to do a job. The job would be completed, with some changes in the process, but no discussion about them. Then I would get a bill for considerably more than the original estimate. When I called to complain, I would hear an annoying litany of what seemed to me minuscule details for which I was being gouged. This threw budgets out of balance and made me look bad with the college departments and offices that I served.

When I became a printing salesperson, I saw the matter in a different light. I learned that some vendors watch in silent glee while inexperienced buyers call for costly changes, and I realized that some of my own "minuscule" changes had involved major adjustments. My boss, the owner of the printing firm, was not about to "eat" such charges—and since I knew my clients would *and should* be charged for them, I resolved that whenever changes were made, I would explain to my clients what was involved and approximately what it would cost.

As a home-based writer and desktop publisher, I follow the same policy, though I probably err toward staying with the estimate and keeping my clients happy—leaving money on the table in the process. But when a client calls for a significant change in either a writing or a desktop publishing job, I do not hesitate to charge for it—making it a point to let the client know at the time the change is made that what he or she has asked for will cost extra.

It's good policy to keep a written record of all job changes as you go along since a simple hourly record of the time you and your staff or subcontractors spent on the job may not highlight such changes. Suppose you promised one set of revisions, but in fact you did three; suppose you had estimated five interviews would be required, but in fact you had to do seven; suppose you did not expect to have to spend an extra two hours designing an illustrated pie chart. In order to charge your client fairly, you will need this data, and, of course, you may also need it to justify charges if your clients question them. If you learned from my example, however, your clients won't question added charges because they will have been forewarned!

When a job comes in under budget. What if a job costs less to do than you originally estimated? Following a policy of charging for every extra expense would, it seems to me, obligate you to pass the savings along to your clients when the job turns out to be less costly to produce. But again, it's up to you. My impression is that few of us do pass such savings along, unless they are significant and the client is likely to ask about them. ("You bid on a forty-eight-page instruction manual and then we cut it back to twelve pages. How come you didn't charge me any less?")

The final invoice. Establish a special format for your invoices, even if it's just the word "invoice" added to your letterhead. It's preferable, especially when dealing with large corporations, to give each invoice a number. I don't do this, although every year I promise myself I will. When I did a series of newsletters for Kaiser Permanente, their accounts payable people called and told me they required a number, so I started a series of "K" invoices just for them.

Your invoice must show the name of the client, the client's purchase order number if applicable (very important when dealing with large organizations), a brief description of the job, and the amount due. You might also include the date the job was delivered. Any variations from the original estimate should be detailed. If you do not state your terms, most clients will assume your terms are "net thirty"—meaning the full amount is due in thirty days.

Bill promptly. No matter how busy you are, make it a rule to bill as soon as you deliver the job—or according to whatever payment schedule has been agreed upon. This is probably the most vital part of your office paperwork routine because, obviously, if you don't bill, you won't get paid. But it's more subtle than that. If you don't bill promptly, your client will assume you don't care about being paid promptly, and your bill may go on the bottom of the pile. Furthermore, if you don't bill promptly, both you and your client will forget about details of the job, which may lead to your receiving less than you deserve or to disagreements with your client about what you do deserve.

Getting paid on time

I am often surprised to discover that some seemingly aggressive writers are reluctant to go after their money when they are not paid on time. As a commissioned printing salesperson, I was expected to collect late payments in order to get paid myself—which was a very strong motivation. As a result, I never hesitate to call about my freelance invoices. No invoice should be allowed to go unpaid for more than thirty days without action on your part.

Is your invoice in order? It may help you to know that checking on payment is a standard business procedure and if you call to "make sure everything is in order," no one takes offense and the vast majority of your payment problems can be solved. Calling when the invoice has been out about three weeks is a reasonable procedure. Your bill may have gone astray. Some documentation may be missing. Your client may have been holding your invoice because she had a question. Or she may have simply forgotten to submit your invoice for payment. From a psychological perspective, politely showing that you are concerned about payment has the effect of moving your invoice toward the top of the pile.

Accounts payable departments. In large organizations your client probably has nothing to do with payment. You will need to make yourself known to the Accounts Payable Department, which often organizes vendors alphabetically. When I check on payment from large hospitals and corporations, I find myself asking to speak to "the person who handles the P's." Even in small companies, it's usually not your client, but the bookkeeper, who writes the checks. Treat these bill-paying folks with friendliness and respect. Cooperate with them and try to help them do their jobs. Asking for an immediate check is not helpful since it interrupts their routines. If you need extremely fast payment, call in advance to see if a "handmade" check can be arranged.

When payment is late. In the small percentage of cases where the client's intention is to put you off, polite persistence, not rudeness, is the best approach. Once you have determined that everything about your invoice is in order, send regular reminders. When one institution of higher education where I worked hit hard times, bills started going 90 and 120 days and even longer—and vendors were becoming frantic. What I learned from our besieged business office was that the abusive vendors were the very last to get paid.

If possible, try to work out a payment plan with a client who is experiencing financial difficulties. Consider offering to accept in-kind payment if that would be an option. Know the laws regarding collection procedures in your area and be prepared to take further action if the amount justifies it and you have some chance of collecting. Just sending a letter on your attorney's letterhead may result in a check.

BARTERING

The age-old custom of bartering is becoming a viable and popular way for home-based entrepreneurs both to sell and to get paid. These days, however, it's not done vendor-to-vendor, but through barter firms which compile information on goods and services which are sought and/or available, exchanging them over a specific geographic area through a system of credits. For example, you might write a series of promotional articles worth X dollars for a manufacturer in another city and receive X dollars worth of orthodontic care for your kid in your hometown.

With barter, many costs can be avoided, including marketing, billing, collection, and even some taxes—but you can charge your normal price for a writing job.

The bartering vendor whose goods or services you receive in exchange does the same, so everybody wins, including the barter firm. The Internet will quickly put you in touch with many barter exchanges. Check the Web search engines—and check references on the firm you choose before making a commitment.

TOWARD A BUSINESS PLAN

Success Worksheet Twenty-Nine

Estimate accurately, bill promptly, and make sure all your costs are covered.

Estimating and billing go hand-in-hand. Accurate information helps you bid competitively and allows you to get all that is coming to you on every job. Always bill promptly, and follow up until payment is received.

- Do you have good methods for obtaining all the information needed to produce accurate, competitive estimates?

  _____ A specifications form or worksheet

  _____ Assurance that you are dealing with the decision maker

  _____ Analysis of direct costs, including buy-outs

  _____ Analysis of special job requirements

  _____ Analysis of reimbursable expenses

  _____ Other _____

- What points will need to be covered in your customized Estimating Form to describe the kinds of jobs you do?

  _____

  _____

- What negotiating strategies will you have in mind when you present a price to help you win the job?

  _____

  _____

■ How will you determine the creditworthiness of your clients?

_____

_____

_____

■ What terms of payment do you plan to use?

____ Payment due on delivery

____ Payment due on receipt of invoice

____ Net seven days, fifteen days, thirty days

____ Discount for prompt payment

____ Percentage charged for late payment

____ Arrangements for partial payments in advance or during the job

____ Other _____

■ How will you record your time and that of employees or subcontractors for billing purposes? How will you keep track of other job costs?

_____

_____

■ How will you keep track of billable changes or additions to jobs?

_____

_____

■ What systems will you use to assure prompt billing and regular follow-up until each invoice is paid?

_____

_____

Judith Broadhurst
Writer, Ben Lomond, California

Succeeding and Moving on . . .

From her cabin beside a river in northern California's Santa Cruz Mountains, Judith Broadhurst looks back on "about three phases" that define her career as a magazine and book author, newsletter publisher, and teacher. "Now," she says, "I'm going into a fourth phase." As this book stresses, home-based writers can earn a satisfying living writing for local and little-known clients without matching Broadhurst's national accomplishments—but they can also learn from her analysis of the phases in an independent writer's career. As she says: "Most people go through similar phases."

A onetime airline flight attendant who then spent seven years as a jazz and blues concert promoter and columnist before turning to fulltime writing, Broadhurst is twice divorced, has recovered twice from cancer, holds a bachelor's degree plus grad work in psychology, and has lived in more cities than she "cares to remember," including Salt Lake City, Miami, Chicago, Atlanta, Houston, and nearly four years in New York (proving to herself that she "could make it there"). Now, she swears, she's settled for good among her beloved redwoods. Born and raised in Ohio, she has written about online networks, the effects of technology, small business management, writing, the arts, and travel for such magazines as *NetGuide, Glamour, Self, Working Woman, Small Business Computing, Home Office Computing, Writer's Digest, The Writer*, and *The Columbia Journalism Review*. She's the author of *The Woman's Guide to Online Services* (McGraw-Hill, 1995) and chapters in *The Portable Writers Conference* (QuillDriver, 1996) and *The Writer's Handbook* (The Writer, 1992).

In 1992, Broadhurst founded *Freelance Success*, a weekly market-oriented newsletter for freelance writers available in both in E-mail and print versions (see Bibliography). She sold the publication in 1997. A frequent speaker on writing and electronic publishing, she teaches writing classes online and for the University of California Santa Cruz. Her memberships include the American Society of Journalists and Authors and the Authors Guild. Her honors include awards from Women in Communications and the International Association of Business Communicators. She's listed in *International Authors and Writers* and *Who's Who Among American Women*. And she recently popped up in *E-Mail Addresses of the Rich and Famous*—a listing Broadhurst describes as "clearly inaccurate"—yet adding, "I hope it's a good omen."

Which brings us to the phases of a writer's career. "Most of us start out writing for local or regional markets," Broadhurst observes. "That's where we get practice. It's a ladder, and you have to climb up. I think newspaper reporting experience is invaluable for at least a couple of years. Too many people 'just want to write,' and it's flat irresponsible to do that unless you learn the basics of journalistic reporting, principles, and ethics."

In Broadhurst's case, she worked in public relations, marketing, and fund raising for arts, health, and human service agencies, then spent four years writing for regional publications like the *San Jose Mercury News* and *Pacific Magazine*. Part-time and full-time jobs and concert promotion punctuated these years. "I didn't make it fulltime until my second time around freelancing," she recalls.

"My biggest regret," Broadhurst says, "is that I stayed in the local and regional market far longer than I should have because, I guess, I was intimidated. I was afraid I wouldn't succeed at the next level. Yet it came to me that the amount of work I put into some of those stories, for which I got paid a maximum of $650 and sometimes as little as $50 or $150—was going to be about the same at the national level for a story I would get paid ten times that amount for. And it turned out to be absolutely true.

"I think you do have to pay your dues at the local-regional level," the California writer continues, "and then you really ought to start thinking about going on." For a business writer, this move might be to larger corporate or organizational clients—or into a more lucrative writing specialty. Broadhurst's goal was to "write for the national newsstand magazines."

As it happened, a short-term reporting project for a non-profit organization paid for her move to New York about the time she felt she had to go there to prove herself. "It was a real mind-shift," she says. "Everybody there writes for national magazines. They take it for granted. In fact, I'd hate to be a beginning writer trying to start out in New York because there are so few places to write that aren't of national stature."

Broadhurst had already written more than 300 articles on topics like travel, arts, and entertainment—some of which she resold to other markets—but since many were written for newspapers, she often had to produce two or three articles a week. Now, at national rates of one-to-three-dollars a word, she could spend more time on every piece. But this, she discovered, was not always a blessing.

"With some national magazines, you get edited by a committee,"

Broadhurst explains, "and different editors have different ideas of what the article should be about. "What you really have to look at as a writer," she stresses, "is not how much you're getting per word, but how much time you're spending on a story, because time is all you've got. You need to know your hourly rate—how much you're earning per hour or per day. Because you don't work every single hour at that rate and you have expenses. I call New York a lot and my phone bills can run $400 a month." Another problem accompanied her New York success: editors began calling Broadhurst with ideas. "You lose the initiative of what you're writing about," she says.

After producing "women's things and service pieces" for many national markets, Broadhurst began the third phase of her career, starting her newsletter, *Freelance Success*, in 1992, and then writing a book. Since 1990, she had been an avid online communicator, in touch with other professional writers through forums, and she had started writing on computer topics when she was approached by McGraw-Hill to write a book about online services for women.

"I think we get this idea that you're not a real writer until you've done a book," Broadhurst observes. But, having published a nonfiction guidebook, she's in no hurry to write another. "It takes over your life," she says, "so you'd better make enough on the advance to see you through the time it takes you to do it. People said to me, 'Well, you should do that because of the exposure,' but I've never been interested in exposure."

Enter the fourth phase.

"I should be grateful and I really am," Broadhurst reflects. "I've met the goals I had, but now I want to find out if I can do what I call 'real writing.' I'm sick to death of service pieces. It will still be nonfiction and I'll still write magazine articles and I'll still write those lists of lists about the Internet when somebody offers me at least $1,500, but now I'm in the process of making a transition to articles, and possibly books, about things that are more substantive." For one such project, Broadhurst reached back to her experience of being highjacked when she was a flight attendant.

"I'm tired of doing formula telephone interviews—three experts in three different cities. I want to do the kind of writing you do when you hear the pauses and see the look in their eyes and see where they live and work. Call it a midlife crisis, but I've decided that whatever I do for the next decade must matter—to me and to the reader and to someone who can get it from me to the reader."

CHAPTER TEN

TIPS FOR MANAGING YOUR BUSINESS (AND YOURSELF) AND WRITING YOUR BUSINESS PLAN

WHAT ELSE IS INVOLVED IN RUNNING YOUR BUSINESS?

The nine chapters you have just completed cover what you need to know to *open* your home-based writing business—and much of what you need to know to *operate* it. You've analyzed marketing and selling, pricing and bidding, billing and collecting, and finding the jobs most profitable for you. In my own experience and that of many people I have talked with in researching this book, these are the operational activities that will most concern you during your first months in business. The topics we will touch on in this chapter will seem less urgent initially, but they are no less important.

Several legal issues may concern you on a continual basis. You may want to protect yourself from liability with business insurance. If you hire help, you will encounter management issues as well as numerous state and federal requirements. Taxes will always be a major concern.

To keep your business solvent, you must manage your cash flow, do regular income projections, and deal with other financial issues. The organization of your business, your procedures and policies, and on-going systems analysis can significantly impact your profitability.

Another concern will be the set-up and maintenance of your records. You will need to establish methods for purchasing, controlling inventory, and maintaining your equipment and facilities. Your computer system will require administration.

The security of your entire operation, especially your computer system, is important, too.

Many personal issues also affect your business performance—issues such as goal setting; time management; your management style; staying current with knowledge and skills; issues of stress, attitude, and motivation; retirement planning and investing; and the ongoing impact of your business on your family.

My purpose here is to share a few tips that may get you thinking about these important topics.

LEGAL ISSUES

On-going legal issues. Setting up your business involves certain legal issues, discussed in Chapter Four, but your ongoing business operations involve others, among them issues of liability, contracts, collection problems, and rights to intellectual property. Regulations concerning employees represent another important legal area, dealt with later in this chapter.

Many successful home-based writers and desktop publishers give little thought to legal matters, but don't you take that chance. Consider these issues and, at minimum, know an attorney you can turn to for occasional business-related advice.

Will your home owner's policy cover it?

If a business visitor is injured on your property, you are liable, and your home owner's insurance is not likely to cover it unless you have broadened the policy to do so—or obtained separate coverage. If your computer or copier is stolen or destroyed in a fire, the situation is the same. Home owner's policies are not likely to cover business equipment and they certainly will not cover a regular employee injured on the job. I believe most home-based entrepreneurs realize this potential risk, and many of them make sure their home owner's coverage is extended or additional coverage is obtained, including whatever employee disability coverage is required by your state.

Covering general liability

But what if you damage something in a client's office? What if a subject is injured during a photo shoot you are supervising? What if a client sustains a loss because of an inaccuracy in work you have written or produced? General liability insurance will protect you in such situations, and it's something you should consider.

I must admit that sometimes the whole idea seems far-fetched to me. *Moi?*

How could I ever be found liable for some business injury? Then I remember the harrowing experience of a close writer friend. My friend had interviewed a patient and written an article for a hospital publication. The patient had read the article, and it was my friend's understanding that the patient had approved it, but a release was never signed. My friend had kept her client informed, so the hospital knew there was no release. After the material was published, the patient sued both the hospital and my friend, claiming that the article was damaging. My friend was fortunate that the hospital backed her up and covered her court costs.

While the best insurance against such an experience is to scrupulously cover all bases, liability insurance is also a good idea.

Contracts

Most of the writers and desktop publishers I interviewed for this book said they did not deal much with contracts. Those setting up agreements involving the work of others, like technical writers, were the exception—along with ghostwriters and others who do major, long-term projects. Your verbal or written estimate or proposal to do a job is also a form of contract, however. And, of course, a written agreement is safer for both parties. At minimum, this "contract" should include

- A description of the job

- The production schedule

- Delivery instructions

- The amount and terms of payment

Advertising and public relations agencies usually ask clients to return a signed copy of such a proposal before beginning the work—and so can you. If major changes occur during the job, put them in writing and send a copy to the client.

Collections

Collections were discussed in the last chapter. The best way to avoid collection problems is to stay on top of all your outstanding invoices and stay away from clients with questionable credit. Very often, when a colleague has told me how he or she got stiffed, I hear such comments as, "I had my doubts about them from the beginning." Or, "I should have gotten some money up front, but it was a big rush job." Know the small-claims court procedures in your community, and discuss serious collection problems with your attorney.

Copyright

United States copyright law unequivocally recognizes the creator of a work as its owner unless the work was done "for hire" or you otherwise signed away specific rights. Your work, therefore, is copyrighted whether or not you register it with the Copyright Office, a division of the United States Library of Congress (see Source Directory). The Library of Congress does not require you to register each work individually. You can, in fact, register several works in one large group. Although there are some requirements you must follow when submitting groups of work, there is no limit on the number of works that can be included in a group.

Laws governing the use of intellectual property are complex, but read up on this subject regularly if it relates to your work. Since most of the assignments discussed in this book would be considered work for hire, you are selling all rights. Bear in mind, however, that you can establish a different agreement with a client, perhaps arranging to make a noncompetitive use of the material. If you want to do this, it's wise to do it in advance.

Copyright laws could also affect you if you engage in copyright infringement, including illegal copying of software. In October 1992, federal law made it a felony for anyone to steal ten copies of a program or more than $2,500 worth of software—with a maximum penalty of five years in prison and $250,000 in fines. Unauthorized use of copyrighted graphic or written material could also land you—and your client—in trouble. Good copyright-free clip art and stock photos are widely available. If that won't do, it's often surprisingly easy—and inexpensive or free—to get permission to use copyrighted material. Before approaching the copyright holder, think of some way to benefit them, such as giving a generous credit. Major publications and publishers have staffers responsible for handling such requests, but it may take time to track down other sources.

ISSUES CONCERNING EMPLOYEES

Paying federal taxes

In the aftermath of President Clinton's first-term withdrawal of several proposed appointments because the appointees had not paid federal taxes on domestic employees, millions of Americans took a second look at their casual employment practices. IRS rules say that if you pay an "employee" more than $50 in any calendar quarter, you are supposed to obtain an employer identification number (apply using Form SS-4) and fill out a W–2 form. If you pay an individual more than $1,000 a quarter, you will generally have to pay Social Security and Medicare taxes, and state rules may apply as well. How closely you adhere to these regulations is your decision.

Independent contractor vs. employee

The federal government—including the IRS, the Department of Labor, and the Immigration and Naturalization Service—and most states have specific, but differing, definitions for "independent contractors" and "employees." One important point on which they do agree is that the employee has a continuing relationship with the employer, and an independent contractor does not.

Among other goals, federal and state agencies want to prevent employers from defining employees as independent contractors so they can avoid paying withholding taxes and providing required benefits—thus depriving state and federal governments of revenues and employees of their rights. If you hire independent contractors or work as an independent contractor yourself, know the federal rules as well as those in your state.

The IRS uses 20 specific rules to distinguish an employee from an independent contractor, including being supervised vs. working independently, provision of a workplace and setting of hours for employees but not for independent contractors, payment for hours or days worked vs. payment by the job, tools furnished vs. providing own tools, and ability to be fired or to quit (employees can do both while independent contractors can't be fired as long as they fulfill the contract and can't quit because they are legally obligated to do the contracted job).

A Congressional proposal would pare these rules down to three general conditions. Under this proposal, a written contract must exist, laying out the work agreement. The contractor must meet one of five requirements—(1) significant investment in assets or training; (2) significant unreimbursed expenses; (3) agreement to complete a project, liability for potential damages, and possibility of termination without cause; (4) payment on a commission basis; or (5) purchase of products for resale. Finally, an independent contractor must have a principal place of business or must pay rent to the company with whom he or she is contracting.

Technical writers and designers frequently fall into a gray area, carrying out long-term, full-time assignments for a single client. If you handle such assignments, consider the impact of employee versus independent contractor status on your income, business, and taxes, and make sure you are protected.

The IRS's free publication, *Circular E-Employer's Tax Guide*, explains the definition of an employee. The IRS will evaluate your individual situation if you file Form #SS-8.

Full-time employees

Adding a full-time employee is a very serious step for a home-based entrepreneur. It will greatly increase your paperwork, and, of course, you will need to sustain a larger volume of business. Signing regular salary checks without jobs to cover them can be a terrifying drain. Nevertheless, the right employee could be well worth it if he or she provides a vital skill you lack or frees you to do more profitable tasks.

Federal and state regulations governing employees vary according to size and type of business, but in general employers are responsible for federal and state withholding taxes, including Social Security; state disability insurance and unemployment taxes; workers' compensation insurance; health and other benefits; and regulations covering minimum wages, maximum hours to be worked, health and safety, and fair employment practices. Whew! Check with the IRS and state agencies or your local Small Business Administration (SBA) office to find out which requirements apply to your situation. And be aware that your homeowner's insurance will not cover injury to an employee; you must have employee disability insurance.

Having several employees can qualify you for health insurance plans not available to individuals. A group health insurance plan could benefit you and your family as well as your employees, although "employer" policies can be written for companies with just one employee–yourself. I currently have such a policy, written by Humana. Check with your insurer or local SBA office for more information.

Part-time workers

Hiring part-time help is a typical solution to a home-based writer or desktop publisher's labor problems. You have less financial drain and can hire various workers for the skills you need. But unless you and your employee are willing to risk becoming part of the underground cash economy, you cannot escape the basic employer responsibilities of withholding taxes and complying with minimum employment regulations.

Temporary workers

If you have an occasional need for clerical, desktop publishing, or other help, a temporary agency may provide the answer. The cost will be considerably more than you would pay to the worker directly, but workers are prescreened, they are there when you need them, and you have no employer responsibilities except supervision.

Occasional labor

The occasional worker fills in for a few hours on an irregular basis. For example, I've used crews of my daughter's friends to stuff envelopes and stick on labels, paying the workers with checks or cash—and usually pizza—and passing the cost on to my client as labor.

TAXES

The good news is that if you're used to filling out "the long form," paying your income taxes as a home-based entrepreneur will not be much more complex. If you're a sole proprietor, you will deduct your business costs from your gross income, treating what's left as personal income, just as you did before you were self-employed. The bad news is that since no employer is withholding your taxes, you are responsible for making quarterly advance payments of your estimated federal and state income taxes. These payments must also include both the employer's and the employee's portions of your estimated Social Security tax. Payments are due on April 15, June 15, September 15, and January 15, using Form 1040-ES. At the end of the year, you will file a final Form 1040 and a Schedule C—the form on which self-employed individuals report the costs of running their business.

Home office deductions

One of the benefits of working at home is that you can deduct a percentage of your utility, maintenance, and rental costs on Schedule C. If you own your home, you can also depreciate a portion of it (the value of the house times the percent used for your business, divided by the anticipated years of life of the house). But beware! If you sell your house, you could wind up paying capital-gains taxes on the portion you call your office, instead of deferring all gains into your next house, as is usually done with a residence.

Home office deductions have become a hot issue, so check with your tax consultant for the latest rulings. While the IRS denies it, tax authorities say that an individual who takes a home-office deduction has a better-than-average chance of being audited, and some home-based entrepreneurs prefer to avoid potential problems by not taking the deduction. I have always taken such a deduction, however—and so have most home-based writers I interviewed for this book.

The goal of the Internal Revenue Service, of course, is not to keep you from claiming legitimate business expenses, but to stop tax evasion by those who may have a home office, but earn little or nothing from it. Unfortunately, many legitimate businesspeople who work *out of* (rather than *in*) their homes were caught in a January 1993, U.S. Supreme Court ruling that struck down an anesthesiologist's home office deduction because he did not spend the bulk of his workdays there. Home-business advocates immediately began fighting back, claiming that the ruling creates a double standard since other businesses are not required to prove their offices are *where* their revenues are generated. Reading *Home Office Computing* or other publications for home entrepreneurs will help you stay informed on this important issue. And if you can influence laws or regulations, your help will be welcomed.

Federal tax laws enacted in 1996 offered a bit of good news for the self-employed. Deductions for health insurance were scheduled to rise gradually from 40% to 80% after 2005, and larger deductions were allowed for business equipment.

If you decide to take a home-office deduction, here are some things you can do to protect yourself.

- Make sure your home office is used exclusively for business, not for other purposes.

- Install a separate phone for your business. Otherwise, you may be required to produce records showing which calls on your home phone were business calls.

- Make sure your office serves as your place of business at least 50 percent of the time. If this might be an issue for you, keep a log of the hours you spend there as opposed to time you may spend working in your client's office or at other off-site locations.

- Do everything you can to strengthen your status as an independent contractor, if this might be an issue. Avoid working for just one client. Get a written contract for each job.

- If you're still moonlighting and haven't gone full-time with your business yet, take care. Unless your home-based business supplies "a significant portion" (some say half) of your income, tax specialists advise you not to take the deduction. Be aware also that the IRS considers an enterprise to be a hobby if it does not show a profit in three out of five years. In other words, to qualify for deductions, your business should be showing a profit by the third year. Discuss current regulations with your tax consultant.

Deducting other business expenses

Like any businessperson, you are entitled to deduct the costs of doing business. Such expenditures include

- Depreciation on major equipment and furniture
- Supplies and materials
- Labor costs and employee benefits
- Commissions and referral fees
- Consultant fees (sometimes a touchy area, document carefully)
- Professional services (legal, tax preparation, etc.)
- Advertising and promotion

- Postage, shipping, and messenger services

- Electronic mail and other on-line services

- Mileage or a portion of your auto expenses

- Business travel, meals, and lodging (at present, 100 percent of lodging but only 50 percent of meals apply—check current regulations)

- Lobbying

- Gifts (up to $25 per recipient per year)

- Entertainment (strictly regulated, so, again, know the rules)

- Copyright costs

- Training and professional memberships

- Professional information and research

- Business insurance

- Taxes (including 50 percent of your Social Security taxes)

- Bad debts and losses from theft or disaster

- Any other costs directly associated with your work

Sales tax

Obtaining a reseller's permit was discussed in Chapter Four. Having one doesn't require you to collect tax on every job or even on most jobs, but it does require you to file reports to your state tax department several times a year and pay the tax you have collected (or you may file annually if the amount is small).

Must you collect sales tax? Yes, if you are delivering a product; generally no, if you are delivering a service. States vary, however, in how they define these categories. Get information from your local SBA office or state tax department. Discuss the matter with your mentors and colleagues. Being required to pay the state a large sum for taxes you failed to collect could be an unpleasant experience. A gray area that is important to desktop publishers is camera-ready art or film. Is prepress material considered a product in *your* state?

If you are charging sales tax, you do not have to pay sales tax on the supplies you use to produce the job. Your vendors will ask you to fill out a resale card, and they will keep your resale number on file. If you normally collect sales tax on your work and are selling to a client who charges a sales tax—such as a book publisher—you will do the same.

CASH FLOW, INCOME PROJECTION, AND OTHER FINANCIAL ISSUES

Setting up your books

You can ask your accountant or bookkeeper to help you set up a chart of accounts. Or you can set up your books yourself. Your accounting system will need to cover income and expenses and reveal how much you are spending in various categories and how much you are receiving from various sources. For example, you may want to know how much you are making on different types of jobs, as well as how much you are earning from each client. If you design a system yourself, it's wise to get your accountant's feedback on it.

Stationery stores offer a variety of simple bookkeeping systems for small businesses—or you can opt for a software program such as Intuit's popular Quick-Books. While it may be more trouble to learn a computer system, software offers the enormous benefit of generating instant reports and producing the information you need at tax time, totalled in appropriate categories. The system will probably write checks for you and may even include an invoicing capability.

The important thing is to establish a reliable system for keeping track of all the money you spend for your business and all the money you take in—and to establish it right away. What we're talking about is called single-entry bookkeeping, which is probably all you need unless your accountant thinks otherwise.

Business vs. personal funds

Not every home entrepreneur sets up a separate business banking account, but all authorities advise it. Keeping business and personal funds separate is important, not only for tax purposes, but to let you see clearly where your business stands. The same thing applies to credit cards. You don't have to apply for a new business credit card unless you want to. Use one of your personal cards exclusively for business expenses.

Using financial information

Financial information lets you know how you're doing. It allows you to record and project your monthly income, cash flow, profit, and loss. Financial information also keeps track of jobs for billing and estimating purposes. It tells you which jobs and clients are most profitable (very important!) and how much you can afford to pay yourself each month. Failing to stay on top of these numbers is like driving without a road map.

Past financial information is normally the basis for both short- and long-range business planning, and it helps you enter realistic figures when doing "what if" business modeling. "What if I bought another computer and hired an assistant?" "What if I stopped writing trade journal articles and concentrated on writing advertising copy?"

At tax time, your financial records provide the information you need to prepare tax forms and take advantage of legitimate deductions. If you're audited by the IRS, your records will provide back-up data.

Some types of clients require financial information about vendors in order to qualify them before awarding work. Lenders making business loan decisions will require even more data, including a summary of your business' assets, liabilities, and net worth (assets minus liabilities). If your figures are clear, accurate, and complete, lenders will be favorably impressed. The same is true of a potential partner or a person who might be interested in buying your business. The first thing they will want to see will be the books.

Cash flow

A simple way of thinking about cash flow is, "Collect everything that's owed you as soon as you can, and hold onto cash as long as you can." Within the usual 30-day period, you can pay bills at the best time for you. That may include taking advantage of a cash discount for prompt payment, if one is offered. You can also use short-term credit with a business credit card. A business credit card allows you to make 800-number purchases, and it will even out monthly cash flow—but keep it paid up. A cash reserve is a prudent safeguard.

Income projection

What's coming in? There are two ways to keep track of income—cash and accrual. A cash system counts the money you have actually received. An accrual system keeps track of receivables—what you are owed. Obviously, in our work we need to be on top of both. But I'd like to suggest that you take income projection a little further.

Try this:

Each month, review your ongoing jobs, the bids you have presented, the jobs you have discussed with clients, and any other immediate business you have pending or planned. Then, *in writing,* project what you will sell over the next three months—month by month, job by job. Put an estimated amount and a completion date on each project.

If three months is too long, forecast for two months or even one. For writers involved in projects like books and technical manuals, three months may be too short a time to analyze. Either way, give it a serious try and see how helpful it can be.

This income projection exercise can be tremendously motivating. You are hoping to get these jobs. In fact, the numbers show you *need* these jobs. But you have not sold them yet. Better make sure you do sell them! And better make sure you can get them done. If all the jobs in the pipeline are more than you can handle in the next three months, now is the time to work with clients or subcontractors to make sure all deadlines can be met.

POLICIES AND PROCEDURES

An organization chart for a home-based business?

If employees or other family members are involved in your business, their roles and responsibilities need to be defined. How much responsibility and authority do they have? Who is empowered to make what kinds of decisions? You probably don't need an organization chart, but you do need a clear understanding by all concerned. And thinking it through will help you determine the best arrangement.

Think it through and write it down

It's a good idea to have important policies and procedures written down—especially if family members or employees help you in your business. Writing down procedures helps you clarify them and observe them.

Here are some of the day-to-day business questions that your policies and procedures can quickly answer.

- Which tasks take priority?
- Which clients take priority?
- When and in what priority are bills paid each month?
- How often are machines serviced?
- What forms do you use and how are they filled out?

Quality

One of your most important policies involves quality. How important is quality to you? How do you maintain quality? The truth is, quality varies widely in our work since not all clients want or need the same levels of quality. Within your own business framework, however, you must establish and maintain certain quality standards. Systems analysis, discussed below, can help you make sure quality is built into every step of your work.

Professionalism

Hello? Is anyone home? In researching this book, I have been astonished at how often the phones of home-based writers go unanswered or are answered by a casual "Hello." How much does it cost to put in an answering machine? How hard is it to train a spouse or child to give a business salutation? Some of my interview subjects have told me of successfully training even small children to sound professional on the phone. If I were setting up policies and procedures for a home-based business, the first rule I would establish would be: "Make sure the phone is always professionally answered during business hours."

Government requirements

Your state or local regulations may require written policies and procedures covering such topics as employees, safety, and the handling of hazardous materials. Rarely does a business your size have to produce such documents, but thinking through the issues can't hurt.

Systems? What systems?

What steps do you take as you perform specific business tasks? In what order? What tools do you use? Could processes be simplified, combined, eliminated? Who is the best person to do various jobs?

Analyze your systems periodically and try to improve them in terms of both efficiency and quality. For example, even if you have no employees, you may find that buying out certain services, such as bookkeeping or deliveries, makes sense. Or you may decide to hire an employee. Realizing the hourly value of his consulting time, one young home entrepreneur decided to stop doing things like researching personal and business matters on the phone, writing checks, even putting gas in his car. Instead, he hired a student from a nearby university as a personal and business assistant.

Studying your systems in detail will also show you where errors are creeping in.

RECORD KEEPING

Planning your files

Applying systems analysis to the way you organize your records is especially important for writers, since our stock-in-trade is information. Make a list of the kinds of information you keep and analyze it. Can any groups of records be combined? What cross-referencing is needed? How do you basically want to organize things? By client? Subject matter? Type of job? Individual job? Do you use titles or numbers to identify jobs? How and where will your paper data be stored? Your electronic data? Can you computerize material and discard the paper version?

Tracking jobs

How do you keep track of jobs? Consider assigning each job a number that will stay with it through invoicing and storage. Will your job number contain a code for the year? Month? Client? Type of job? A job control form is suggested in this book, to be kept with each job, recording all pertinent information.

How long to keep it?

The sensible answer is keep documents as long as applicable. With regard to your job and client files, that's entirely up to you, based on the kinds of jobs you do and your clients' needs. As a former buyer of writing and graphics services, my suggestion is that before you discard materials relating to client projects—such as art, computer documents, or research files—offer them to the client.

If you are discarding electronic data from your hard disk on a regular basis, be sure to inform clients of your policy in advance or before you delete the last copies of their files. A solution might be to keep a backup file on a low-cost medium, such as tape for several years. File compression programs can also help. If you routinely dump client files after a certain period of time, inform your clients of this policy.

Most writers keep files on subjects in their areas of expertise. Some can craft articles entirely out of these valuable storehouses. Review material periodically (perhaps once a year) and discard what is outdated. Be aware that the Internet with its vast, instant resources makes it unnecessary to keep as much information on file as you might once have done.

As for business-related and personal files, most people keep far more records than they need. While a few records are permanent, most should eventually be discarded.

You can discard copies of your tax return and supporting documents six years after filing, unless the IRS has begun an audit. (Check with your accountant to make sure this is still the current ruling.) Other records in the "as long as applicable" category include business financial records not needed for tax purposes, partnership agreements, corporation papers, employee records, Keogh statements, nondeductible IRA records, insurance policies, brokerage and fund transactions, stock and bond certificates, certificates of deposit, stock-option agreements, loan records, membership records, warranties and receipts for major purchases, and operating instructions for equipment. Also in this category are vehicle documents and real estate records, including deeds, title insurance policies, and documentation of major property improvements.

Not worth saving once you're satisfied they're accurate are credit card bills, bank statements, and cancelled checks (unless needed for tax purposes). You should also toss out receipts for everyday or small purchases unless you need them for tax documentation.

Master Job Log

In the log suggested in this book, the date is the controlling factor. The log is filled in chronologically as you receive your jobs. Tailor a similar log to your needs. You could make the job number the controlling factor. A series of job numbers might be assigned to a long-range project even though all the individual jobs were not yet in hand. The job and invoice number might be the same.

The point of a Master Job Log is to help you capture and control data, and the log can be designed to record any important information. If, for example, you have partners or employees, you will want to know who is in charge of each job. If you do multiple-part jobs, you may want to log in the parts rather than giving each part its own job number, since they will not be separately invoiced. If you invoice a large job in parts (for example, one-third in advance, one-third halfway through, one-third on delivery), you may need room for several invoice numbers.

Your log will help you check on or locate a job or invoice, help you gather and analyze data such as volume of business and client activity, and provide quick answers to questions like "When did I do that job?" or "What was the job we did for Smith & Smith last year?" For specific details on a job, you will go to the job control form.

This log, as shown, is designed to serve a writer who normally receives an assignment before starting a project. Writers who submit finished articles to publications might create a log with such headings as "Date," "Title," "Job Number," "Sold to," "Date of Sale," and "Date Paid."

If you are a writer who often re-writes the same material for different markets, you might add a heading such as "Re-write of Job # ____." If you sell reprint rights to published articles, you might add a heading to record additional sales. If you normally query editors before starting an article, a separate log might help you

JOB CONTROL FORM

Printing this form on the outside of a large envelope or attaching it to a manila folder can facilitate handling a job. The envelope or folder contains working materials for the job and will eventually hold the documentation and a few job samples that will be kept on file–usually by job number or name of client.

Job name _____ Job. # _____

Client _____

Address _____

City _____ State _____ Zipcode _____

Contact _____

Title _____

Phone (_____) _____ Ext. _____ Fax (_____) _____

Bill to _____ P.O. #_____

Address if different _____

Ship to _____ Attn._____

Address if different _____

Via _____

PRODUCTION SCHEDULE

Job received _____ Date due _____ Date delivered _____

Allow space below for dates due and actual completion dates of major steps in production, including client approvals. Briefly describe the steps.

Step 1 _____ Step 2 _____ Step 3 _____

Date due _____ Date due _____ Date due _____

Completed _____ Completed _____ Completed _____

JOB DESCRIPTION

Design this space to fit your needs. Writers might want blanks for sections, length, and reader level. If you're also doing desktop publishing, you might want blanks for number of pages, dimensions, halftone screen line specifications, paper type and color, ink colors, finishing and bindery instructions. This job description can be less detailed than the Estimating Form job description, but be sure that final choices on such points as paper and ink are recorded for future reference.

Special instructions _____

continued on next page

RECORD OF COSTS

Date	Task/Item	Source (if buy-out)	No. hrs./ Qty.	Rate/ Price ea.	Amount
_____	_____	_____	_____	_____	$_____
_____	_____	_____	_____	_____	_____
_____	_____	_____	_____	_____	_____
_____	_____	_____	_____	_____	_____
_____	_____	_____	_____	_____	_____
_____	_____	_____	_____	_____	_____
_____	_____	_____	_____	_____	_____
_____	_____	_____	_____	_____	_____
_____	_____	_____	_____	_____	_____
_____	_____	_____	_____	_____	_____
_____	_____	_____	_____	_____	_____
_____	_____	_____	_____	_____	_____
_____	_____	_____	_____	_____	_____
_____	_____	_____	_____	_____	_____
_____	_____	_____	_____	_____	_____
_____	_____	_____	_____	_____	_____
_____	_____	_____	_____	_____	_____
_____	_____	_____	_____	_____	_____
_____	_____	_____	_____	_____	_____
_____	_____	_____	_____	_____	_____

BILLING

Original estimate $ _____   Changes to estimate _____

_____

Sales tax _____%   Applies to _____

Invoice # _____   Date _____   Amount $ _____

Payment received date _____

Payment received date _____

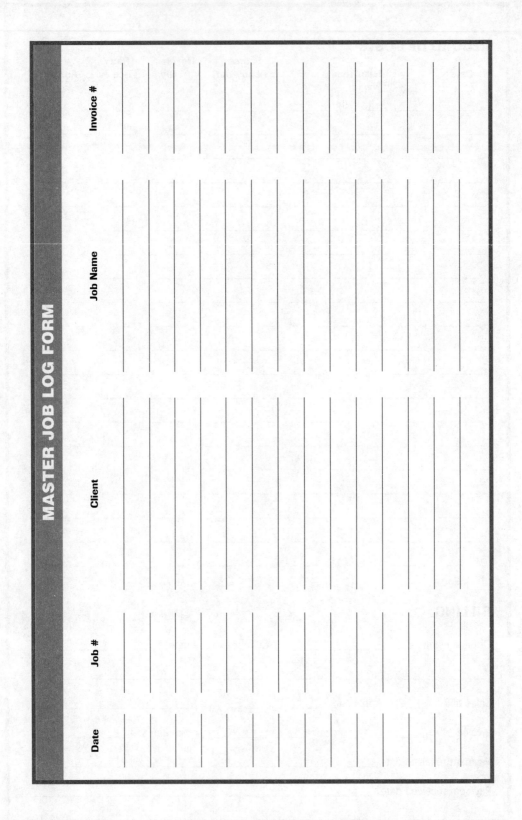

MASTER JOB LOG FORM

Date	Job #	Client	Job Name	Invoice #

keep track of queries. The CD-ROM version of the *1997 Writer's Market* includes "Submission Tracker™," a software program to handle this type of record-keeping (see Bibliography).

PURCHASING AND INVENTORY CONTROL

Establish business credit

Early on, set up credit with several vendors, such as an office supply store or desktop publishing service bureau. Establishing business credit will help your general business profile, especially when you need credit in the future. Credit with your major vendors will also help you even out your cash flow.

Pay on time

Regardless of what your personal credit history has been, it's important to maintain good business credit. Don't let bills go unpaid over thirty days. If you have a cash-flow problem, discuss it promptly with your vendor.

Try for business discounts

When dealing with firms that serve the general public, such as art supply and stationery stores, ask for a business discount. Many will comply.

Value vendor relationships

Build good relationships with key vendors. You may save money at a giant discount store, but the owner won't stay open for you when you realize a few minutes before closing that you need some supplies. And the young guy indifferently putting up stock along the endless warehouse rows can't solve your technical problem and doesn't care to try.

Respond to all bids

When you have requested a bid, perhaps from a printer or a designer, extend the same courtesy you would like from your own clients. Bids take effort to prepare, and the vendor may even be tentatively reserving time to do your work. As soon as you have made a decision, let each bidder know whether that firm did or did not get the job. Rarely will you be harangued to change your mind. Rather, your courtesy will be appreciated.

Control your inventory

Be aware of the supplies you use regularly and develop a method for reminding yourself to buy more when your stock gets low. Losing production time because you were out of materials is money out of your pocket—since the lost time can't be regained.

Beware of bargains.

"Conserve cash" is good advice in the early years of any business, so if you see a bargain on supplies or equipment, balance any savings you might achieve with the usefulness of ready cash. Stock up only when you can afford it—and when you have room to store it.

MAINTENANCE OF EQUIPMENT AND FACILITIES

Using business services

Just because you're working at home doesn't mean you can't have business services to maintain your equipment. I keep a service contract on my Sharp copier (currently $280 per 20,000 copies), and the repairman is at my office within one to three hours whenever I have a problem—just like in a "real" office. I've replaced the drum once in four and a half years, and the quality I get from this machine is still as good as from a new machine. Equally valuable to me is the peace of mind I get from knowing I can avoid lost productivity following a copier breakdown. Similarly, the firm that delivers laser printer cartridges to my home office provides prompt printer repairs. Look for such services for small businesspeople in your community.

Keeping clutter at bay

What about office maintenance—keeping your work space clean, neat, and in repair? If you were a clean-desk person when you were employed outside your home, chances are you'll remain one, but my guess is that many of us are clutterers. (I base this impression on the long list of anti-clutter books offered by the Writer's Digest Book Club—not, of course, on visits to the offices of writer friends.)

In the interest of making a good impression on business visitors, finding materials when you need them, and maintaining your own sanity, I suggest you have some plan for regular cleaning, straightening, and repairs in your home office. This is something another family member might help you with to make sure it gets done. In my own case, I find having to "clean up for the cleaning people" every other week tends to restore order.

COMPUTER SYSTEM ADMINISTRATION AND SECURITY

Saving and backing up documents

Save your documents regularly as you work. Do it automatically, without fail. Back up your hard drive on a regular schedule, using whatever media you choose—floppies, removable cartridges, rewritable optical disks, another hard drive, or tape. It's a good idea to keep these backups in a separate location.

System administration

Allow regular time in your schedule—and in your pricing structure—for computer system administration. Solving problems and installing new equipment and software need to be done when there's time to do it properly, not under crisis conditions. Include time for learning new software. If the installations and troubleshooting are beyond you, get help.

Getting help

Build a computer support network before you need it. This should include a reliable computer repair service (possibly a maintenance contract on key items like your computer and printer), a consultant for occasional heavy-duty service and advice, and some knowledgeable colleagues on whom you can call for quick troubleshooting. Your local computer user group may be a valuable resource. Desktop publishers may get free or low-cost advice from their service bureaus.

Have a contingency plan that will let you continue working if your computer goes down for an extended period. You might have a second computer on your premises—or know of one you can borrow or rent. Copy centers often rent Macs and PCs by the hour—a possible emergency solution.

Computer security

Do you need to keep others out of your system or to secure certain documents? Do your clients require security safeguards? Working at home, we're likely to overlook issues of computer security (unless young computer users are a problem). But think about it. Unix and Windows NT have built in security provisions, but DOS, Windows, and the Macintosh operating system don't, unless you add passwords to protect certain files.

Security in general

You have some valuable equipment in your home office and you certainly don't want the loss and work disruption that a security problem could cause. Do what you can in advance to keep your property secure.

When guarding against theft, experts say the best security is the *appearance* of security. Any home can be broken into, but thieves will pass by homes where windows and doors are closed and properly locked (especially sliding patio doors), lights are on in the evening, people are seen coming and going, mail and newspapers are picked up, the yard is tended, and security night lights are installed. A dog that barks at strangers can help, too.

Since we work out of our homes, we have an advantage over our neighbors who go away to work, but be aware that in "safe" suburban neighborhoods, many break-ins are carried out by kids skipping school and sometimes high on drugs. Such kids are often willfully destructive and can be unpredictable. Don't let your residence appear inviting.

Do a safety audit

Fire and water damage pose dangers. Once a year, look over your facilities with security in mind. How would you evacuate your office in an emergency? Do stored materials or temporary electric wiring pose fire hazards? Could water leak in? In the basement office I formerly occupied, I realized that my computer was directly under the washing machine, and water leaking through the floor following an overflow would be bad news. Home safety experts tell us never to leave the house with the washing machine on, but how many of us pay attention?

TOWARD A BUSINESS PLAN

Success Worksheet Thirty

Systems solve management problems.

Knowledge and advance planning will help you establish systems and policies to keep your business running smoothly.

- **Legal issues and business insurance**

    Do you have insurance to cover injury, theft, fire, or other disaster in your home office?

    _____

    Do you have insurance to cover general liability? Employee disability?

    _____

How do you handle job agreements? Do you view them as contracts?

_____

If you joint venture with other vendors, how are all parties protected?

_____

How do you handle collection problems?

_____

Is copyright an issue for you and, if so, how do you handle it? How do you stay informed on copyright regulations, especially electronic rights?

_____

Do you ever infringe on the copyrights of others? How can you avoid doing so?

_____

■ **Issues concerning employees**

Do you know the difference between an employee and an independent contractor? Could this be an issue for you in obtaining outside services or in offering your own services to clients?

_____

If you hire employees, what kind will you hire? Full-time? Part-time? Occasional labor?

_____

How will you inform yourself of and carry out federal and state regulations regarding your employees?

_____

■ **Taxes**

How have you arranged to pay your income and Social Security taxes?

_____

If you take your home office as a deduction, do you have an area of your house used exclusively for your office? What records do you keep to substantiate your claims?

_____

What records do you keep to identify and substantiate other legal business deductions?

_____

Does your state require you to collect sales tax on products you sell? If so, have you completed state re-sale registration forms? How do you handle sales tax records? Are you on file with vendors as sales-tax exempt when buying items for resale?

_____

■ **Cash flow, income projection, other financial issues**

How will you set up your financial records? Will you use paper or a computer program? Will you use professional help?

_____

How will you keep business and personal funds separate?

_____

How will you handle cash flow problems?

_____

How will you do income projections?

_____

■ **Organization, policies and procedures, system analysis**

If others are involved in your business, what authority and responsibilities do they have?

_____

What policies and procedures do you have to define priorities and keep routine matters running smoothly? Have you put them in writing?

_____

How do you define and maintain quality standards in your work?

_____

What are the steps in your production process? Can they be simplified or improved?

_____

- **Record-keeping**

  How do you track jobs, invoices, client materials?

  _____

  What systems and schedules do you use to retain and discard paper and electronic records?

  _____

  What special record-keeping systems do you need to meet specific requirements in your business?

  _____

- **Purchasing and inventory control**

  How do you establish business credit and develop vendor relationships?

  _____

  How do you assure that business bills are paid on time?

  _____

  How do you maintain inventory control?

  _____

- **Maintenance of equipment and facilities**

  Do you use professional services to maintain key office equipment? Who do you use? What is the cost?

  _____

  How do you keep your office neat, clean, and in repair on a regular basis?

  _____

- **Computer system administration, security**

  What procedures do you use for backing up computer data? When working, do you save documents frequently? Do you store backup data in a separate location?

  _____

How do you handle normal system administration, such as installing and learning new software programs and correcting system problems?

_____

What will you do if your computer is out of commission?

_____

If you require computer security, what system do you use?

_____

How do you assure security for all your business equipment, supplies, and files against theft, fire, water, and other damage?

_____

SETTING GOALS AND MANAGING TIME WITHIN YOUR MANAGEMENT STYLE

I was well along in my professional career before I fully realized that personal and business goals should be aligned with each other—and with daily behavior. I got this message by listening to a series of tapes called *Time Power* by the time-management expert, Charles R. Hobbs. Hobbs maintains that goals grow out of our underlying personal values—what he calls "unifying principles"—and that the whole personal management process is one of self-unification.

Success is based on goals

Hobbs's system is one of many good programs that will teach you what should be self-evident, but often isn't: "Success is based upon goals." Goals guide the way you organize your time, the projects you undertake, the purchases you make, the training you seek, the people you associate with. And if you have no goals, that, too, is a choice. But you wouldn't be starting a business if you didn't have goals. And perhaps your most important long-range business goal is "growth."

Many of your key business decisions will be based on the goals you set for the growth of your business. But what is your definition of business growth? Will you have "grown" when you can charge more per hour for your services? Or does growth mean having a larger organization? Do you want both? If you plan to become larger, how big do you want to be?

Time Management

Time management is the secret to achieving your goals, and there are many popular time-management techniques. If you're not already using one of them, do some research—find a book, tape, desk, or pocket organizer or computer scheduling system that appeals to you, and put it to work! Here's an added benefit: In the early months of operating your home business, you may often be struck by a pit-of-the-stomach anxiety that urgently cries, "Right now, you're not earning any money!" On one level, this is probably healthy. But on another, it can produce panic or even paralysis. I believe consistent time management reduces "new entrepreneur panic" because it puts you in control. "No, I may not be earning money at this moment, but I'm doing what I need to do now."

To me, the main characteristics of time management are

- Doing regular planning
- Listing tasks (or subtasks)
- Prioritizing them
- Following through
- Rewarding yourself for achievement

Setting priorities

Many systems for prioritizing employ some variant of the "ABC Priority System" described by Alan Lakein in his 1973 classic, *How to Get Control of Your Time and Your Life*. Once you have listed the tasks that need doing, you assign an A to those that have high value in terms of your long-range goals, B to those that have medium value, and C to those with low value. Then you do the As first, saving the Bs and Cs for later, realizing that many Cs and some Bs may never get done.

But why bring in your long-range goals? Why not assign an A to those tasks that are urgent or important today? One reason for managing your time is so that you don't spend it "putting out fires." For example, to avoid paying a penalty on an overdue bill, you may find yourself canceling an appointment with a potential client so you can deliver the late payment to your creditor's office. That's "time out of control"—and it can damage or destroy your business.

Following through and rewarding yourself

Good time management systems have many techniques for overcoming procrastination and getting started on the As—breaking big tasks into smaller tasks, working on a task for a short period of time, analyzing your motives, trying to match some phase of the task to your current mood, doing more detailed planning, and combining pleasant tasks with difficult ones. Experts also advise you to reward yourself for priorities accomplished—a practice I strongly endorse. If you've gotten this far in this book—and in planning your business—you deserve at least a weekend in the mountains. Develop a series of big and little rewards that mean something special to you. Hey, we're all human!

Avoiding interruptions at home

According to home-business gurus Paul and Sarah Edwards, "one or two out of ten people" have trouble running businesses from their homes because of family and household demands and interruptions. My gut-level feeling is that 10–20 percent is a very low estimate, so be on the alert for your own solutions to these problems.

Isolating your office. If you can isolate your office in a separate room or section of the house, that's great. If not, establish a symbolic isolation—some signal that lets the rest of the family know you are at work and not to be disturbed. This could be drawing a curtain, putting up a sign, even the way you dress—whatever carries the message that you are now open for business.

Phone interruptions. An early problem will be friends and relatives who will call to chat, knowing you are at home. Stop this practice from the start by saying something like, "Sorry, I can't talk. I'm at work right now. Could you call back after five?"

Child care. If you have small children at home, you may need to arrange for child care during certain periods of the day in order to do work that requires heavy concentration. Some work is almost impossible to do piecemeal. Consider the hourly cost of child care versus what you can bill for productive time, and you'll see the value of getting help.

Your Management Style

There is no ideal management style, but it's wise to know what your style is. Often an authoritarian, *micro-management* style in which the owner has a say in every business decision makes a small business successful. But it's the very thing that hampers the business when it starts to grow. Successful entrepreneurs face such issues squarely—sometimes changing their styles, sometimes changing their management structure so that problem areas are handled by others. Here are some questions that will help you identify your management style—

- As the business owner, you must make final decisions. But how do you arrive at those decisions? Do you invite others to participate or do you have your mind made up before you talk with them?

- Do you focus primarily on products or on relationships?

- Do you focus primarily on processes or on outcomes?

- Do you like joint ventures or do you prefer to work alone?

- When you work with other professionals, do you team, or do you want to be in charge?

- Do you get things done in advance or do you need deadlines to keep you going?

TOWARD A BUSINESS PLAN

Success Worksheet Thirty-One

Identify your management style and work with it for success.

Setting goals and managing time to accomplish priority tasks are essential to success as a home-based writer—but the overall key is your management style. Know what it is and don't work against yourself.

- **Goal setting**

  What goals have you established for your business? Do they correspond with your underlying values and your goals for family and personal life?

  _____

  _____

  How do you define "growth" for your business?

  _____

  _____

- **Time management**

  What time management system do you use?

  _____

  _____

  How do you make sure you are working on priority projects?

  _____

  _____

How do you reward yourself for having managed time well?

_____

_____

How do you control interruptions in your home office?

_____

_____

■ **Management style**

Check the statements that most closely fit the way you prefer to operate in business.

_____ I make up my mind, then tell others. If necessary, I'll make a change.

_____ I listen to all persons involved, then make a decision.

_____ I am primarily interested in products, then in relationships.

_____ I am primarily interested in relationships, then in products.

_____ I am primarily interested in outcomes, then in the process of achieving them.

_____ I am interested in outcomes, but I am more interested in how they are achieved.

_____ When I work with others, I prefer to be in charge.

_____ I enjoy teaming with others and sharing responsibility for a project.

_____ I generally do work for which I am responsible well in advance.

_____ I work best under deadlines. Without a deadline, I have a hard time getting started.

What do your answers suggest to you about a partner or joint venture situation for your business?

_____

_____

What do your answers suggest about how you should manage employees?

_____

_____

If you have problems cooperating with others, what techniques can help you?

_____

_____

What do your answers suggest about making commitments?

_____

_____

If you have problems meeting deadlines, what techniques can help you?

_____

_____

YOUR BUSINESS AND YOUR LIFE

Staying Current with Knowledge and Skills

My friend, Polly Pattison, who recently retired to Utah from a long career in California as an internationally-known trainer in newsletter design, had reached the top of her field when the desktop publishing revolution hit. Instead of resisting new developments, she jumped in with both feet, even writing a book on the subject. Learning about computers and helping to guide their impact on design gave a whole new impetus to her career.

We all learn in our own way—whether it's through reading, audio and video tapes, meetings and seminars, conversations with colleagues, or experimenting on our own. Whatever works for you, it's vital that you continue learning—not only to keep up with the competition but to stay creatively alive.

Read the profiles of Donna Donovan in Chapter Three and Judith Broadhurst in Chapter Nine to see this principle in action. Donovan draws creatively from a group studying _The Artists' Way_ to refresh her work and business relationships. Broadhurst's entire career has been one of moving on to new levels. You, too, will grow your business by growing your knowledge and skills!

Job-related stress

Aside from the stress of having to find new clients and new jobs, which is just part of being an entrepreneur, home-based writers often experience stress because jobs come in bunches. There's nothing to do one day, and too much the next—and with one or two workers, it's tough to even out the flow. Advanced scheduling and personal time management can solve the majority of these problems. When confronted with several As to do, for example, many people start on Cs because the As just seem too overwhelming. This strategy will, of course, compound rather than solve the problem.

When deadlines stack up, you can reduce stress by taking a moment to examine the situation, asking, "What really must be done now and what might be delayed?" When I was selling printing, our production manager occasionally asked me to "try to get us a little more time on this job." At first I hated making such calls, fearing that my clients would be annoyed, but I was surprised to find that often they had no problem with a moderate delay. People frequently say they want something as soon as possible when the job is not really urgent. If you find yourself routinely asking for extra time, however, take a look at the production estimates you're giving your clients. Telling them what they want to hear makes you look good when estimating but bad at delivery time.

Get help. In a real work-flow crisis, having trusted colleagues you can call on for help is a solution, even though subcontracting the job may take most of your profit. For an entrepreneur with a "can-do" attitude, the important thing is to get the job done. And, who knows? When your colleague gets overloaded, he or she may send a job your way.

Loneliness

Feeling lonely a few months into your new business? Isolation is a problem that many home-based entrepreneurs complain about—especially when they're used to being surrounded by fellow workers. As you adapt to working at home, this feeling will probably decrease, but don't ignore it. Arrange what Paul and Sarah Edwards describe as "people breaks." This could be a trip to a vendor or a client's office, instead of using a delivery service. It could be lunch with a friend or business colleague. Even a phone call will help when you're feeling disconnected from the world. I often receive such calls from home-based business friends (and I make them, too). But be sure your colleague has time for the ego-reviving chat you have in mind.

Rekindling motivation

When your motivation drops, as it will from time to time, make a list of the benefits of running a home business—or keep one handy to review. There will be days when you will wonder why you ever started your business, when you long for the security of a full-time job, when you want to escape from the continuing search for new clients or from vendors demanding payment while cash is just not flowing. It shouldn't take you long to come up with arguments to counter these negative feelings. Remind yourself how important it is to be in command of your own destiny and how good it feels to be away from office politics. A trick I use is one I picked up from the motivation expert, Anthony Robbins. Robbins tells of feeling overwhelmed and discouraged by business demands, then jumping into his home spa during business hours and returning phone calls as the bubbles massaged away his troubles. I've tried it in my own home spa, and he's right. It works!

Retirement planning

Running a One-Person Business by Whitmyer, Rasberry, and Phillips, an otherwise exemplary book, advises new entrepreneurs that, "On the whole, the idea of retirement should probably seem ridiculous to you. Salaried people retire to do the things they have always dreamed of. . . . But you are already doing what you dream of."

Sorry, but I couldn't disagree more! And I can't believe these authors ever cared for an infirm, destitute relative. Guess what? We don't always get to spend our old age doing "the things we dream of," and we need to prepare for what may be ahead.

Perhaps you don't want to hear this now—as you're starting your business. Sure, it's nice to know you can't be forced to retire. It's nice to be able to say, "I love what I'm doing, and I'll do it as long as I can." But one day you *will* want to slow down. Or health problems will slow you down. Or your spouse will want to move to Arizona. And even though the government gives small business owners tax incentives to save for retirement, many creative entrepreneurs pay no attention.

"Well, what about selling my business?" you ask. "Won't that be a source of funds?" Unfortunately, as creative workers, our businesses are not as saleable as a store, repair shop, or medical practice. In fact, few home-based writing businesses would be saleable at all, unless you have a staff who can carry on. What clients are buying, primarily, is *you*.

Start investing

Don't let your final years be less than rosy. Take pro-active measures now. Unfortunately, there's no automatic retirement deduction. We have to set one up. And with no generous "employer contribution," we have to pay it all. Furthermore, there rarely is a large sum left over to invest each month when we finish balancing the books. Instead, we must do as financial planners advise: Pay yourself first. In other words, invest a fixed portion of your income every month *before* you pay your bills—no matter how small the amount. Look into government Keogh and IRA plans. Look into stocks, mutual funds, bonds, real estate. Or perhaps you can continue adding to a plan you are in already.

Don't wait until a few years before retirement to deal with this. When it comes to investing, time is money's best friend, and you cannot catch up ten or twenty years from now with where you would have been if you had started today.

The impact of your business on your family

Early in this book, we discussed the cooperation you must have from those you live with in order to open and operate a home business. But even when you have strong cooperation at home, it's important to stay alert for the impact—both positive and negative—of your business on your family. Common problems are access to the phone, parking, or certain parts of the house; sound control; visitors; even your own hours and accessibility. If a problem is developing, don't let it fester. Catch it early by discussing it and seeking a solution.

Business vs. personal time

One of the key advantages of a home-based business—your ability to integrate your business and personal life—can sometimes become one of its key disadvantages. If you tend to get deeply involved in your work, your home-based business can take over your personal life. You will never "go home." You will never stop thinking about business. Basically, you will never leave the office. Added to this, if you tend to let deadlines turn into crises, your business crises may start to dominate the entire household.

I realize that deeply ingrained work traits cannot be changed with pat advice, but I urge you to think about the damage that can result to relationships and to young lives if all the needs and priorities of the family become subservient to THE BUSINESS. For an ounce of prevention, set aside inviolable "family time" and "personal time" every week. Sports? Hobbies? Entertainment? Talking? Walking? Whatever it is, spend time with the family and create an escape valve for yourself.

Chip off the old block

There's another kind of influence a home business can have on your family—and that's the example you set. Not long out of college, my son started his own home-based computer consulting business. And my daughter just opened her own body piercing business with future plans for owning an alternative clothing store. Seeing me enjoy my home-based business—financial worries and all—must have had some impact, even though I'm not sure they're ready to be self-employed. Watch out! If you have kids, nieces, or nephews, the same thing may happen to you.

Success Worksheet Thirty-Two

Manage yourself.

Find ways to deal with stress, loneliness, and motivation. Plan and invest for retirement. Make time for your family and yourself.

■ **Stress, loneliness, motivation**

How do you recognize and handle stress on the job?

_____

_____

If loneliness is a problem, how do you recognize and deal with it?

_____

_____

How do you keep your motivation strong?

_____

_____

■ **Retirement planning, investing**

When and how do you plan to retire?

_____

_____

What investments can/do you make now to be sure you will be able to retire comfortably some day? Do you "pay yourself first"?

_____

_____

■ **The impact of your business on your family**

How will you know if your business is causing problems for family members?

_____

_____

Do you regularly clear quality time for family members? How do you spend it?

_____

_____

Do you regularly make personal time for yourself? How do you spend it?

_____

_____

WRITING YOUR BUSINESS PLAN

Back in Chapter One, I presented the concept of "writing a business plan," so you might keep that important task in mind as you worked your way through these pages. I presented a seven-part formulation for a business plan which I particularly like for its clarity and simplicity. It includes the topics any business plan must cover, regardless which of many possible formulations you finally decide to use. These topics are:

1. The executive summary

2. The management plan

3. The organizational plan

4. The service and product plan

5. The marketing plan

6. The financial plan

7. The forecasting plan

Please take a moment to re-read pages 19 to 21 .

Now you're ready

It's not within the scope of this book to guide you through writing your business plan. What this book attempts to do is to get you *ready* to write your business plan by presenting information, asking questions, and encouraging you to complete the thirty-two Success Worksheets provided. If you have completed all or even part of them, you have already done much of the work.

You have made many key decisions about your home-based writing business. You may have tried out treasured ideas and found them wanting, discarding them in favor of services or clients that you believe will be more profitable or appropriate to your interests or capabilities. You probably have talked your plans over with mentors or colleagues and your spouse or significant other. You may have approached creative professionals, such as desktop publishers, web page designers, photographers, with whom you can team to expand your services. You may have filled pages with numbers, determining your startup costs and how you will support yourself until your business shows a profit. Of particular importance are the financial worksheets at the end of Chapter Six.

Get a business plan book or software program

In the Bibliography you will find books on writing a business plan. In the Source Directory you will find software for doing the same. I urge you to review this material and select a book or software program that you like. No, you probably won't have to present your business plan to a lender for funding (the reason many business plans actually find their way onto paper). Few home-based writing businesses are launched with a business loan unless it's from a relative. But your business plan should be your most important working document—a roadmap, a reality gauge, a timetable. It will contain success measurements to be evaluated and adjusted over time. If you are using it correctly, it will keep you on target. You will turn to it often in the months and even years ahead.

Good luck! Starting a home-based business near the end of this incredible century puts you into an historic trend that may give us a very different business landscape in the years to come. With new information technology, homes are once again becoming the site of much of the world's work—just as they were for centuries before the Industrial Revolution.

Let's hope your home-based business is one of the leaders in this extraordinary movement! Writer and publisher Bob Brenner, whose profile ends this book, is a futurist who has studied these developments for many years.

Robert C Brenner
Brenner Information Group, San Diego, California

Riding the Wave of 'Change'

In his 1970 classic, *Future Shock,* Alvin Toffler compares staying abreast of social and technological change with riding the crest of a wave. Writer/publisher/consultant and spare-time futurist Robert Brenner handles that task like a veteran surfer. In so doing, he sets an example for writers who are establishing new businesses during an era of massive change in the information industry.

Today such concepts as "electronic publishing," "information super-highway," "online," "interactive," and "virtual reality" suggest a communications world we are only beginning to imagine. Yet it is one all of us will be required to deal with if we are to stay competitive.

What can Brenner teach us?

From a kid who made his own comic books—using the reverse sides of cereal boxes as covers and sewing them together with yarn—Brenner grew up dreaming of being a writer. Instead, as a freshman in college and out of money, he enlisted in the Active Navy Reserve. He got married and, after earning a degree in electrical engineering, was commissioned in the regular Navy. He went on to earn graduate degrees in systems management and electrical engineering.

Then in 1981, while serving as an engineering duty officer in San Diego, Brenner took leave and spent $700 on a three-day seminar that would change his life. It focused on right-brain thinking and money.

"The seminar was designed by futurist Buckminster Fuller," he recalls "It taught me how to bring the left and right sides of my brain to the same operating level. After that, I was constantly wired. I discovered that the only barriers to my success were those I imagined and created."

Still an aspiring writer and entrepreneur, Brenner began writing church newsletters and volunteer articles to gain experience. Soon he was being paid for his work. In 1983, he proposed a series of books on troubleshooting and repair of popular computers to a major publisher and got a seven-book contract with Howard W. Sams/McMillan. Recently, he co-wrote a book on VCR repair for the same publisher. He also started several businesses, including a technical writing business in his home.

In 1984, Brenner retired from the Navy—he calls it "changing careers"—and worked for a seminar presentation company supporting the Department of Defense until he joined TRW as a senior staff engineer. There he rose to technical marketing manager, flying 143,000 miles one year, and worked with many large U.S. defense firms. When he proposed a commercial application for a TRW research product, however, he was rebuffed because "they wanted to remain in defense R&D." Frustrated with senior management's lack of vision, he left the company in 1987.

"The next day I bought a Mac II, PageMaker software, and a LaserWriter NTX," he recalls.

Brenner became fascinated with what were then called "microcomputers" and their potential for self-publishing, and once more he started on the ground floor, designing business cards and fliers. "I knew the only way to master desktop publishing was to get in the trenches," he says, "so I forced myself to learn, working fourteen-hour days."

Soon he was writing and designing manuals for clients, and by 1990, he self-published his first book, *The Silent Speech of Politicians*, written by a psychologist colleague. Brenner lost money on the venture, which he now calls "a good book with poor design." He was still learning the ropes.

"I've experienced almost every pitfall in desktop publishing," he admits, "but I've learned from them." One mistake was moving into a suite of offices to create a "company image." When the costly lease was up, he moved back into his San Diego home—just months before a major recession hit California.

From the beginning, Brenner collected information about the emerging desktop market. In 1990, as requests came from clients for desktop publishing jobs, he realized he "didn't have a clue" what to charge, and he began doing research. What he discovered was that few owner-operators in the new industry seemed to have a clear idea of costs and pricing—and the concept for his book, *Pricing Guide: Desktop Publishing Services,* was born.

"It took all of 1991," Brenner recalls. He compiled a list of almost 15,000 desktop publishers from Yellow Pages, trade magazine ads, and other sources, and began surveying them to collect pricing information. He analyzed the data with the help of a statistician; wrote a tutorial on cost, pricing strategies, and estimating; and published the first edition of the *Pricing Guide* in January 1992. Industry reaction was positive.

By 1996, with the 4th edition under way (now two books: *Pricing Guide: for Desktop Services* and *Pricing Tables: for Desktop Services*), Brenner was established as an industry expert, and his firm, Brenner Information Group, had moved back into an office for order-taking, fulfillment, shipping, and invoicing.

"I really prefer to work out of my home," he says. "But our business has grown so much we just couldn't handle it that way. Now I do all my writing and personal entrepreneur creativity out of my home in the early morning."

For his new *Pricing Tables,* Brenner surveyed more than 26,000 small businesses and collected more than 200,000 pricing-related data points. He also uses the information to publish related materials and to speak at industry gatherings. In addition, he offers consulting services on a wide range of technical and business information needs.

To stay current and spot trends, Brenner monitors more than 120 publications a month with the aid of his wife, who is a banker, and his grown children, who work with him in related ventures. Sometimes he consults with clients over coffee at Denny's or McDonald's "to reduce anxiety for a frightened entrepreneur." Sometimes it's via modem or fax with clients as far away as Argentina and Japan.

"I see people in our country traumatized by downsizing in the workplace, so discouraged and upset," he says, "and *I'm* saying, 'Let's see. How shall I have fun working and making money today?'"

For instance, Brenner cites an Oregon entrepreneur he surveyed who makes "a very comfortable living" at home, collecting "junk mail."

"I called him up and said, 'You only work three hours a day, what do you do?' And he said, 'Well, I collect junk mail. I look for the poorly-designed, poorly-written pieces. And I re-write it, re-design the graphics and send it back under my copyright and offer to do work for them.' 'Yes,' I said, 'but why do you work only three hours a day?' And he said, 'Because the fishing's good up here!'"

Offering another example, Brenner says he participates in a "virtual corporation" with a home-based entrepreneur in the Midwest who produces log books, both pocket and electronic versions, for sports and outdoor enthusiasts who want to record information. "There are countless ways to make money in a home office!" he insists.

On a theoretical note, the writer-futurist observes, "The workplace paradigm is changing and power is shifting from money to knowledge—driven by microelectronics. The old hierarchical corporate structure is changing forever. Information now flows horizontally and vertically so fast that you no longer need the middle level. New jobs are being born every day, but they are totally different jobs involving the processing and movement of information. For example, opportunities for writers—'content providers'—are expanding significantly because many, many businesses are going online. I see opportunities like never before in history for those who know how to generate and move information."

BIBLIOGRAPHY

BOOKS ON BUSINESS

Attard, Janet. *Home Office & Small Business Success Book: How to Run Your Business More Profitably With Less Effort*. New York: Henry Holt & Co., Inc., 1996. Money-making advice from a pro.

Attard, Janet. *The Home Office & Small Business Answer Book: Solutions to the Most Frequently Asked Questions about Starting & Running Home Offices & Small Businesses*. New York: Henry Holt & Co., Inc., l993. Like a long talk with a good mentor.

Blake, Gary, and Robert W. Bly. *How to Promote Your Own Business*. New York: New American Library-Dutton, 1983. Practical advice with lots of examples. Includes a chapter on marketing with newsletters, one on trade shows and expositions, plus many promotional ideas.

Bly, Robert W. *Selling Your Services: Proven Strategies for Getting Clients to Hire You (Or Your Firm)*. New York: Henry Holt & Co., Inc., 1992. Techniques to help you through tough sales situations.

Bly, Robert W. *Targeted Public Relations How to Get Thousands of Dollars of Free Publicity for Your Product, Service, Organization, or Idea*. New York: Henry Holt & Co., Inc., 1994. Useful techniques for promoting your services.

Boyan, Lee. *Successful Cold Call Selling*. New York: Amacom, A Division of American Management Association, 1989. A useful and thoughtful book on a difficult subject. still in print after many years.

Brabec, Barbara. *Homemade Money: How to Select, Start, Manage, Market & Multiply the Profits of a Business at Home*, 5th ed. Cincinnati: F & W Publications, Inc., 1994. This has become a classic. Workbook approach to starting a home-based business. Includes instructions for writing a business plan. Provides an A-Z glossary of business terms, advice on personal and business management, and an extensive resource directory.

Breen, George, and Albert B. Blankenship. *Do-It-Yourself Marketing Research*, 3rd ed. New York: McGraw-Hill, 1992. Guides you through the arcane mysteries of marketing research with clear writing and instructive examples. Suggests low-cost methods.

Brenner, Robert. *Pricing Guide for Desktop Services*, 4th ed. Brenner Information Group, P.O. Box 721000, San Diego, CA 92172-1000. Whether you sell desktop services or buy them for yourself or your clients, this $34.95 book by writer/publisher/consultant Bob Brenner (profiled in Chapter Ten) can help. The Brenner group publishes several other volumes on the subject.

Davidson, Jeffrey P. *Marketing for the Home-Based Business*. Holbrook: Adams Publishing, 1990. (260 Center St., Holbrook, MA 02343.) Includes launch plan for a home business, ideas for creating an image, marketing tools, marketing with newsletters, telephone marketing, hiring parttime help. Lists home business organizations, periodicals, marketing directories.

Edwards, Paul and Sarah. *Getting Business to Come to You*. Los Angeles: Jeremy P. Tarcher Inc., 1991. An original marketing twist from the gurus of home business.

Edwards, Paul and Sarah, and Rick Benzel. *Teaming-Up: The Small Business Guide to Collaborating with Others to Increase Your Earnings, Reduce Your Costs, & Boost Your Business to New Levels*. New York: Putnam Publishing Group, 1996. The home business experts discuss a significant trend.

Edwards, Paul and Sarah. *Working from Home: Everything You Need to Know about Living & Working under the Same Roof*, 4th ed. New York: Putnam Publishing Group, 1994. The "bible" of our industry. While part of this book is devoted to identifying work you can do from home, many sections apply to those who already know what they want to do. Emphasis is on the human side of business.

Eyler, David R. *The Home Business Bible*. New York: John Wiley & Sons, 1994. A useful A-Z reference of key business topics. Appendices provide business forms; tax guidelines; and sources of information, software, and supplies.

Fisher, Lionel L. *On Your Own: A Guide to Working Happily, Productively & Successfully form Home*. Englewood Cliffs: Prentice Hall, 1995. The personal side of home business, including self-understanding and self-motivation, organizational skills, productivity, office/home boundaries, and procrastination. Excellent bibliography on these and related topics.

Floyd, Elaine. *Marketing with Newsletters. How to Boost Sales, Add Members, Raise Donations & Further Your Cause with a Printed, Faxed, or Web Site Newsletter,* 2nd ed. Hollywood: LIFETIME Books, Inc., 1996. An update of Floyd's useful 1991 book with new emphasis on electronic formats. Covers newsletters from planning to production. Good bibliography. Valuable not only for your own marketing, but to help you produce marketing newsletters for clients. (See her book on writing newsletters in the writing books section below.)

Hill, Napoleon. *Think & Grow Rich.* New York: Fawcett Book Group, 1996. First published in 1937, this classic still offers inspiring, practical advice to new entrepreneurs.

Kamoroff, Bernard. *Small-Time Operator: How to Start Your Own Small Business, Keep Your Books, Pay Your Taxes & Stay Out of Trouble,* 21st ed. Bell Springs Publishing, 1996. (Box 640, Bell Springs Rd., Laytonville, CA 95454.) Revised and enlarged, this perennial seller is a fine introduction to starting and running a small business. Emphasis on financial records and planning. Includes valuable advice on setting up your accounts.

Kanarek, Lisa. *One Hundred-One Home Office Success Secrets.* Franklin Lakes: Career Press, Inc., 1994. Helpful insider tips based on the author's experience and that of 30 other successful home-based professionals. Featured on the Public Broadcast Series, "Small Business Today."

Levinson, Jay C., and Charles Rubin. *Guerrilla Advertising: Cost-Effective Tactics for Small Business Success.* Boston: Houghton Mifflin Co., 1994. Practical and lively, full of examples of low-cost ads.

Levinson, Jay C. *Guerrilla Marketing Handbook.* Boston: Houghton Mifflin Co., 1994. A classic for over a decade, "guerrilla marketing" relies on bold, imaginative, money-saving strategies.

Levinson, Jay C. *Guerrilla Marketing Attack: New Strategies, Tactics, & Weapons for Winning Big Profits.* Boston: Houghton Mifflin Co., 1989. Here Levinson explodes thirty-three marketing myths and puts his ideas to work, offering many specific programs readers can try.

Levinson, Jay C. *Guerrilla Marketing Excellence: The 50 Golden Rules for Small Business Success.* Boston: Houghton Mifflin Co., 1993. More good tips and techniques.

Levinson, Jay C., and Seth Godin. *Guerrilla Marketing for the Home-Based Business.* Boston:

Houghton Mifflin Co., 1995. Lots of emphasis on creative workers—e.g., a business plan writer's three-tiered direct marketing campaign; a marketing consultant/writer who built her business primarily through CompuServe classifieds. Covers positioning, customer service, word of mouth, publicity, printed materials, direct mail, newsletters, classified ads, networking, telephone techniques, closing the sale. Levinson runs a profitable writing/consulting business from his home. Godin also ran a home-based business until it outgrew his residence.

Levinson, Jay C., and Charles Rubin. *Guerrilla Marketing Online Weapons: 100 Low-Cost, High-Impact Weapons for Online Profits & Prosperity*. Boston: Houghton Mifflin Co., 1996. The "guerrilla marketers" take on the Internet.

Levinson, Jay C. *Guerrilla Marketing Weapons: 100 Affordable Marketing Methods for Maximizing Profits from Your Small Business*. New York: New American Library-Dutton, 1990. Levinson fires off more specific techniques under ten "weapons groups." A solid idea-builder.

Lonier, Terri. *Working Solo: The Real Guide to Freedom & Financial Success with your Own Business*. New York: Portico Press, 1994. A *What Color Is Your Parachute* for prospective entrepreneurs. Lonier, a consultant and seminar leader, helps you conceptualize your business and provides planning guidelines.

Lulow, Kalia. *The Freelancer's Business Book*. New York: Ballantine Books, Inc., 1984. Practical start-up advice for all freelancers. Writing a business plan. Negotiating with clients.

Morganstern, Steve. *Grow Your Business with Desktop Marketing*. New York: Random House, 1996. Joint production of Random House Reference & Information Publishing and Home Office Computing magazine. Practical general marketing advice. Techniques for list-building at your desk. Advice on self-promotion. Overview of desktop publishing with samples of creative printed promos and newsletter design. Information on online marketing, including autoresponders (for E-mail), using the World Wide Web, and "spamming" (sending commercial messages to newsgroups) without being "flamed" (having your E-mail logjammed with angry replies). Product recommendations.

Phillips, Michael, and Salli Rasberry, Peter Turner, and Emily Bower. *Honest Business: A Superior Strategy for Starting & Managing Your Own Business*. East Lansing: Shambala Publications, 1996. Inspirational approach to business ethics combined with practical advice on small-business success.

Phillips, Michael, and Salli Rasberry. *Marketing Without Advertising.* Berkeley: Nolo Press, 1996. Emphasizing customer loyalty and personal recommendations, this volume offers practical steps for building and expanding a small business while spending little or nothing on ads.

Sorenson, George. *Power Freelancing: Home-Based Careers for Writers, Designers, & Consultants.* Minneapolis: Mid-List Press, 1995. (P.O. Box 20292, Denver, CO 80220.) Education and guidance for creative professionals on starting and running a home-based business.

Urquhart, James R., III. *The IRS, Independent Contractors and You.* Irvine: Fidelity Publishing, 1993. (2061 Business Center Dr., No. 112, Irvine, CA 92715). Tax attorney who gives seminars nationwide on use of independent contractors explains how to avoid pitfalls, discusses common law factors that define an independent contractor, and provides model agreement and IRS forms.

Whitmyer, Claude, and Salli Rasberry and Michael Phillips. *Running a One-Person Business*, revised ed.. Berkeley: Ten Speed Press, 1994. Covers the basics, including legal, financial, and human factors. Presents profiles of several one-person business successes. Appendix provides a tight summary of steps in starting a business.

Yudkin, Marcia. *Marketing Online: Low-Cost, High-Yield Strategies for Small Businesses & Professionals.* New York: A Plume Book, The Penguin Group, 1995. One of many recent books on a new topic, this one is thorough and is focused on small and solo businesses.

BOOKS AND BOOKLETS ON WRITING A BUSINESS PLAN

Abrams, Rhonda M. *Successful Business Plan Secrets & Strategies*, 2nd ed. Grants Pass: Oasis Press, 1993. Ringbound workbook to help the entrepreneur write a business plan.

Covello, Joseph A. and Brian J. Hazelgren. *The Complete Book of Business Plans.* Naperville: Sourcebooks, Inc., 1996. (P.O. Box 372, Naperville, IL 60566). Provides 101 questions to structure your business plan. Includes actual business plans. A useful guide, though aimed more at services, retail, and recreation businesses than individuals selling creative skills. Other books in this Sourcebook Series include: *The Internet Business Planner, Mancuso's Small Business Resource Guide, Your First Business Plan,* and *The Small Business Start-up Guide.*

Gumpert, David E. *How to Really Create a Successful Business Plan.* 3rd ed., revised. Boston: Inc. Publishing, 1996. A revised edition of this long-popular book.

McKeever, Mike. *How to Write a Business Plan*, 3rd ed., revised. Berkeley: Nolo Press, 1995. A good overview with help in clarifying your "financials," suggestions for drafting your own "business accomplishment resume," advice on organizing your plan, ideas about how to use it, and a strong resources section. Clear, friendly writing. Sample business plans.

SBA BOOKLETS: "The Business Plan for Home-Based Businesses" has sections on preparing the financial aspects of a business plan. "Business Plan for Small Service Firms" contains worksheets for cash flow and income projections. Both are available from the Small Business Administration, 409 3rd St. SW, Washington, DC 20476, (800) U-ASK-SBA (827-5722), or through your local SBA office.

BOOKS ON TIME MANAGEMENT AND ORGANIZATION

Lakein, Alan. *How to Get Control of Your Time and Your Life*. New York: New American Library-Dutton, 1973, 1989. A classic. You'll find many of Lakein's ideas in other books on time management.

Hobbs, Charles R. *Time Power: The Revolutionary Time Management System That Can Change Your Professional and Personal Life*. New York: HarperCollins, 1988. Emphasis is on prioritizing, unifying, and taking action. Hobbs' organization does seminars and sells tapes and is tied in with the popular Day-Timer scheduling systems available from Day-Timers, Inc.

Kanarek, Lisa. *Organizing Your Home Office for Success: Expert Strategies That Can Work for You*. New York: New American Library-Dutton, 1994. Kanarak shows you how to set up your office to best advantage.

BOOKS ON THE BUSINESS OF WRITING

American Society of Journalists & Authors Staff and Dodi Schultz. *Tools of the Writer's Trade: Successful Writers Tell All about the Equipment & Services They Find the Best*. New York: HarperCollins Publishers, Inc., 1991. Over 300 pages of concise tips on working as a writer contributed by members of The American Society of Journalists & Authors. Annotated lists of professional writers' organizations and mail order sources of writers' supplies and services.

Bly, Robert W. *Secrets of a Freelance Writer: How to Make $85,000 A Year*, revised ed. New York: Henry Holt & Co., Inc., 1995. A guru of the freelance writing business, Bly focuses on writing for business and government, with advice on setting fees and ideas for adding to your writing income through self-publishing, training, and consulting. Originally published in the 1980s, this is one of the first books (and still one of the few) to deal with what the book you're reading calls "the hidden market for freelance writers."

Burack, Sylvia K. *The Writer's Handbook 1997 Edition* (61st ed., revised and enlarged). Boston: The Writer, Inc., 1996. Published annually. Articles by distinguished professionals, advice on the creative process, information on writing techniques. Directory of over 3,000 current markets, including magazines and publishers. Listings of literary agents, writers' organizations, contests, and awards.

Crawford, Tag. *Business and Legal Forms for Authors and Self-Publishers*. New York: Allworth Press, 1996. Allworth Communications, Inc., 10 E. 23rd St., New York, NY 10010. Twenty forms including estimating, confirming an assignment, invoicing, book publishing, collaboration, privacy release, and electronic rights. Details on how to use them. Emphasis is on traditional writing (articles, books), rather than on "work-for-hire" business assignments.

Floyd, Elaine. *Making Money Writing Newsletters: From Moonlighting to Full-Time Work, How to Set-up & Run a Newsletter Production Service*. Saint Louis: Newsletter Resources, 1994. If newsletters interest you, don't miss this volume, full of practical advice. (See her book on marketing with newsletters in the business books section above.)

Holm, Kirsten C., and Mark Garvey. *1997 Writer's Market: Where & How to Sell What You Write*. Cincinnati: F & W Publications, Inc., 1996. Published annually. Contains 4,000 mostly traditional markets for writers—invaluable if you're submitting to editors and publishers. Front of book contains helpful information on research, new freelance opportunities, contracts, copyright, setting prices, and other topics. (Also available on CD-ROM.)

Holtz, Herman R. *How to Start & Run a Writing & Editing Business*. New York: John Wiley & Sons, Inc., 1992. Offers advice on penetrating business and government markets and serving individuals. Covers writing and marketing special reports. Suggests good work habits and techniques. Discusses research via electronic databases. Good coverage of copyright issues and writers' organizations. (See Holtz' Webpage at *http://www.bellicose.com/freelance/.*)

Kopelman, Alexander, writer/editor. *National Writers Union Guide to Freelance Rates & Standard Practice*. New York: National Writers Union, 1995. (873 Broadway, Suite 203, New York, NY 10003.) Also distributed by Writers Digest Books. Includes rates and practices in journalism, book publishing, technical writing, and corporate/non-profit writing. Discusses copyrights, contracts, electronic rights.

Sorenson, George. *Writing for the Corporate Market: How to Make Big Money Freelancing for Business*. Minneapolis: Mid-List Press, 1990. (P.O. Box 20292, Denver, CO 80220.) Covers major types of business writing and strategies for obtaining business.

Suzanne, Claudia. *This Business of Books: A Complete Overview of the Industry from Concept through Sales*. Tustin, CA: WAMBTAC, 1996. (WAMBTAC, 17300 17th St., Suite J276, Tustin, CA 92680). Longtime California ghostwriter Claudia Suzanne explains the difference between collaborating, ghostwriting, and working-for-hire; how to tell a subsidy publisher from a vanity press; industry standards and formats for contracts, fees, advances, royalties; pros and cons of self-publishing; and more. Can be purchased at on the Internet at *http://bookzone.com/bookzone/indexed/ 10000804.html*.

Writer's Digest Editors. *The Writer's Essential Desk Reference: A Companion to the Writer's Market*, 2nd ed. Cincinnati: F & W Publications, Inc., 1996. Useful information for writers on finances, taxes, law, writers' groups, conferences, workshops, instruction, research techniques, working with others, book publishing, and sales.

BOOK ON BENEFITS

Janecek, Lenore. *Health Insurance: A Guide for Artists, Consultants, Entrepreneurs & Other Self-Employed*. New York: American Council for the Arts, co-published with Allworth Press, 1993. Giving up employee benefits doesn't mean you'll give up personal and family coverage. Janecek examines every aspect of finding and selecting health insurance, including types of plans, alternative medicine issues, and selecting a physician. The book also deals with disability insurance, long-term care insurance, life insurance, and saving for retirement. The appendix offers a list of creative professional organizations which provide member insurance.

MEDIA GUIDES

Bacon's Information, Inc.. *Newspaper/Magazine Directory* (2 volumes), *Radio/TV/Cable Directory* (2 volumes), *Media Calendar Directory, Business Media Directory, International Media Directory, New York Media Directory*, and *California Media Directory*. Chicago: Bacon's Information, Inc. (332 S. Michigan Ave., Suite 900, Chicago, CA 60604, (800) 621-0561.) Seven directories published annually. Also available on CD-ROM. Expensive. Check your local library. Bacon's also offers a national clipping service and a press release distribution service.

Weber, Hilary. *Gale Directory of Publications & Broadcast Media 1996 & Update*, 96th ed. Detroit: Gale Research, Inc., 1995. Published annually. Expensive. Check your local library.

SMALL/HOME BUSINESS PERIODICALS

If any of these periodicals interests you, write for a sample copy.

At Home Professional Magazine, At Home Professional, Inc.. 708 Millifold Pl., Brandon, Florida 33510, Website: *http://www.homeprofessionals.com/.* Semi-monthly, $9.95/yr. Four-color magazine for home-based business owners and telecommuters. Edited by "an independent team of professionals joined together by virtual offices."

Creative Business, 275 Newbury St., Boston, MA 02116-9643, (617) 424-1368, edited by Cameron S. Foote. Six bi-monthly issues and four special reports a year, $89/yr. Covers practical aspects of running a small creative business. Information based on real-life experiences of copywriters, graphic designers, and illustrators around the country.

Entrepreneur, Subscription Department, P.O. Box 58808, Boulder CO 80321, (800) 274-6229. Monthly, $19.97/yr. Covers all aspects of small business, including home-based business. Sold on newsstands.

Home Business Communiqué: A Publication for Home-Based Business Owners, P.O. Box 3644, Lakewood, CA 90711-3644, (310) 867-0505. Monthly, $18/yr. Home-based entrepreneur Carol Tober edits this newsletter, focusing primarily on southern California and western U.S. activities. Strong emphasis on networking.

Home Office Computing, Subscription Department, P.O. Box 51344, Boulder, CO 80321-1344, (800) 288-7812, *http://www.smalloffice.com.* Monthly, $19.97/yr. Success stories, new products, tax and legal issues for home entrepreneurs, office design, monthly column by home office experts Paul and Sarah Edwards. A valuable resource. Sold on newsstands.

Income Opportunities: The Original Small Business/Home Office Magazine, Subscription Department, P.O. Box 55206, Boulder, CO 80322. Monthly, $17.89/yr. (may also be sent free). Articles of general interest, but heavy on business opportunities that involve outlay of funds.

PERIODICALS FOR PROFESSIONAL WRITERS

Freelance Success: The Marketing and Management Guide for Experienced Journalists, 801 NE 70th St., Miami, FL 33138, (305) 757-8854, fax (305) 757-8857, E-mail: freelance-success@usa.net. Monthly, $97/yr. print version, $77/yr. weekly E-mail version. Founded by Judith Broadhurst out of northern California. (She's profiled in Chapter Nine) and recently sold to Teresa Mears of Miami. Full of concise, in-depth articles to help traditional working journalists sell and earn. Not aimed at corporate writers.

Freelance Writers Report, Cassell Network of Writers, P.O. Box A, North Stratford, NH 03290, (800) 351-9278. The network represents several freelance writers associations and publishes a national newsletter monthly, available to non-members for $39 a year. Price includes a listing in the network writers data bank.

Publishing Entrepreneur: Profit Strategies for the Information and Publishing Industries. 121 E. Front St., 4th Floor, P.O. Box 192, Traverse City, MI 49685-0192, (616) 933-0445. http://www.smallpress.com/ Semi-monthly, $28/yr. A lively, online-savvy journal of interest to writers involved in independent publishing.

The Working Communicator, Ragan Communications, 212 W. Superior St., Suite 200, Chicago, IL 60610, (800) 878-5331, fax (312) 335-9583. Monthly eight-page newsletter plus seven free books, reg. $129/yr. (New subscribers pay $89/yr. if ordered by phone.) Aimed at public relations pros, editors, writers, speech writers, information specialists—mainly in the corporate world. New ideas, trends, and techniques. Useful in sharpening your skills and serving clients.

Today's $85,000 Freelance Writer, BSK Communications, P.O. Box 543, Oradell, NJ 07649, voice(201) 262-3277, Fax (201) 599-2635, E-mail bskcom@internexus.net. Semi-monthly $23.70/yr. A magazine expansion of owner-editor Brian S. Konradt's newsletter, The Prolific Freelancer. Online-savvy articles covering many types of commercial writing, including corporate writing, direct marketing, Website production, ad agency copy—plus general information on marketing and business procedures for writers.

The Travel Writer's International Network Newsletter, P.O. Box 8822, Madeira Beach, FL 33738. Monthly, $50/yr. or $65/yr. outside North America. Marketing and networking information from Carol J. Perry, prolific Florida writer and writing instructor. As Perry put it in her inaugural issue (January, 1996), "Let's face it. We're not all going to sell our words to the big, high-paying markets like Travel & Leisure or Condé Nast Traveler. But there are literally hundreds of other good-paying national, regional, and international publications buying articles from freelancers every day!"

Writer's Digest, Subscription Dept. P.O. Box 2124, Harlan, IA 51593-2313. Monthly, $23.96/yr. One of the oldest writer's magazines. Covers all aspects, but places more emphasis on traditional markets. Lists writers' conferences and market news. Sold on news stands.

The Writer, 120 Boylston St., Boston, MA 02116-4615. Monthly, $27/yr. Emphasis on traditional markets and techniques. Lists writers' conferences and market news. Sold on news stands.

Writing for Money: Where to Sell What You Write, Blue Dolphin Communications, 83 Boston Post Rd., Sudbury, MA 01776, (800) 477-8088. 17 times a year, $78/yr. (But don't pay that much. One promotion offered $49/yr., including three special reports. Another touted $29.97 for six issues and 24 reports, plus a guidebook.) Edited by John Clausen out of Hendersonville, NC. Up-to-date profiles of publications readers of this book can realistically expect to sell to. Concise articles on strategy, multiple sales, personal experiences. Not aimed at corporate writers.

AUDIO-VISUAL RESOURCES

How to Get Paid What You Are Worth, videotape by author, lecturer, and creative services consultant Maria Piscopo. (See Chapter Eight). Other titles in this series are *How to Find & Keep New Clients, How to Create More Time & Less Stress,* and *How to Get Clients to Call You*. Turner Video Communications, P.O. Box 8252, Newport Beach, CA 92658, (714) 644-0939, (800) 382-9417, fax (714) 644-5820. $29.95 each or $99.95 for all four videos, plus $2.95 shipping and handling per video.

SOFTWARE—BUSINESS PLANS

Automate Your Business Plan. Tustin, CA: Out of Your Mind and Into the Marketplace. (714) 544-0248. Praised by Inc. Magazine. Helps entrepreneurs develop accurate projections.

BizPlan Builder. Mountain View, CA: Jian Tools for Sales. (800) 346-5426. Provides a structured framework to use with your word processor and spreadsheet. Prompts ask questions and make suggestions.

Business Plan Pro. Eugene, OR: Palo Alto Software. (800) 229-7526, http://www.pasware.com. Highly-rated program. Provides a prompted text writer that takes you step-by-step with your own words. Compatible with many popular spreadsheet programs. Helps you estimate cash flow, profit and loss, and other financials. Provides a table for tracking date and budget milestones. Allows you to keep three versions of your numbers: plan and actual—and the difference between them.

PFS: Business Plan. Cambridge, MA: SoftKey International. (800) 227-5609, http://www.softkey.com.

PlanMaker. St. Louis: POWERSolutions for Business. (800) 955-3337, http://www.planmaker.com.

PlanWrite, Business Insight, and Quick Insight. Austin, TX: Business Resource Software. (800) 423-1228, http://www.brs-inc.com.

Success, Inc. Newport Beach, CA: Dynamic Pathways. (800) 543-7788.

SOFTWARE—MEDIA GUIDES, MARKETING

Bacon's Information, Inc.. *MediaSource Software, Media Calendar Software*, and *Clip Scanning and Analysis Reports Software* (Windows only). Chicago: Bacon's Information, Inc., 1996. (332 S. Michigan Ave., Suite 900, Chicago, CA 60604, (800) 621-0561) Published annually. CD-ROM for Windows and Macintosh. Expensive. Check your local library. Bacon's also offers a national clipping service and a press release distribution service.

Digital Directory Assistance, Inc., (800) 284-8353, sells CD-ROM products for marketing research.

Dolphin Software Solutions, *The Working Writer* (DOS and Windows only). 1917 W. 4th Ave., Suite 256, Vancouver, BC V6J 1M7, (604) 739-1336, fax (604) 739-1188, email: dss—com@hotmail.com. Software system tracks the business of freelance writing "from query letter to paycheck."

Edwards, Paul and Sarah. *Getting Business to Come to You*. Orem: Infobusiness, Inc., 1996. An update of the Edwards' 1991 handbook. Includes information on computer network resources. CD-ROM, Audio.

Holm, Kirsten C., and Mark Garvey. *1997 Writer's Market: Where & How to Sell What You Write*. Cincinnati: F & W Publications, Inc., 1996. Published annually. Contains 4,000 mostly traditional markets for writers—invaluable if you're submitting to editors and publishers. Also contains helpful information on research, new freelance opportunities, contracts, copyright, setting prices, and other topics. CD-ROM for both Windows and Macintosh includes manuscript submission-tracking software.

Marketing Plan Pro. Eugene, OR: Palo Alto Software. (800) 229-7526, http://www.pasware.com. Windows and dialogues guide you through your marketing plan, linking strategies to tactics to specific activity budgets.

Marketplace Information Corp., (800) 999-9497, sell CD-ROM products for marketing research and planning.

SOURCE DIRECTORY

SOURCES FOR SPECIALIZED BOOKS

LSI Educational Technologies, 1436 Bugle Ln., Clearwater, FL 34624, (813) 531-2637. Owner Katie Lachance sells books and booklets of interest to entrepreneurs in the SOHO (small office/home office) movement. Special emphasis on online marketing.

The Writers' Computer Store, 11317 Santa Monica Blvd., Los Angeles, CA 90025-3118, (310) 479-7774. Mail order service at 2631 Bridgeway Ave., Sausalito, CA 94965, (800) 272-8927 or (415) 332-7005. Publishes a catalog of books, software, and videos of interest to writers. Special emphasis on film and television. Website: *http://www.writerscomputer.com/.*

Writer's Digest Book Club, P.O. Box 12948, Cincinnati, OH 45212-0948, (513) 531-8250. Monthly catalogs for members list books on the craft and business of writing, as well as on time management and organization. Most books are offered at a discount; bonus books can be earned.

INSURANCE RESOURCES

Many business and professional organizations provide access to health, disability, and life insurance; retirement plans; credit unions; and other benefits as a service to their members. Shop carefully and check performance with entrepreneurs already enrolled.

Alliance for Affordable Health Care, 1725 K St. NW, Suite 310, Washington, D.C. 20006. Focuses primarily on health insurance.

Council of Writers Organizations, Dixie Franklin, Executive Director, 972 Valley Rd., Marquette, MI 49855. Offers major medical, term life, and accidental death and dismemberment insurance through an outside provider to members of twenty member organizations.

National Association for the Self-Employed, 2121 Precinct Line Rd., Hurst, TX 75054, (800) 827-9990. Emphasizes health insurance, along with purchasing and travel benefits.

National Association of Socially Responsible Organizations, 1925 K St., Suite 310, Washington, DC 20006, (800) 638-8113. Provides "alternatives to the health care crisis for non-profits, small businesses, and the self-employed."

TRAINING

This directory cannot begin to cover the training opportunities offered in adult school and college classrooms, through commercial seminars, by mail, and online—any of which may help you become a successful commercial writer. However, if you're writing articles for small and mid-sized markets, I recommend Dr. John McCollister, best known for his book, *Writing for Dollars*, who gives seminars nationally and sells books and tapes on his techniques. I've attended his affordable seminars and found them full of useful information, primarily for beginners. Write or call American Writers Institute, 26 Lazy Eight Dr., Daytona Beach, FL 32124, (800) 283-3050, or check his Website at *http://members.aol.com/WriterDoc/*.

Another expert to follow up on is Gordon Burgett, author of *How to Sell 75% of Your Free-lance Writing*, *The Writer's Guide to Query Letters and Cover Letters*, and *The Travel Writer's Guide* (available from Writer's Digest Book Club), plus other books and tapes on writing, speaking, and consulting. I've attended Burgett's programs also and found them worthwhile. For information, contact Communications Unlimited, P.O. Box 6405, Santa Maria, CA 93456, (805) 937-8711, fax (805) 937-3035, E-mail: gburgett@aol.com. Check his Website at *http://speakers.com/spkr1161.html*.

Florida business writer Steve Morrill, profiled in Chapter Six, offers online classes on article writing and marketing. E-mail him at writers@gte.com regarding his Internet classes or at stevemoril@aol.com regarding his classes on America Online.

WEBSITES FOR SMALL/HOME BUSINESS

Don't forget to check Internet newsgroups and America Online and CompuServe chat rooms and forums for more online home business resources.

CHH Business Owners' Toolkit, *http://www.toolkit.com/*. Multilevel site with resources ranging from downloadable worksheets to model policies on smoking.

Home Business Review, *http://www.tab.com/Home.Business/*. Monthly online newspaper designed to "educate and promote" home-based businesses. Includes The Home Based Business Yellow Pages.

Internal Revenue Service, *http://irs.ustreas.gov/*.

The Internet for Small Business: Bellicose Industries, *http://www.bellicose.com /* Help for small business from Website hosting firm. Provides advice for doing business on the Internet and Website evaluation.

SOHO Trend: Small Office Home Office Resource, *http://hbnet.com/*. Resources, trends, news.

Small & Home-Based Business Links, *http://www.ro.com/small—business/home-based.html*. References, opportunities, newsgroups, marketing, and more.

Small Business Administration, *http://www.sba.gov/*.

Smart Business Supersite, *http://www.smartbiz.com/*. Downloadable fact sheets on starting and operating a business in each of the 50 states—and much more info. Less commercial than many small office/home office sites.

Your Small Office, *http://www.smalloffice.com/*. From the editors of Small Office Computing and Home Office Computing. Wide variety of current info for small/home businesses. Editorial index.

WEBSITES FOR WRITERS

Don't forget to check Internet newsgroups and America Online and CompuServe chat rooms and forums for more online writing resources. Also watch for bulletin boards (BBSs), often listed in local publications. These dial-in forums preceded the Internet's popularity and still allow writers to exchange views.

A Few Tips on Marketing and Writing Marketing Materials, *http://www.bellicose.com/freelance/*. Webpage of Herman Holtz, author of *How to Start & Run a Writing & Editing Business* and other books on writing and marketing.

BookZone, *http://www.bookzone.com/*. This award-winning site is an online source for books, audiobooks, and more. Resources section for writers.

Creative Directory Services, *http://www.creativedir.com/*. Lists creative services with heavy emphasis on film, TV, music, multimedia. Brainchild of Beverly Hansen and David M. Hansen. Grew out of print version of the Chicago Creative Directory, published since 1975. Includes a long list of freelance writers at *http://www.creativedir.com/html/92.html*.

Creative Freelancers, *http://www.freelancers.com/*. New York-based registry for artists, writers, and other talent.

Creative Freelancers Registry, *http://www.ghgcorp.com/cfr/index.html*. "A multi-faceted resource for the creation of books." Includes a freelancers database.

Freelance Online Jobs Available, *http://www.FreelanceOnline.com/jobsavail .html*. Lists writing-related jobs available, both freelance and fulltime.

Inklings, *http://www.inkspot.com/~ohi/ink/inklings.html*. Semi-weekly newsletter for writers on the Net. Inklings has over 6,000 subscribers with a wide range of writing interests. Check out other services available at this site *(inkspot.com)*.For example, advice on how to start an online newsletter is offered at *http://www.inkspot.com/~ohi/ink/newsletterinfo.html*. Links to resources for writers are offered at *http://www.inkspot.com/~ohi/inkspot/*.

The Internet for Business Writers and Communicators, *http://www.sfu.ca /continuing-studies/CAPPs/WPtext/BWNet.html*. Provides relevant resources and links. Site maintained by Simon Fraser University.

Online Advertising Systems Network, *http://www.oasysnet.com/*. Matches freelancers with clients, sponsored by the American Association of Advertising Agencies.

Tips for Writers and Designers, *http://www.dsiegel.com/tips/index.html*. Valuable info if you do Web authoring.

Working Writers, *http://www.working-writers.com/*. New York-based registry with emphasis on technical writing. Also showcases writers' work.

Writer Resources, *http://www.writers.net/*. Fine compilation of links for writers.

Writers & Editors Island Net, *http://www.shorewood.bc.ca/mall-writers.html*. Links to sites of interest to writers and editors, both fiction and non-fiction.

Writers Resource Listing, *http://www.gi.net/NET/PM-1996/96-02/96-02-15/0042.html*. Many useful links, including resources for journalists and technical writers.

Writing for the Web: A New Resource for Writers, *http://homepage.interaccess.com/~kejohns/web1.htm*. A how-to on writing for the Web, presented at 7th Annual Writers Institute (1996), University of Wisconsin, Madison.

Writers Organizations, *http://www.writeonmag.com:80/org.html*. Compiled by Write On Magazine.

OTHER RESOURCES

Copyright. U.S. copyright law unequivocally recognizes the creator of a work as its owner—unless the work was done "for hire" or you otherwise signed away specific rights. Thus, your work is copyrighted whether or not you register it. However, registration is necessary before you can bring an infringement suit to court. Contact the Copyright Office, Library of Congress, Washington, DC 20559, (202) 479-0700, for a free Copyright Information Kit or registrations forms. The office will answer specific questions, but will not provide legal advice. It is not necessary for you to register each work individually. In fact, there is no limit on the number of works that can be copyrighted in a group, although there are some requirements for submitting a group of works.

Service Core of Retired Executives Association (SCORE), 409 3rd St. SW, Suite 5900, Washington, DC 20476, (202) 205-6759. SCORE, a service of the Small Business Administration (SBA), is made up of some 12,500 volunteer members nationwide, retired businesspersons who give seminars to entrepreneurs and provide free assistance to small businesses. Check with your local SBA office or Chamber of Commerce.

Small Business Administration, 409 3rd St. SW, Washington, DC 20476, (800) U-ASK-SBA (827-5722). Personnel locator (202) 205-6600. See current U.S. Government Manual, usually available at libraries, for the address and phone number of the SBA field office in your region, or check the phone book or the SBA Website.

Tax Information. "Business Use of Your Home," Internal Revenue Service Publication 587, may be obtained by calling (800) TAX-FORM. So may Publication 334, which deals with taxes for small business, including regulations regarding tax-sheltered retirement accounts for the self-employed. Specific questions about home office tax regulations can be answered by the IRS' tax information hot line, (800) TAX-1040.

Trademarks and Servicemarks. For information on registering a trademark nationally, contact the Office of Public Affairs, Patent and Trademark Office, Washington, DC 20231, (703) 305-8341. Offices are located at 2011 Crystal Dr., Arlington, VA 22202. A trademark includes "any distinctive word, name, symbol, device, or any combination thereof adopted and used, or intended to be used, by a manufacturer or merchant to identify his goods or services and distinguish them (from others)." The term of registration or renewal is 10 years. For information on registering a trademark or servicemark in your state, contact your State Department of Commerce.

ORGANIZATIONS FOR HOME-BASED ENTREPRENEURS

Each organization has a different emphasis and offers different services. Write or call for information—and beware of organizations that exist only to promote business opportunities offered for sale. These opportunities may be valid, but the organization's goal is more to promote them than to help fledgling entrepreneurs.

American Association of Home-Based Businesses, P.O. Box 10023, Rockville, MD 20849, (800) 447-9710, fax (301) 963-7042, e-mail: aahbb@crosslink.net, Website: *http://www.aahbb.org*. A non-profit organization run by and for home-based business owners with chapters nationwide.

Home Business Institute, Inc., P. O. Box 301, White Plains, NY 10605-0301, (888) DIAL HBI, fax (914) 946-6694. Information services and benefits for home-based businesses.

The Home Office and Business Opportunities Association (HOBO), 92 Corporate Park, Suite C-250, Irvine, CA 92714, (714) 589-3232, fax. (714) 757-4626. California's foremost non-profit home-business organization.

Home Office Association of America, Inc., 909 Third Avenue, Suite 990, New York, NY 10022. Website: *http://www.hoaa.com/*. Offers insurance programs and discounts on prescription drugs, UPS, Kinko's Copy Centers, and more. Website features news, information, links, ideas, and a member Website directory.

International Association of Home-Based Businesses, 8333 Ralston Rd., Suite 4, Arvada, CO 80002-2355, (800) 41-IAHBB, fax (303) 425-9675. Support and networking, mostly in Colorado.

National Association of Home Based Businesses, 10451 Mill Run Circle, Owings Mills, MD 21117, (410) 363-3698, E-mail: nahbb@ix.netcom.com, Website: *http://www.usahomebusiness.com/*. Private organization founded in 1984 to encourage home-based businesses. Recent thrusts include an Information Superhighway for home-based businesses and formation of a Worldwide Home Based Business Alliance.

Nebraska Home-Based Business Association, P.O. Box 2136, Kearney, NE 68848. Helps Nebraskans develop home-based business.

Oklahoma Home-Based Business Association, P.O. Box 1335, Durant, OK 74702, (405) 924-5094, (800) 658-2823, fax (405) 920-2745. Fifteen chapters across the state.

The Rocky Mountain Home-Based Business Association, 9905 E. Colfax Ave., Aurora, CO 80010, (303) 367-1918, fax (303) 361-2953, Website: *http://www.edonnet.com\rmhbba*. Non-profit, offers networking and educational opportunities to nearly 400 members from Colorado, Wyoming, New Mexico.

SOHO (Small Office/Home Office) America, 10800 Lyndale Ave. South, Suite 200, Minneapolis, MN 55420, (800) 495-SOHO, fax (612) 887-2823, Website: *http://www.soho.org*. Electronic access to information and benefits, including weekly E-mail newsletter and 24-hour computer help, plus discounts and travel assistance.

ORGANIZATIONS FOR PROFESSIONAL WRITERS

American Medical Writers Association, 9650 Rockville Pike, Bethesda, MD 20816, (301) 493-0003.

American Society of Indexers, P.O. Box 386, Port Aransas, TX 78373, (512) 749-4052, fax (512) 749-6634.

American Society of Journalists and Authors, 1501 Broadway, Suite 302, New York, NY 10036, (212) 997-0947.

Associated Business Writers of America, Suite 620, 1450 S. Havana, Aurora, CO 80012, (303) 751-7844.

Association of Desktop Publishers, 4507 30th St., Suite 800, San Diego, CA 92116-4239, (619) 563-9714.

Association of Great Lakes Outdoor Writers, 301 Cross, Sullivan, IN 47882-1419, phone/fax (812) 268-6232.

Aviation/Space Writers Association, 17 S. High St., Suite 1200, Columbus, OH 43215, (614) 221-1900.

Cassell Network of Writers, Cassell Network of Writers, P.O. Box A, North Stratford, NH 03290, (800) 351-9278. Represents the Freelance Writers Associations of Florida, Georgia, and Texas. (See periodicals for writers.)

Computer Press Association, Michele Zatorski, Administrator, 631 Henmar Dr., Landing, NJ 07850, (201) 398-7300, fax (201) 398-3888, E-mail: 102751, e-mail: 1445@compuserve.com, Website:*http://ourworld.compuserve.com/homepages/Computer—Press—Association/*.

Copywriters Council of America, Freelance, Linick Building 102, 7 Putter Ln., Middle Island, NY 11953-0102, (516) 924-8555.

Editorial Freelancers Association, 71 W. 23rd St., Suite 1504, New York, NY 10014, (212) 929-5400.

Freelance Editorial Association, P.O. Box 380835, Cambridge, MA 02238-0835, (617) 634-8626.

Garden Writers Association of America, 10210 Leatherleaf Ct., Manassas, VA 22111, (703) 257-1032.

The HTML Writers Guild, *http://www.hwg.com*. With over 10,000 members in 56 countries, The HTML Writers Guild "continues to grow as the World Wide Web becomes established as an alternative to print and other mass marketing media." Highly technical, but a great place to learn and share online if you do Web authoring. What these "writers" write is usually programming code.

Independent Writers of Chicago, 7855 Gross Point Rd., Unit M, Skokie, IL 60077, (847) 676-3784.

Independent Writers of Southern California, P.O. Box 34279, Los Angeles, CA 90034, (310) 558-4090.

International Association of Business Communicators, One Hallidie Plaza, Suite 600, San Francisco, CA 94102, (415) 433-3400, fax (415) 362-8762, *http://www.iabc.com/*. Chapters around the world, many throughout the U.S. Excellent for networking in corporate and organizational communications.

International Food, Wine & Travel Writers Association, P.O. Box 13110, Long Beach, CA 90803, (310) 433-5969, fax (310) 438-6384.

The International Women's Writing Guild, P.O. Box 810, Gracie Station, New York, NY 10028-0082, (212) 737-7536.

Midwest Travel Writers Association, P.O. Box 3535, Omaha, NE 68103, (402) 571-4097.

National Association of Science Writers, P.O. Box 294, Greenlawn, NY 11740, (516) 757-5664.

National Writers Association, 1450 S. Havana Suite 620, Aurora, CO 80012, (303) 751-7844. Not-for-profit corporation founded in 1937. $50 a year for general membership, $60 for qualified professional membership (plus set-up fee). Monthly magazine, *Authorship*; chapters around the United States; literary agent service; bookstore.

National Writers Union, 873 Broadway, Suite 203, New York, NY 10003, (212) 254-0279.

New York Business Press Editors, 68-38 Yellowstone Blvd., Forest Hills, NY 11375, phone/fax (718) 275-8396.

North American Ski Journalists Association, P.O. Box 5334, Takoma Park, MD 20913, (301) 864-6428.

Outdoor Writers Association of America, 2017 Cato Ave., Suite 101, State College, PA 16801, (814) 234-1011.

Public Relations Society of America, 33 Irving Pl, 3rd Floor, New York, NY 10003-2376, (212) 995-2230, fax (212) 995-0797. National organization with chapters nationwide. Excellent for networking in corporate, organizational, and agency communications.

Society for Technical Communication, 901 N. Stuart St., Arlington, VA 22203, (703) 522-4114. National organization with chapters nationwide.

Society of American Business Editors and Writers, c/o Janine Latus-Musick, University of Missouri School of Journalism, 76 Jannett Hall, Columbia, MO 65211, (314) 882-7862.

Society of American Travel Writers, 4101 Lake Boon Trail, Suite 201, Raleigh, NC 27607, (919) 787-5181.

Society of Professional Journalists, 16 S. Jackson, Greencastle, IN 46135, (317) 653-3333.

Travel Journalists Guild, P.O. Box 10643, Chicago, IL 60610, (312) 664-9279.

Washington Independent Writers, 220 Woodward Blvd., 733 15th St. NW, Washington, DC 20005, (202) 347-4973, fax (202) 628-0298.

Women in Communications, Inc., 2101 Wilson Blvd., Suite 417, Arlington, VA 22201, (703) 528-4200, fax (703) 528-4205. National organization with chapters nationwide. Serves all branches of communications. Great networking.

Writers Connection, 1601 Saratoga-Sunnyvale Rd., Suite 180, Cupertino, CA 95014, (408) 973-0227.

INDEX

ABOUT THE AUTHOR

Lucy V. Parker is a writer and desktop publisher who works out of her home in Land O' Lakes, FL, where she moved in 1994 after many years in southern California. Her previous experience was in higher education public relations and publications and in commerical printing sales. A graduate of Northwestern University Medill School of Journalism, Parker lectures on writing, newsletters, and graphics design and has taught graphic design at the college level. Her recent interests include Internet Webpage creation. She's also working on a long-planned novel.

A veteran networker in such organizations as the Independent Writers of Southern California, the International Association of Business Communicators, and Women in Communications, Inc., she is currently active in the Tampa Writers Alliance and the American Association of Home Based Businesses–Tampa Bay.